Unprecedented

PLI
PRESS

PLI PRESS is Practising Law Institute's highly regarded publishing division. Our team of dedicated publishing and information professionals is committed to providing you the highest-quality analysis and practice guidance while keeping you updated on current legal developments.

Each year, **PLI PRESS** publishes more than 100 treatises, practice guides, books on lawyering skills, yearbooks, answer books, and journals—written and updated by leading practitioners in their respective practice areas, and edited and managed by our in-house legal editors. We also produce more than 200 Course Handbook titles annually, each corresponding to one of PLI's award-winning CLE programs.

QUESTIONS ABOUT THIS PUBLICATION?

If you have questions about updates to this publication, billing, or shipments, or would like information about our other products, please contact **PLI customer service** at info@pli.edu or at (800) 260-4PLI.

For any other questions or suggestions about this book, please contact the PLI Press **editorial department** at plipress@pli.edu.

For general information about Practising Law Institute, please visit **www.pli.edu**.

To view a full list of PLI Press publications,
visit **www.pli.edu/plipress**.

Practising Law Institute • 1177 Avenue of the Americas • New York, NY 10036

Unprecedented

Designing a Human-Centered Law Firm When Everything Is Changing

Jennifer A. Leonard

PLI Press • New York City • #447974

The views and opinions expressed herein do not necessarily represent those of Practising Law Institute. This work is designed to provide practical and useful information on the subject matter covered. However, it is provided with the understanding that neither the publisher nor the author is engaged in rendering legal, accounting, or other professional services. If legal advice or other expert assistance is required, the services of a competent professional should be sought.

Legal Editor: Lori Wood

LCCN: 2026936556

ISBN: 978-1-4024-5006-8

For Julian and Lucy, who share their names with two people trying to transform a law firm, and who transformed their mom into an author by refusing to let her quit.

About the Author

JENNIFER A. LEONARD has spent over twenty years at the intersection of law practice and legal innovation. She is the Founder of Creative Lawyers, a consultancy she leads with her favorite creative collaborator and fellow Penn Carey Law graduate, Mariel Staszewski. Through their work, Creative Lawyers has partnered with law firms of all sizes, from boutiques to global firms, and their clients in corporate legal departments to navigate the competitive, technological, and cultural forces transforming the profession. Their work focuses on the questions at the heart of this book: How do law firms evolve? What does it take to move a tradition-bound institution toward something better? And what makes law firm partnerships particularly challenging organizations to lead through change?

Before launching Creative Lawyers, Jen was Penn Carey Law's first Chief Innovation Officer and Executive Director of the Future of the Profession Initiative. During her time at Penn, she also built a nationally recognized law student professional development program and devoted herself to improving the way new lawyers form their professional identities in her role as a legal educator.

She began her career as a litigation associate with a Center City Philadelphia law firm before serving as Chief of Staff to the City of Philadelphia Law Department, where she developed a front-row perspective on how legal institutions really operate.

Jen has taught generative AI in law practice, design thinking, and law firm business models to students at the University of Pennsylvania Carey Law School and to executives in the Wharton School's Executive MBA program. She is a frequent speaker and thought leader on the future of the legal profession, including through *AI and the Future of Law*, a popular podcast she co-hosts with the American Arbitration Association's President, the brilliant and incomparable Bridget McCormack. Jen also serves on the board of the Pro Bono Institute.

Jen lives in Philadelphia's Art Museum neighborhood—right across from the Rocky steps—with her husband, Jim, her two children, Julian and Lucy, and a clownish French Bulldog named Elvis.

Unprecedented is her first book.

Table of Chapters

Table of Contents

Foreword

This book lives up to its name. It is ground-breaking. It is a bold, insightful assessment of the magnitude of the challenges facing the legal profession. And it provides a roadmap that is both extraordinarily creative and powerfully pragmatic for law firm leaders who have the vision and the fortitude to tackle those challenges.

This is a book about change management in a profession that is stubbornly resistant to change. It is about confronting an unprecedented convergence of threatening trends: heightened client expectations, an increasingly archaic pricing model, the rapid emergence of a technology—generative artificial intelligence—that upends traditional law firm service assumptions, a misalignment of personal compensation incentives and urgent institutional needs, new lawyers' insistence on more effective professional development and better lives, and a business environment that feels incompatible with important values and beloved cultures.

Unprecedented is the story of a law firm's five-day retreat to rethink its future in the face of these trends. Although the firm and the characters are fictional, the plot and the casting are spot-on realistic. I know this firm. I know these people. The story's authenticity is attributable to the brilliance and breadth of experience of its author, Jennifer Leonard, a former Big Law attorney and Chief Innovation Officer at the University of Pennsylvania Carey Law School who now heads one of the nation's leading consultancies for legal innovators.

The greatest virtue of *Unprecedented* is its optimism—its message that these threats are not only manageable, but opportunities for creating a better, more client-centric, more fulfilling profession. Without blinking at the complexity of the challenges, the legitimacy of some skepticism, and the tenacity of change-resistors, Jen Leonard plots a path to success. It is a path illuminated by multiple outside perspectives, genuine internal inclusivity, and proven business practices. It is a path that leads to business success while promoting professionalism and accommodating the best of institutional culture.

Many books on change management are big on theory and short on practicality. Not this one. *Unprecedented* recognizes that the hardest part of change management is implementation—the work of turning decisions into action. Here you will find concrete, no-nonsense advice on how to accomplish the change you need. You will find comfort in the candid acknowledgement that even if your progress is slower than you wanted, even if you lose some people along the way, and even if some initiatives don't prove out, you can still succeed. This book offers you a detailed, adaptive process that will reward your perseverance.

Unprecedented is ultimately a book about the importance of leadership. The fictional firm that is its subject has a leader who can see a future requiring significant change for the firm to survive. The leader rises to the occasion despite the skepticism of important colleagues. He resists the pulls of the three greatest obstacles to necessary change: insularity, complacency, and orthodoxy. He risks his leadership for the good of the institution he loves. I won't give away the ending, but I think he is the model of a great leader.

JAMES J. SANDMAN
Distinguished Lecturer, University of Pennsylvania Carey Law School
President Emeritus, Legal Services Corporation
Former Managing Partner, Arnold & Porter

Acknowledgments

No book is written alone, and this one is no exception.

To my husband, Jim, for your unwavering support throughout this process. You never once questioned the late nights, the weekend writing sessions, or the moments when I wasn't sure I could finish. You simply believed I would.

To my parents, for every opportunity you created for me, both the ones I recognized at the time and the countless ones I didn't. You set me on a path that led to a career in law and, eventually, to having something worth saying about a profession undergoing massive change. This book exists because of the foundation you built.

To Jim Sandman, for writing the foreword and, more importantly, for inspiring me to think differently about how the legal profession can be better for lawyers and clients alike. Your example gave me the courage to believe that a book like this could matter.

To Genevieve Tung, who read earlier (terrible) versions of this manuscript and somehow found kind and constructive things to say about every one of them. You were my commitment device, my first reader, and the reason I learned to accept criticism without spiraling. Every first-time author should be so lucky.

To David Ackert, who helped me untangle two competing narrative arcs I'd wrestled with for months in the space of a single ten-minute Zoom call. Some people just see the story you're trying to tell more clearly than you do.

To Marjorie Ferris, Jessica Grayson, Maya Markovich, and Shelley Smith, who generously shared their time and insights in interviews that shaped the characters and challenges in this book. Your real-world perspectives kept the fiction grounded in truth.

To Mariel Staszewski, the "special sauce" of Creative Lawyers. Every wild idea we chase somehow becomes smarter, sharper, and actually workable once you get your hands on it. I'm so grateful for a true partner who elevates everything we do, and who does it with gobsmacking talent, attention to detail, and good humor.

To Alexa Robertson, who was the first person to suggest I write a book—a completely absurd proposition. Encouraging others to take on ambitious feats is one of the most powerful ways to impact the world. Without your thoughtful prompting, I would *never* have had the confidence to start.

To the many fantastic people at Practising Law Institute who work tirelessly to bring fresh ideas and new perspectives to a profession undergoing massive changes. PLI's leadership under President Sharon Crane is a beacon during an exciting but foggy time as legal professionals at all levels seek to chart a new future.

And to Lori Wood, for your patience, encouraging feedback, and steady hand in guiding a first-time author from rough draft to finished book. What could have been a very intimidating experience was, because of you, genuinely delightful.

How to Use This Book

This is not a traditional business book. It is not designed to be an academic treatise or easy step-by-step guide to change in a law firm. And there are no promises of transformation in thirty days. Instead, you're about to spend a week inside a law firm wrestling with questions that have no easy answers.

Unprecedented follows the partners, associates, and staff of McNamee, Weiss & Oh as they gather for a five-day retreat to confront an uncomfortable truth: the model that made their firm successful is breaking down. Through their conversations, conflicts, and occasional breakthroughs, you'll encounter real frameworks for change, including design thinking, empathy mapping, innovation tournaments. Through the story, these models are embedded in the messy human reality of people trying to transform while still serving clients, managing egos, and protecting what they've built.

Why a Story?

Change is hard, and reading about change frameworks in the abstract rarely makes it easier. What helps is seeing how real people, who sound like your colleagues, who share your doubts, who protect the same practices as your firm leaders, navigate the gap between knowing they need to change and actually doing it.

Julian Justice isn't a hero. He's a managing partner who isn't sure he's doing the right thing. Lucy Lex isn't a guru. She's a facilitator who worries constantly that her design is too ambitious. William Klept isn't a villain. He's a rainmaker who built tremendous value under the old rules and doesn't want to see it redistributed. By following these characters through their week, you'll see your own firm's dynamics reflected. And perhaps you'll find new ways to think about your own transformation challenges.

How to Read This Book

You can read *Unprecedented* in several ways:

As a straight narrative: Follow the story from Monday morning to Friday afternoon (and six months beyond in the Epilogue). Let the frameworks emerge naturally through the characters' experiences. The appendices to this book provide additional detail about the characters and the main takeaways from each chapter.

As a workshop companion: If you're planning your own retreat or transformation initiative, use the chapters as a preview of what different sessions might look like. The ***Reader Reflection*** questions that appear at the end of many chapters can become discussion prompts for your team. For your convenience and to stimulate your own retreat ideas, you can find the agenda for the weeklong firm retreat that Lucy designed in Appendix B at the end of the book.

As a book club selection: The chapter-end ***Reader Reflection*** questions are designed to spark conversation. A leadership team reading this together will find plenty to debate, especially around compensation, associate development, and the tension between individual achievement and collective success.

As a reference: The ***Cast of Characters*** (see Appendix C) and the ***Bibliography*** let you dip in and out. If you're interested in a specific topic, like AI's impact on firms, you can skip to chapter 9. If you want to see how the characters think through changes to partner compensation, chapter 17 is waiting. For easy reference, the ***Main Takeaways*** in Appendix A summarize each chapter's major points.

About the Reader Reflections

The ***Reader Reflection*** questions aren't comprehension questions; you won't find the answers by re-reading the chapter. They're designed to help you connect what you've read to your own organization's reality.

Some questions will feel immediately relevant. Others might not apply to your situation. That's fine. The goal isn't to answer every question but to find the ones that make you uncomfortable. Those are probably the ones worth sitting with.

What This Book Won't Do

This book won't give you a paint-by-numbers guide to transforming your firm. McNamee, Weiss & Oh is fictional, and what works for them might not work for you. The Epilogue makes clear that even with the best intentions, transformation is messy, partial, and ongoing.

But it might give you something more valuable than a template: permission to try. Permission to run a retreat that asks hard questions. Permission to prototype ideas before they're perfect. Permission to fail at some initiatives while succeeding at others. Permission to believe that the culture you want to build is worth fighting for, even when the easier path is right in front of you.

One Last Thing

As you read, pay attention to which character you identify with. Are you Julian, the managing partner, carrying the weight of decisions that affect everyone? Lucy, the firm's Chief Information Officer, pushing for change while worrying she's asking too much? Robert, a senior partner, skeptical but open to being convinced? William, another skeptical partner, protecting what he's built? Jessica, a senior associate, wondering if there's a future for her at the firm?

The answer might tell you something about where you are in your own transformation journey, and what you need to move forward.

Prologue

In 1906, Paul Cravath became the authoritative head of the firm that would become Cravath, Swaine & Moore. He developed the "Cravath System" that defined the core of most large American law firm business models for over a hundred years.

* * *

On November 30, 2022, OpenAI CEO Sam Altman hovered over his laptop and hit post, sharing this message with his followers: "today we launched ChatGPT. try talking with it here: http://chat.openai.com."

Chapter 1

The Reckoning

Julian Justice had built his career on certainty. Twenty-eight years at McNamee, Weiss & Oh, eight as managing partner, and he could read the firm's vital signs like the back of his hand. Revenue per lawyer, profit per partner, associate utilization rates, and client retention metrics. The numbers had always told a story he understood. Until now.

He stared at the spreadsheet glowing on his monitor on January 27, 2027, at 11:47 p.m., the Charlotte office empty except for the security guard and the soft hum of computers that never slept. The numbers should have been reassuring. Gross revenue was holding steady. The firm's 300 lawyers across fifteen offices had billed nearly $325 million this fiscal year. By traditional measures, McNamee Weiss was thriving.

But Julian had learned to read between the lines, and what he saw there kept him awake at night.

The realization rate, or percentage of billed hours that clients actually paid, had dropped from 92% to 82% over the past eighteen months. At first, he'd attributed it to the usual belt-tightening. Clients had been scrutinizing bills more carefully since all the way back in 2008, and the pandemic had only intensified their focus on efficiency. But this felt different.

But the client feedback was more pointed and attributable to a very specific dynamic now. "Our AI completed a similar analysis in two hours," one pharmaceutical GC had written in response to a $28,000 research memo. "Your team's work is thorough, but we're struggling to justify the time your lawyers spent on it." Another client had questioned why due diligence for a relatively straightforward acquisition had required six associates when their internal AI could flag issues in minutes. In other cases, clients complained about confusing handoffs from one attorney to another or delays in communications. As technology improved while lateral hiring accelerated, clients were feeling lost in the shuffle, frustrated by what they perceived as decreasing quality and increasing rates.

The budget conversations had become downright contentious. All law firms were accustomed to conversations about lower rates, but these conversations were different. Clients were now setting matter budgets based on AI benchmarks. "Our systems estimate this should require forty hours of attorney time, not eighty," had become a common refrain. When Julian and his colleagues pushed back, explaining the nuances that AI missed, the complexities that required human judgment, they were often met with polite but firm responses: "We understand, but we need to see more efficiency."

The associate utilization crisis was perhaps the most immediate concern. Junior lawyers, traditionally the engine of law firm profitability, were struggling to find enough substantive work. Clients were increasingly handling preliminary research, initial document drafts, and basic due diligence in-house with AI tools that seemed to become more sophisticated by the hour. What remained was complex, high-level work that clients expected partners to handle personally, but at a fraction of the total engagement value.

Julian's cell phone glowed with a text from Sandy Miller, managing partner at Wagner, Lee & Morse: "Any thoughts on our conversation last week? The offer stands, but timing matters. Happy to discuss next steps whenever works for you."

The merger offer. Seven hundred fifty lawyers, prestigious New York and Los Angeles offices, a sophisticated financial services practice that would complement McNamee's environmental and regulatory focus. On paper, it was a perfect fit. The combined firm would give McNamee Weiss the scale to compete with the true global players, the resources to invest in cutting-edge technology, and the geographic footprint to serve its clients' growing global ambitions seamlessly.

And it was also the end of everything Julian loved about his firm.

The firm had been founded in 1960 by three WWII veterans who believed that excellent legal work could be delivered with genuine care for clients and respect for lawyers' lives outside the office. That ethos had survived the growth of the 1980s, the dot-com boom and bust, the 2008 financial crisis, and even the pandemic's upheaval. McNamee Weiss lawyers stayed. Clients stayed. The professionals knew and cared about one another. One of the stories the firm loved to tell was of a client who sent an embroidered blanket to a female partner who was on leave after adopting a baby, a counter tale to the horror stories of BigLaw chewing up and spitting out women who chose to start families. The culture was collaborative rather than competitive, progressive rather than traditional, family-friendly in ways that most firms only pretended to be.

Wagner, Lee & Morse was different. Prestigious, profitable, and relentlessly ambitious. Their lawyers were brilliant, but Julian had heard the stories about hundred-hour weeks, associates burning out before their third year, partners who measured success solely in billable hours and profits per equity partner. Sure, their partners owned second homes in the Hamptons, but few of the partners who owned them could even enjoy them as they were married to the all-consuming need to generate more and more business. The culture that had made McNamee Weiss special would disappear into Wagner's machine within eighteen months of the merger, if not sooner.

But what choice did Julian have? The financial pressures were real and accelerating. Julian felt like he was trying to outrun a tidal wave and he was growing tired. If the trends continued, McNamee would face the same fate as dozens of mid-sized firms over the past decade: steady decline, lateral defections, and eventual absorption by a larger competitor on less favorable terms.

He closed the spreadsheet and walked down the hall toward the innovation lab. Lucy Lex often worked late, and he could see light spilling from under her office door. He knocked softly.

"Come in," came the familiar voice.

Lucy looked up from her laptop, her LinkedIn profile glowing on the screen. She quickly minimized the window, but not before Julian caught sight of job postings for positions like "Director of Innovation, Healthcare Technology Startup" and "Chief Operating Officer, Legal Tech Company."

"Burning the midnight oil, too?" Julian asked, settling into the chair across from her desk.

"Just doing some reading," Lucy said, though they both knew better. "You?"

"Running numbers. Again." Julian rubbed his temples. "Lucy, I need to ask you something, and I need you to be completely honest with me."

She leaned back in her chair, studying his face. In the eight years since she'd moved from the litigation department to lead the firm's innovation efforts, she'd learned to read Julian's moods well. This wasn't his usual late-night check-in.

"How much time do you think we have?" he asked.

"Before what?"

"Before we're forced to make a choice we don't want to make."

Lucy was quiet for a long moment. She'd been tracking the same trends Julian had. She had sensed the growing client pushback, the associate utilization problems, the growing sophistication of AI tools that were reshaping how legal work got done. But she'd also been watching her colleagues' responses to these changes. They were in denial, focused on incremental adjustments, wrapped in the belief that legal services are too special to be disrupted and hoping that traditional approaches would again allow them to weather another upheaval.

"If we keep doing what we're doing?" she said finally. "Two years. Maybe three if we're lucky."

Julian nodded slowly. It matched his own assessment.

"Sandy Miller reached out again today," he said. "Wagner wants to move forward with the merger talks."

Lucy's stomach dropped. She'd known this was coming and had been expecting it for months, but hearing Julian say it out loud made it real. "What did you tell her?"

"That I needed more time to think." Julian stood and moved to the window, looking out at the Charlotte skyline. "But the truth is, I don't think time is going to change the fundamentals. Either we find a way to transform this firm into something that can compete in the world that's coming, or we accept that our best option is to become part of someone else's vision."

"And you're leaning toward the merger."

"I'm leaning toward keeping this firm alive," Julian said. "Whether that's through merger or miracle, I honestly don't know anymore."

Lucy had spent the last fifteen years thinking about transformation. She had studied design thinking, innovation frameworks, change management principles that other industries had used to navigate disruption. She'd run workshops, built prototypes, launched pilot programs. All valuable, all incremental, all insufficient for the scale of change that was coming.

"What if we had one chance to really do it?" she asked. "To build the firm we've always talked about building?"

Julian turned back to her. "What do you mean?"

"I mean what if we stopped thinking about innovation as something we do on the margins and started thinking about it as fundamental redesign? What if we took everything we've learned about what's broken in law firms, from the billable hour to the associate development model to the way we structure partnerships to how we price our services to how we work with clients, all of it . . . and built something completely different?"

"Lucy, we've talked about this before. The partners—"

"Would resist. I know. They always have." Lucy stood and began pacing, her mind racing through possibilities she'd been sketching for years. "But what if we could show them that transformation is about building something better, not about surviving the next downturn or tech advancement? It's something that serves clients better, develops lawyers better, and creates more sustainable careers?"

Julian watched her carefully. Lucy's passion for reimagining legal practice had always been one of her greatest strengths and, from a partnership perspective, one of her biggest liabilities. She pushed too hard, moved too fast, challenged too many revered assumptions. But she also saw possibilities that others missed.

"What would that look like?" he asked.

Lucy stopped pacing and looked directly at him. "Give me four weeks to design a retreat. Not a weekend planning session or a half-day strategic discussion. A real retreat. We need five days, mandatory attendance for all of the firm's committees. Every member of our leadership teams and committees."

"Lucy . . ."

"Let me build the programming I've always wanted to build," she continued, her voice gaining momentum. "A deep dive into how we got to the structures that constrain us, from the history of legal education to the rise of the billable hour, and the fundamental and irreversible leverage shift between firms and their clients. Show them how design thinking holds the key to developing empathy-based client services, how AI impacts everything lawyers do and how to elevate the human superpowers of lawyers. Reimagining the associate development program of the future, structuring strong change leadership programs, redesigning succession planning. Everything."

Lucy felt her pace quicken and she knew she was getting a bit overexcited. But she also knew everything she was saying was exactly why firms like McNamee Weiss were in the position they were. All the deferred modernization had made them vulnerable and she wanted the chance to fix it.

Julian was quiet for a long moment, weighing the risks. A week-long retreat would cost significant money, disrupt client service, and potentially expose the firm's vulnerabilities to competitors if word got out. But the alternative of a slow decline or absorption into Wagner's culture felt worse.

"And if it doesn't work?" he asked. "If we go through this process and the partners decide they'd rather stick with the status quo or go through with the merger?"

"Then we'll know we tried," Lucy said. "And you can call Sandy with a clear conscience."

Julian looked around Lucy's office. He saw whiteboards covered with innovation frameworks, a bookshelf filled with design thinking guides and business transformation case studies, a wall of client feedback that Lucy used to fuel her improvement projects. She'd been preparing for this moment for fifteen years, even if neither of them had realized it.

"All right. One week," he said finally. "But Lucy, I need you to understand something, and I'm not trying to add undue pressure here. But this can't just be an innovation session. We need to help our colleagues see this is about the survival of everything we've built here. If we're going to do this, we have to do it right. I'll help you, but we need to bring in other voices, too, to underscore the urgency of what we're facing and to lend legitimacy to our message. The message can't just come from inside the house."

Lucy was already reaching for her notebook, her mind spinning through the retreat design that had been taking shape in her head for years. She'd been studying these topics for what felt like forever. The more she learned about the history of the profession, the psychology of change, the frameworks that other industries had used to reinvent themselves, the more she knew how poorly the legal industry was designed to do what it was intended to do: serve clients and develop lawyers. She'd always wanted the runway to put it all into motion so other people could do it too and build something better. Now was her chance to do it with people she cared about in the firm where she had grown up as a professional.

"I know you've put so much thought into what a law firm could look like if you could build it from scratch," Julian continued, "and we've only been able to move the needle so much within our current structure. But now . . ."

"Now we get to find out what's possible," Lucy finished.

As Julian headed back to his office, Lucy opened a new document and began typing: "McNamee, Weiss & Oh Transformation Retreat: A Blueprint for the Future."

Outside her window, Charlotte slept. But inside the innovation lab, the future of the firm, whatever that would be, was just beginning to take shape.

Reader Reflection

What This Means for Your Firm

The pressures facing McNamee, Weiss & Oh are the same forces reshaping every law firm today. If you're reading this story and recognizing familiar challenges in your own practice, you're not alone. Change has arrived in the legal industry. How will you respond as a practitioner, practice group leader, business department chair, or firm leader?

1. **What would your firm's "spreadsheet at midnight" reveal?** Are your realization rates, associate utilization numbers, and client feedback telling a story you're ready to hear?

2. **What's your merger offer?** Every firm faces the choice between transformation and consolidation. What external pressures or opportunities are forcing your hand?

3. **Who is your Lucy?** Innovation requires champions who can see beyond current constraints. Does your firm have leaders positioned to design and drive fundamental change?

4. **How much time do you really have?** Julian and Lucy estimated two or three years. What's your honest assessment of your firm's runway for transformation?

The retreat Lucy is about to design is a story device, but it's also a roadmap. The frameworks, case studies, and practical tools that emerge from McNamee Weiss's week of intensive planning can be adapted to your firm's unique culture, practice areas, and challenges. Throughout the book, exercises and reflection questions will provide you with ways you can adapt the work Lucy will lead at McNamee Weiss to your own context.

Chapter 2

The Call to Action

The next morning, Julian sent an email to everyone in the firm who held a leadership role.

FROM: Julian Justice jjustice@mcnameeweissoh.com

TO: All Chairs—McNamee, Weiss & Oh; All Committees—McNamee, Weiss & Oh

DATE: February 4, 2027

SUBJECT: Mandatory Retreat for Firm Leaders: Designing Our Future

Dear Colleagues,

As we approach the close of our fiscal year, I want to share some thoughts about where our firm stands and where we need to go.

McNamee, Weiss & Oh has weathered significant changes over the past two decades. Together, we've navigated the 2008 financial crisis, the pandemic's disruption of how we work, the evolution of client expectations, and the emergence of new competitive pressures. Through each of these challenges, we've adapted while preserving what makes our firm special: our commitment to excellent client service, our collaborative culture, and our belief that practicing law should be both professionally rewarding and personally sustainable.

Today, we face what I believe is the beginning of a new era for law firms. The convergence of artificial intelligence, changing workforce expectations, hybrid work models, regulatory shifts, and evolving client demands is reshaping the legal industry in ways that demand solutions that go far beyond incremental adjustment. Some of you have already experienced this directly in client conversations about efficiency, in questions about billing practices, and in the changing nature of the work we're being asked to do.

Rather than respond to these changes reactively, we have an opportunity to lead. Instead of waiting to see what the industry becomes, we can help shape it.

To that end, I am announcing a mandatory retreat for firm professionals who serve in roles on our various committees scheduled for March 8–12, 2027, at The Omni Grove Park Inn in Asheville. Every attorney and business leader on a committee in the firm will participate. This is not optional, and it is not a traditional strategic planning session. This is an intensive, week-long program designed to reimagine how we deliver legal services, develop our people, and build sustainable competitive advantage.

Why a Full Week?

Real change requires real commitment. The challenges we face are too complex for quick fixes or surface-level adjustments. We need time to understand how we got to where we are, examine successful transformation models from other industries, and develop a comprehensive blueprint for our future. This retreat will be intensive by design because the stakes demand nothing less.

The Program

Lucy Lex, our Chief Innovation Officer, has designed a comprehensive curriculum that will challenge our assumptions while providing practical frameworks for change. The week will include:

- **Historical Context:** Understanding how legal education, firm structures, and pricing models evolved and why those legacy systems may no longer serve us
- **External Forces:** Analysis of the five key drivers reshaping our industry and their implications for how we practice

- **Design Thinking Workshop:** Learning human-centric innovation approaches that have transformed other professional services industries
- **AI and the Future of Legal Work:** A non-technical literacy experience to help us think about how to leverage this shape-shifting technology while elevating our uniquely human legal skills
- **Reimagining Associate Development:** Building career paths that align with both firm needs and modern practitioner expectations
- **New Economic Models:** Exploring alternatives to billable hour pricing that better align our interests with client outcomes
- **Change Leadership:** Developing the skills and mindsets needed to guide transformation at every level of the firm

What This Means

This retreat represents a significant investment of our firm time, resources, and intellectual energy. We are doing this because I believe McNamee Weiss has the potential to become a model for what law firms can be in the next decade. But that potential will only be realized if we're willing to examine our practices honestly and commit to the fundamental change the future demands.

Some of you may be skeptical about the need for such comprehensive change. Others may worry about the disruption to client service or the time away from billable work. I understand those concerns, but I ask you to consider the inadequacy of the alternative of continuing with incremental adjustments while the foundation of our industry shifts beneath us.

Your Role

Come prepared to think differently. Bring your best ideas, your toughest questions, and your willingness to challenge assumptions, including your own. Do not expect pronouncements from me or anyone else about how we should change. The truth is no single person has the answer to that question. These are complex challenges that require the collaborative design of a shared future.

Lucy will be sending additional details about logistics, pre-work assignments, and what to expect. Block your calendars now.

Arrange for client coverage. This is the most important week our firm will spend this year. I know I am asking for a great deal from you. I hope you know how crucial this time together is to warrant such a request.

The legal profession is changing whether we participate or not. Our choice is whether to help lead that change or simply hope to survive it. I believe we can do better than survive, I believe we can thrive. But only if we're willing to do the work.

See you in Asheville.

Julian

P.S. For those wondering about precedent, there isn't any. We've never attempted anything quite like this. That's exactly why we all need to be together and fully engaged.

As Julian's email landed in inboxes across fifteen offices, reactions ranged from excitement to anxiety to outright resistance. In conference rooms and hallways, around coffee machines and in Slack channels, the conversations began immediately. Senior partners questioned the cost and timing. Associates wondered if this signaled layoffs or expansion. Parents agonized over childcare coverage. Practice group leaders worried about client reactions to a week of reduced availability.

But in her innovation lab, Lucy was already deep into retreat design, her whiteboards filled with session outlines, learning objectives, and facilitation notes.

The email was just the beginning. The real work would start in Asheville.

Chapter 3

Welcome to the Retreat

The March morning was cold and bright as the first attendees made their way into the Sunset Terrace breakfast area, most clutching coffee cups and glancing occasionally at the retreat agenda they'd received the night before. The Omni Grove Park Inn's mountain views were spectacular, but few seemed to be admiring the scenery. Instead, conversations clustered around the same questions: What exactly was Julian planning? And what did "designing our future" actually mean?

Robert Kim stood near the coffee station, methodically adding cream to his second cup while scanning the room. As a sixty-two-year-old Real Estate practice group chair, he'd seen plenty of firm retreats. He remembered team-building exercises in the '90s (complete with cringeworthy and liability-inducing "trust falls"), technology workshops in the 2000s, "efficiency initiatives" after 2008, and retreats focused on health, well-being, and belonging in the late 2010s and early 2020s. This agenda felt different, though he couldn't decide if that was good or bad. The phrase "collaborative design" from Julian's email particularly bothered him. In his experience, the best transformations happened quietly, through good work and satisfied clients, not through weeklong workshops with external facilitators. And he *really* didn't think involving associates and counsel made any sense, though he knew he couldn't say that out loud because "radical transparency" and such nonsense was the corporate rallying cry of the day. But what does a second-year associate know about the business of law? Certainly no one asked him *his* opinion when he was at that level, and why should they have?? In reality, most associates wouldn't stick around long enough to be partners, so they could afford to have reckless ideas. What do they care? It's not their money at stake. They'll be long gone when their bad ideas crash and burn. It's the partners left holding the bag.

"Morning, Robert." Dwarkesh Jones approached with a plate of fruit and pastry. At forty-five, Dwarkesh occupied the firm's practical middle. He was old enough to understand the traditional business model, young enough to recognize that something had to change. "Beautiful location for whatever we're about to experience."

"Indeed." Robert took another sip. "Though I notice Lucy's name is all over this agenda. I hope Julian knows what he's doing, putting our Chief Innovation Officer instead of an equity partner in charge of a retreat about the firm's business."

Dwarkesh chose his words carefully. Robert was a major rainmaker, but he could be . . . challenging when he felt the firm was moving too quickly. "I've worked with Lucy on a few client matters. She's thoughtful. Not likely to recommend anything too dramatic."

Before Robert could respond, a burst of laughter drew their attention to a corner table where Alex Rivera was animated in conversation with Priya Patel and Jessica Park. Priya and Jessica were shaking their heads in skeptical disbelief at something Alex had said. At twenty-nine, Alex was an energetic litigation associate who brought an energy that made even breakfast feel like a networking event.

"I'm just saying," Alex was saying to his colleagues, "look at what happened to travel agencies, to bookstores, to taxi companies. Every industry thinks they're different until they're not."

"But law isn't travel booking," Jessica replied, though her tone was more curious than dismissive. At thirty-five and on the cusp of partnership in the firm's corporate group, she'd been asking herself hard questions about the profession lately. Those questions had intensified when she received Julian's email about this retreat. "We're dealing with people's most important problems. That requires judgment, not just efficiency."

Priya, a twenty-eight-year-old tax associate nodded but added, "True, but how much of what we do actually requires that level of judgment? I spent fourteen hours last week reviewing new parts of the tax code for implications in an ongoing deal for a client. A well-trained AI could have flagged the same issues in minutes."

Alex leaned forward. "Exactly! And that's not taking away from lawyering. Getting rid of the mundane stuff a machine could do can free us up to do more actual lawyering. Isn't that why we went to law school in the first place?"

Their conversation was drawing attention from other tables. Sarah Williams, balancing her coffee and a notebook while navigating between chairs, paused to listen. As an employment law partner and working parent, she was always interested in conversations about efficiency. Anything that could give her more time with her family while still serving clients well had her attention. But efficiency alone couldn't help her generate business and serve clients. With a law firm business model and young kids, the math just always seemed torturously unworkable. It seemed too much to hope that this time could be different. Instead, it seemed like the technology would inevitably benefit people without kids . . . again.

Across the room, Tom Brennan sat alone at a small table, working through what appeared to be spreadsheets on his laptop. The firm's CFO rarely looked comfortable at social gatherings, preferring numbers to networking. But these particular numbers were troubling. The projections he and Julian had been exchanging made clear the firm would be facing some difficult decisions in the next two years unless something fundamentally changed.

"Tom, you look like a man who's solving the world's problems before 9 a.m." Maggie McNamee approached with her characteristic warmth. As the granddaughter of one of the name partners and now a partner herself, she'd grown up around the firm and had developed an ability to put people at ease. "Mind if I join you?"

Tom looked up, grateful for the interruption. "Just reviewing some financials. Nothing that a good keynote speaker can't solve, I'm sure."

Maggie smiled as she sat down. "My grandfather used to say that the best solutions usually came from the most unlikely places. Maybe Julian's onto something with this format."

"I hope so. Because the alternative . . ." Tom gestured vaguely at his laptop screen.

Near the windows overlooking the mountains, Lisa Martinez was having a quieter conversation with Michael Solomon. As the Director of Legal Operations, Lisa had implemented dozens of efficiency initiatives over her five years at the firm. Some had succeeded, others had died quiet deaths when partners lost interest. But the scope of this retreat felt different.

"What's your read on all this?" Michael asked. As a counsel-level attorney who'd been at the firm for eight years, he'd positioned himself as someone who understood both the associate perspective and partner concerns. It was a useful place to be, though sometimes it left him feeling like he didn't belong fully in either camp.

"Honestly? I think Julian's more serious about change than he's ever been," Lisa replied. "The fact that he made this mandatory for all committee members, brought in outside facilitators, booked a week away from the office . . . this isn't a symbolic gesture."

Michael nodded thoughtfully. "The question is whether everyone else is ready for serious change."

They both glanced around the room, taking in the various conversations and clusters. Some people looked energized, others wary, most somewhere in between.

As 9:00 approached, people began gravitating toward the main conference room. The mountain views were beautiful, but everyone's real focus was Julian's vision for the firm's future.

Reader Reflection

Identifying Your Role

As the retreat begins, we see characters adopting different postures toward the week ahead.

1. **Which character represents you?** Are you the Skeptic (Robert), the Realist (Tom), the Optimist (Maggie), or the eager Futurist (Alex)?

2. **The Breakfast Conversation:** If your firm held a mandatory retreat tomorrow, what would be the dominant topic of conversation at the coffee station? Excitement about the future, or cynicism about "another management initiative"?

Chapter 4

The Keynote

Julian Justice stood at the front of the conference room, looking out at sixty-three faces that represented the leadership backbone of McNamee, Weiss & Oh. Partners, associates, counsel, key business leaders. The group gathered represented everyone who would need to be part of whatever came next. The morning sun streamed through the floor-to-ceiling windows, casting long shadows across the room, and Julian found himself thinking that this was either the beginning of something extraordinary or the most expensive mistake of his eight-year tenure as managing partner.

He'd rehearsed this speech a dozen times, but now, facing his colleagues in person, he wasn't sure how his words would land.

"Good morning," he began, his voice carrying the authority that had made him a successful litigator and trusted leader. "Thank you for being here. I know this represents a significant investment of time for all of you, and I don't take that lightly."

He paused, scanning the room. Robert Kim sat with his arms crossed, but his attention was focused. Maggie McNamee leaned forward slightly, her expression encouraging. The younger attorneys, including Alex, Priya, Jessica, looked alert and curious. Tom Brennan had closed his laptop. All eyes were fixed on Julian.

"Eight years ago, when I became managing partner, just as we were about to face the chaos of the pandemic, I thought I understood the challenges facing our profession. Economic uncertainty, client pressure on fees, generational differences in work expectations. I believed that with good leadership, sound financial management, and continued excellence in client service, we could navigate whatever changes came our way."

Julian moved away from the podium, a habit from his courtroom days. "I was partially right. We have navigated those challenges. Our revenue has grown. Our client satisfaction scores remain strong. By most measures, McNamee, Weiss & Oh is a successful firm."

He let that sink in for a moment. "But success in 2020 doesn't guarantee success in 2030. And the forces reshaping our profession are both multiplying and accelerating."

On the screen behind him, a simple timeline appeared, showing five major disruptions to legal practice over the past twenty years.

"The 2008 financial crisis changed the relationship between law firms and general counsel forever. Clients learned they could demand more for less, and we learned that our traditional pricing models weren't as unassailable as we'd believed."

Several heads nodded. Many in the room remembered those years.

"The growth of the most intergenerational workforce in history has challenged every assumption about career progression, work-life integration, and what motivates talented lawyers to stay and thrive at a firm."

Julian saw Sarah Williams glance at Jessica Park, both working parents navigating different stages of career and family integration. They had commiserated frequently about the impossibility of trying to balance success in a law firm with the demands of caregiving.

"The COVID pandemic forced us to discover that much of what we do can happen remotely, undermining a business model built on physical proximity, apprenticeship learning, and shared cultural spaces.

"Regulatory changes in some jurisdictions and ambitious, VC-backed entrepreneurial endeavors, and rapidly growing interest of private equity investment in law firms, have opened doors for alternative business structures that can compete directly with traditional law firms for corporate legal work."

Julian paused at the fifth point on his timeline. "And now, generative artificial intelligence is challenging fundamental assumptions about how legal work gets done, how we develop lawyers, and what clients are willing to pay for."

He clicked to the next slide: a simple graph showing the exponential improvement in AI capabilities over the past few years.

"Three months ago, I asked our largest client what percentage of their routine legal work they thought could be handled by AI within the next five years. The answer was 60%. Not 60% assisted by AI; 60% handled *primarily* by AI, with lawyer oversight."

A murmur went through the room.

"Two weeks ago, I had coffee with the managing partner of a firm similar to ours in Chicago. They've just announced they're laying off 30% of their associates and reimagining their leverage model entirely. Not because business is down, but because the nature of the work is changing faster than their business model can adapt and they want to adapt for the future."

Julian returned to the center of the room. "We have choices to make. We can continue to operate as we have, making incremental adjustments and hoping that our reputation and relationships will carry us through whatever comes next."

He looked directly at Tom Brennan. "Tom has run the numbers on that approach. The projections aren't encouraging."

Tom nodded grimly. "If the current trends of client fee pressure, efficiency expectations, and AI adoption in other firms continue, we're looking at a steep revenue decline, maybe as much as 15–20%, over the next three years, assuming we maintain our current cost structure."

The room was completely quiet now.

"Or," Julian continued, "we can choose to be architects of our own future. We can decide what kind of firm we want to be in an AI-augmented world, what kinds of value we want to create for clients, and how we want to develop and retain the best legal talent."

He gestured toward Lucy, who was seated near the front. "A month ago, I went to Lucy's office and asked for her help in designing a process that would let us reimagine our firm's future together. Because I don't have all the answers, and I believe our best answers will come from this room and from your collective wisdom and creativity."

Julian clicked to a final slide: a simple question mark.

"We cannot ask whether our profession is changing. I know lawyers are natural skeptics and I know I've asked you to bring your questions and skepticism with you this week, and I meant it. But this is the one question I don't want to spend time debating. Everything from our firm financials to our client conversations to our conversations with new talent show clear change. So now the question is whether we'll lead that change or be shaped by it. Whether we'll make thoughtful, strategic choices about our future, or have those choices made for us by market forces we failed to respond to when they were all around us."

He looked around the room one more time. "Over the next five days, we're going to explore what it means to build a law firm for 2030 and beyond. We're going to challenge assumptions, experiment with new ideas, and yes, we're going to be uncomfortable sometimes. Because comfortable doesn't get us where we need to go."

Julian smiled slightly. "I've spent eight years as your managing partner trying to preserve what makes this firm special. This week, I'm asking you to help me take what makes us special and adapt it for a changed world. Because the best way to honor what we've built is to ensure it survives and thrives in whatever comes next."

The room was silent for a moment, then Maggie McNamee began applauding. Others joined in, though Julian noticed the applause was thoughtful rather than enthusiastic. That was exactly what he'd hoped for. Enthusiasm could fade by Tuesday afternoon. Thoughtful engagement would carry them through the week.

"Lucy," Julian said, turning to his Chief Innovation Officer, "I believe it's time to begin."

Reader Reflection

The Case for Change

Julian presented a timeline of disruption following his "Spreadsheet at Midnight" reality check about his firm's health.

1. **Your "Spreadsheet at Midnight":** If you looked beyond your firm's gross revenue, what "hidden" metric would keep you awake at night? (e.g., realization rates, associate attrition, client loyalty, or tech adoption).
2. **The Five Forces:** Of the five forces Julian outlined (2008 Aftershocks, Intergenerational Workforce, Pandemic/Hybrid Work, Regulatory Change, Generative AI), which one is currently exerting the most pressure on your specific practice group?
3. **The Choice:** Julian framed the retreat as a choice between being "architects of the future" or "victims of market forces." Can you identify one specific area where your firm is currently letting external forces dictate your strategy?

Chapter 5

Leading Change—ADKAR in Our Firm

Lucy Lex stood where Julian had been just moments before, but her presence filled the space differently. Where Julian commanded attention through authority and gravitas, Lucy invited engagement through curiosity and possibility. Julian had donned a blazer, but Lucy wore a sweater and jeans, a small signal that the formal presentation portion of their time together was over.

"Thank you, Julian," she began, her voice warm but purposeful. "Before we dive into the work ahead of us this week, I want to share something with you. Every successful transformation I've studied, whether in law firms, in other professional services, or in completely different industries, follows a surprisingly similar pattern. Not because someone planned it that way, but because human beings change in predictable ways."

She clicked to her first slide: a simple graphic showing five connected stages.

"We're going to learn a framework developed by change management expert Jeffrey Hiatt called ADKAR this week because it gives us a common language for the journey we're on together. As Hiatt notes, organizations don't change; people do, and ADKAR tells us the process through which people change."

Lucy moved away from the screen, making eye contact around the room. "ADKAR stands for Awareness, Desire, Knowledge, Ability, and Reinforcement. It's how individuals move through change, and since organizations are made up of individuals, it's how organizations change too."

She paused, scanning faces. Some looked intrigued, others politely attentive. Robert Kim was taking notes, which surprised her.

"But what resonates for me about this framework is how familiar it is. Every major change we've successfully navigated in our lives has followed this pattern."

Lucy clicked to the next slide, showing the five stages with brief descriptions:

- **Awareness**: Understanding why change is necessary
- **Desire**: Wanting to participate and support the change
- **Knowledge**: Knowing how to change
- **Ability**: Having the skills and behaviors to implement change
- **Reinforcement**: Sustaining the change over time

"Julian just spent fifteen minutes building awareness," Lucy continued. "He showed us data, trends, and consequences. He helped us understand why change isn't optional anymore. We'll continue building awareness this week through our guest speakers, but awareness alone doesn't create transformation."

She gestured toward the tables where people were seated in groups of six to eight, mixing partners, counsel, associates, and business professionals across practice areas and seniority levels.

"So we're going to start with something that has changed for us at the individual level to remind ourselves of the many ways we are constantly changing. Because before we can lead change in our firm, we need to understand how change actually works in our own lives."

Lucy distributed a worksheet to each table. "I want you to think about a significant change you've made in the past five years. It could be something professional, like changing practice areas, joining this firm, taking on a leadership role. Or it could be personal, like moving cities, getting married, having children, learning a new skill. Something that mattered to you and required you to be different than you were before."

Personal Change Reflection

Think of a significant change you successfully navigated in the past 5 years.

1. **What was the change?**
2. **What made you first realize change was necessary? (Awareness)**
    - What information or experience created the "aha" moment?
    - How long did it take you to fully understand why change was needed?
3. **What made you want to make the change? (Desire)**
    - What were you moving toward? Moving away from?
    - Who or what influenced your motivation?
    - How or why did you overcome your natural resistance to changing?
4. **How did you figure out what to do differently? (Knowledge)**
    - Where did you get information about how to change?
    - Who helped you understand the new way of being/doing?
5. **What was hardest about actually implementing the change? (Ability)**
    - What new skills did you have to develop?
    - What old habits did you have to break?
    - What support did you need?
6. **How do you maintain the change now? (Reinforcement)**
    - What keeps you from sliding back to the old way?
    - How do you measure success in the new way?

"Take about ten minutes to work through this individually," Lucy instructed. "Then I want you to share your stories at your tables. Not just the what, but the how. How did change actually happen for you?"

The room filled with the rustle of papers and the quiet scratching of pens. Lucy walked among the tables, noting the concentration on faces, the occasional smile as someone remembered a particularly meaningful transition.

At Table 3, Robert Kim was writing steadily. His change, he realized as he reflected, had been becoming chair of the real estate group five years ago. He'd resisted the role initially, preferring his client work to administrative responsibilities. But the firm had needed his leadership, and gradually he'd discovered he was actually better at developing younger lawyers than he had expected and he enjoyed building something larger than his individual practice.

Two tables over, Priya Patel was thinking about her decision to specialize in tax law during her second year. She'd initially planned on corporate work, but a rotation in the tax group had opened her eyes to the intellectual complexity and constant evolution of the field. The change had required learning an entirely new vocabulary and way of thinking about business problems.

Jessica Park found herself writing about becoming a working parent. The change had forced her to become more efficient, more strategic about which projects to take on, and more intentional about building systems that didn't depend solely on her physical presence.

As the ten minutes concluded, Lucy called for attention. "Now comes the real learning. Share your stories at your tables. But I want you to listen for patterns. How did awareness happen for people? What created desire? Where did knowledge come from?"

The room transformed into many small conversations, voices rising with engagement, recognition, and even some laughter.

At Table 1, Alex Rivera was explaining his decision to leave a BigLaw firm for McNamee, Weiss & Oh. "The awareness was gradual," he said. "But the desire was sudden—I had one too many nights where I realized I hadn't talked to anyone except other lawyers in three days. I knew I needed to be somewhere that felt more human."

Dwarkesh Jones nodded. "The knowledge piece is interesting. For me, learning to be a lateral partner meant understanding not just the technical work, but the culture, the unwritten rules. That took months."

"And ability is ongoing," added Sarah Williams. "I'm still figuring out how to be the kind of leader I want to be. Some days I nail it, some days I don't."

At Table 5, Michael Solomon was sharing his transition from associate to counsel. "The hardest part was the identity shift," he admitted. "I had to stop thinking like someone climbing toward partnership and start thinking like someone building a different kind of career."

Lisa Martinez leaned forward. "That's exactly what organizations struggle with. The technical changes are usually the easy part. It's the identity and culture shifts that trip people up."

Maggie McNamee, listening to the conversation, found herself thinking about her grandfather's legacy and her own role in preserving versus transforming the firm's culture. "It makes me wonder," she said, "what identity shifts we might be asking people to make this week."

After fifteen minutes of animated discussion, Lucy called the room back together. The energy was noticeably higher than it had been after Julian's keynote. People were leaning back in their chairs, more relaxed but also more engaged.

"What are you noticing?" Lucy asked. "What patterns are emerging?"

Tom Brennan raised his hand. "Awareness often came from outside pressure or a crisis moment. But desire seemed to come from internal drive and seeing a possibility, not just understanding a problem."

"Excellent observation," Lucy responded. "What else?"

Jessica Park spoke up. "Knowledge almost always came from other people. Even when we researched things ourselves, we needed mentors, guides, people who'd done it before."

"And ability took longer than anyone expected," added Dwarkesh Jones. "We kept thinking we'd figured it out, then realizing we had more to learn."

Lucy nodded, moving to her next slide. "These insights are going to be crucial this week. Because now I want you to apply this same framework to our current situation."

She distributed a second worksheet.

ADKAR Assessment: Firm Transformation

Think about the changes Julian described in his keynote.

For each of the following, rate yourself on a scale of 1-5.

AWARENESS

- I understand why our current business model needs to change: ______
- I understand the specific risks of not changing: _____
- I understand the urgency of making changes now rather than later: _____

DESIRE

- I want to be part of creating our firm's future: _____
- I believe the benefits of changing outweigh the risks: _____
- I'm willing to invest time and energy in transformation work: _____

KNOWLEDGE

- I know what our firm should look like in 2035: _____
- I understand what specific changes we need to make: _____
- I know what role I should play in our transformation: _____

ABILITY

- I have the skills needed to work in new ways: _____
- I can adapt my practice to serve clients differently: _____
- I can help others navigate changes successfully: _____

REINFORCEMENT

- I know how we'll measure success in our new model: _____
- I believe our firm will support people through changes: _____
- I'm confident we can sustain changes over time: _____

"Be honest," Lucy said. "This is for your own reflection, not for sharing. But after you complete the assessment, I want you to discuss two questions at your tables: Where do we seem to be strongest as a group? Where do we have the most work to do?"

The room grew quiet again as people worked through the ratings. Lucy noticed different body language this time; people appeared more thoughtful, sometimes uncomfortably shifting in their seats and screwing up their faces as they confronted their own uncertainty.

At his table, Robert Kim found himself surprised by his own responses. His awareness scores were high because Julian's presentation had been compelling and because he'd been in the profession long enough to know it was changing. But his knowledge and ability scores were much lower. He knew change was necessary but felt unclear about what good solutions looked like.

Priya Patel, meanwhile, rated herself high on desire and ability but realized her awareness of the business implications was limited. She understood the technology disruption but not the financial pressures Tom had referenced.

The table discussions revealed fascinating patterns. The younger associates generally scored high on desire and ability but lower on awareness of the broader industry forces. Senior partners had high awareness but more mixed scores on desire and knowledge about specific solutions.

"Time," Lucy called, and conversations gradually subsided. "One insight from each table about our collective strengths and challenges."

Table 1: "We're strong on awareness. Julian's message definitely landed. But we're all over the map on what actually needs to change."

Table 2: "High desire to be part of the solution, but we need more knowledge about what other firms are doing successfully." Lucy rolled her eyes internally. Lawyers *always* want to know what other firms are doing instead of designing their own paths.

Table 3: "The partners feel confident about their ability to adapt, but the associates aren't sure the firm will really support new ways of working."

Table 4: "We're worried about reinforcement. We've seen initiatives launch and then fade when daily pressures take over."

Lucy listened, taking notes on a flip chart. When all tables had reported, she turned back to the group.

"This is exactly where successful transformations begin," she said. "Not with perfect alignment, but with honest assessment and shared commitment to the journey."

She clicked to a final slide showing their week ahead mapped to the ADKAR stages.

"Here's how our five days together will build on what Julian started:

Monday afternoon and Tuesday: We'll continue building awareness with a deep dive into how we got to this moment and the forces driving transformation, then explore what human-centricity really means.

Tuesday and Wednesday: We'll build knowledge by learning design thinking methods and seeing how other organizations have navigated similar changes.

Wednesday and Thursday: We'll develop ability by practicing new approaches to talent development, client service, and business development through empathy, ideation, and prototyping activities.

Friday: We'll create reinforcement systems by planning implementation, assigning responsibilities, and designing accountability measures."

Lucy paused, looking around the room. The faces she saw were more thoughtful than when she'd started, more personally engaged with the challenge ahead.

Priya Patel raised her hand.

"Yes, Priya?," Lucy said.

"Where is the 'D' in our agenda?"

"Ah, the Desire. Maybe I'll toss that question to Julian as we close for the morning."

Julian again faced his colleagues. "Thanks, Lucy, and thank you all for your engagement this morning. As some of you already noted during the exercises, we can equip you with awareness, knowledge, skill building, and work together to create a culture that reinforces change. But the desire is something that has to come from each of you and from all of us. This week is largely about whether we have the desire to do the hard work change requires. And no one can make that decision but you.

"Lucy?," Julian turned the focus back to his chief facilitator.

"Change is hard," she said. "But it's also how we grow. How we become more than we thought we could be. Julian asked us to be architects of our future rather than victims of forces we can't control."

"But," she smiled slyly, "a wise friend once told me, an army crawls on its belly, so first we eat!"

Reader Reflection

Assessing Your Change Readiness

You just walked through the ADKAR model (Awareness, Desire, Knowledge, Ability, Reinforcement).

1. **Locating the Barrier:** Think about a recent failed initiative at your firm (a new software rollout, a diversity initiative, a pricing change). At which stage of ADKAR did it fail? Did you jump to *Ability* (training) before establishing *Desire*?

2. **The "D" Challenge:** As the group noted, *Desire* is the hardest variable to solve. In your firm, what is the single biggest barrier to Desire? Is it compensation incentives, fear of failure, or simple exhaustion?

3. **Your Personal Score:** If you were to rate yourself honestly on the ADKAR scale regarding AI adoption, where is your lowest score? What do you need to raise it?

Chapter 6

What Comes Next

The dining room buzzed with conversation as retreat participants filled their plates from the buffet and found their assigned seats. Lucy had orchestrated the seating carefully to avoid practice group and seniority clusters. Partners found themselves next to second-year associates, litigators sat with corporate attorneys and attorneys with business group colleagues. Everyone was curious about what the afternoon would bring.

At Table 4, Jessica Park was cutting into her salmon while trying to process the morning's revelations. "I keep thinking about those numbers Tom shared," she said to the group. "Major revenue decline if we don't change. That's grim."

Dwarkesh Jones, seated across from her, nodded. "What gets me is how quickly it could happen. I've been assuming we had years to figure this out."

"But figure out what, exactly?" asked Priya Patel, looking around the table. "Julian made the case for change, Lucy gave us a framework for how change happens, but I'm still not clear on what we're actually going to change into."

Alex Rivera leaned forward, energized by the question. "That's what I'm hoping we discover this week. I mean, we can't just decide to become a different kind of firm in five days, but maybe we can figure out what experiments to try."

Michael Solomon, who had been listening quietly, spoke up. "I keep thinking about that client who told Julian 60% of routine legal work could be handled by AI. What does that mean for someone like me? Do I need to completely reinvent my practice?"

Across the room at Table 7, the conversation had taken a more tactical turn. Tom Brennan was explaining the financial projections to a group that included Sarah Williams and two associates from the tax group.

"The challenge isn't just lost revenue," Tom was saying. "It's the timing. If we wait too long to adapt, we'll be making changes from a position of weakness instead of strength."

Sarah Williams nodded. "I've seen that in other contexts. It's much harder to retrain people and restructure when you're under financial pressure."

"So what do you think the solution looks like?" asked one of the associates. "Are we talking about layoffs? Salary cuts? Or is there actually a growth scenario here?"

Tom considered the question carefully. "That's what I'm hoping to understand better this week. Julian seems to think there's a path to growth, but it requires fundamental changes to how we work."

Meanwhile, at Table 2, Robert Kim found himself in an unexpectedly engaging conversation with Lisa Martinez and two younger partners about the practical challenges of transformation.

"I've been through plenty of change initiatives," Robert said, cutting his chicken methodically. "Most of them generate lots of excitement in the short term and then quietly fade away when people get busy with client work."

Lisa Martinez smiled wryly. "That's actually why I'm optimistic about this approach. Hiatt's ADKAR framework Lucy shared recognizes that implementation *is* the hard part. Most change efforts skip right to the 'let's do something different' phase without building the foundation."

"But what's the something different?" pressed one of the younger partners. "I mean, I'm all for innovation, but I need to understand what we're innovating toward."

Robert found himself nodding. "Exactly. I can get behind changing how we work if I understand what we're changing to and why it'll be better for clients."

At the front of the room, Julian sat with Lucy and a few other members of the leadership team, fielding similar questions.

"How much of the solution do you already have in mind?" asked one of the practice group leaders. "Are we here to help you implement a plan, or are we here to create the plan together?"

Julian exchanged a glance with Lucy before answering. "Honestly? We have broad ideas about areas that we think have been broken for some time, but we don't have a blueprint for what replaces them. That's why we're here. I could have announced a set of changes and asked people to implement them, but I don't have the answers and that's not a culture we want to build even if I knew."

Lucy added, "The afternoon sessions are designed to help us understand how our profession evolved to this point and what forces are driving the current disruption. We need to see the bigger picture before we can design our response to it."

"And then what?" the practice leader continued. "Do we vote on changes? Does leadership make the final decisions? How do we actually get from ideas to implementation?"

"That's a great question for Friday," Julian replied. "But I *can* tell you that whatever we decide needs to be something this group can actually execute together. There's no point in designing solutions that nobody's willing to implement."

As lunch wound down, people began clustering in smaller conversations, many gravitating toward the floor-to-ceiling windows overlooking the Blue Ridge Mountains. The morning's sessions had created a shared sense of urgency, but also a shared uncertainty about what came next.

Near the coffee station, Maggie McNamee found herself talking with Alex Rivera and Jessica Park about the generational differences she'd noticed in the morning's discussions.

"I was struck by how differently people responded to Lucy's change assessment," Maggie said. "The associates seemed more focused on whether they'd have the skills to adapt. The partners were more concerned about whether the changes would actually work."

Alex nodded. "I think we're less invested in the current model, so change feels less risky. But you're right that we're worried about our own capabilities. Everything's changing so fast."

Jessica looked thoughtful. "What interests me is that we might need different things from this week. I'm hoping to understand what new career paths might look like." Then she lowered her voice, "but Robert Kim probably wants to know how to preserve what's working as he gets closer to retirement."

"Is that possible?" Alex asked. "Can you preserve culture while changing everything about how you work?"

Maggie smiled. "That's probably the most important question we'll tackle this week."

People began filtering back toward the main conference room. The morning had established why change was necessary and how change happens. Now everyone wanted to know what change might look like and what role they'd play in creating it. But first, Lucy wanted the group to have a shared understanding of how the structures that had led to their current success–and blind spots–had developed.

She stood at the front of the room, watching people take their seats. The afternoon's deep dive into the forces that had brought them to this moment would help them see their situation as part of a larger story of professional transformation. This was the A of the firm's ADKAR journey.

Then tomorrow, they could start imagining their own chapter of that story. As Lucy started, Julian looked around and wondered whether the group would develop the D they needed to undertake change in the years ahead. They wouldn't be able to answer that question this week. Only time would tell.

Chapter 7

How We Got Here—The Evolution of Legal Practice

Lucy addressed the group with a different energy. She was relieved to be stepping back for the afternoon from her role as facilitator as she prepared to introduce their first guest expert. "This afternoon, we're going to do something that might feel like going back to school, which, if you're a nerd like me, might be a lot of fun and a break from the norm" she began. "We're going to examine how the modern law firm became what it is today. Not to assign blame or wallow in criticism, but to understand the forces that shaped our profession so we can make intentional choices about what to preserve and what to evolve."

She smiled. "And because I'm smart enough to know that I'm not the right person to tell this story, I've invited someone who's dedicated his career to understanding the legal profession's evolution."

The screen behind her displayed a name and title: **Professor Ethan Rover, Stanford Law School.**

A man in his early sixties, wearing slacks and a button-down shirt with no tie, walked to the front. His manner was more casual than Julian's or even Lucy's had been. He had the relaxed confidence of someone who spent his days studying institutions rather than running them.

"Thank you, Lucy. And thank you all for inviting me to be part of this conversation." He looked around the room. "I've spent thirty years researching how law firms work, why they resist change, and what happens when they try to evolve. So when Lucy called and described what you're attempting this week, I jumped at the chance to be here."

He clicked to his first slide, which showed a simple timeline stretching from 1870 to 2025.

"The modern law firm you're trying to transform didn't spring up the year you were admitted to the bar, fully formed. It evolved through a series of innovations that solved real problems in their time. But those very innovations now create the interconnected constraints you're struggling against. Indeed, taken together, they serve as a kind of straitjacket that prevents any sort of real change."

The Sacred Distinction: Profession vs. Business

"Let's start with a fundamental question that shapes everything else: Is law a profession or a business?" Rover paused, letting the question hang. "Most of you would probably say 'both,' and you'd be right. But the way we answer that question, and which one we prioritize when they conflict, determines almost every strategic decision law firms make."

He advanced to the next slide, showing images from the late 1800s.

"The legal profession's modern identity crisis traces back to the late nineteenth century. Before then, lawyers were tradespeople. They were skilled, certainly, but not fundamentally different from other commercial service providers. But in the 1870s and 1880s, a movement swept through law."

Robert Kim found himself leaning forward, interested despite himself. He'd never thought much about why the profession was structured the way it was.

"The American Bar Association, founded in 1878, led this movement," Rover continued. "Lawyers worked to distinguish themselves from mere businesspeople. They established that law was a learned profession requiring specialized education, ethical obligations, and self-regulation. Not just anyone could practice law. Lawyers needed credentials, training, and adherence to professional standards.

"This professionalization brought real benefits for lawyers," he said. "They gained social status, commanded higher fees, and enjoyed considerable autonomy. Professional self-regulation meant lawyers, not market forces or government agencies, would determine the standards for practice."

Sarah Williams raised her hand. "But that sounds like it worked well, and we want the public and our clients to be able to trust in our training, expertise, and ethical judgment. Why is that a problem?"

"Excellent question," Rover replied. "Because professionalization also embedded assumptions that increasingly conflict with modern realities and also served as a justification for preventing better ways to serve a broader swath of the marketplace and the public. Professional identity traditionally emphasizes precedent over innovation, autonomy over collaboration, and craft over efficiency."

He clicked to a new slide showing a Venn diagram with "Professional Values" and "Business Imperatives" overlapping.

"Today's law firm leaders often frame this as a choice between ethical integrity and commercial success. But that's a false dichotomy that prevents firms from pursuing strategies that serve both objectives."

He walked away from the podium, his tone becoming more direct. "Consider pricing. Law firms resist outcome-based pricing not because it's inherently unethical, but because professional identity suggests legal work is too complex and valuable to be commoditized. This resistance persists even when clients explicitly request predictable pricing."

Tom Brennan nodded. He'd had this exact conversation with clients countless times.

"There are more insidious problems with the early professionalism efforts, as well. First, much of this credentialing was explicitly and publicly designed to prevent immigrants, racial minorities, and women from entering the field, and, of course, we continue to see the echoes of that structural exclusion to this day."

Professor Rover continued, "And a problem that grew exponentially as the twentieth century unfolded is the civil justice crisis. Remarkably, American lawyers currently address only about 8–10% of American civil level needs. Let that sink in: 8–10%!"

Dwarkesh Jones couldn't help but cry out, "How is that even possible?! What about the other 92%?!"

"It's possible because the public largely has not pressured lawyers to develop better systems, and modern firms have largely been uninterested in serving clients outside of very large corporations. But as Jim Sandman, President Emeritus of Legal Services Corporation, has noted, a heavily regulated profession that enjoys the privilege of self-regulation but fails to serve over 90% of its consumers is a dysfunctional market."

Tom Brennan perked up. As a "non-lawyer" (a term he despised), he always felt intimidated in spite of his business training in conversations with the firm's partners about the opportunities untapped markets created, but he couldn't help himself; his business instincts were kicking into overdrive. "Isn't there a huge opportunity if no one is serving most of the market?"

Professor Rover beamed, "Precisely! This is what business thinking in law is all about. There is *enormous* opportunity, but culture eats strategy for breakfast, as they say, and most firms think they are too "elite" to create new markets to serve, so they continue to fight in the red waters with the rest of the sharks instead of swimming to blue water."

Tom sat a little higher and Julian looked around as he saw the lightbulbs go on for his colleagues. Opportunities for growth are out there, so why had no firm figured out how to capture them? Could his firm actually be that different from the rest?

"Or technology adoption," Rover continued. "Many firms approach legal technology as a necessary evil rather than a tool for better client service. Partially this is because the partnership model and its distribution of profits disincentivizes tech investments, and partially it's because the underlying assumption is that human judgment cannot be systematically enhanced through technology, a view that increasingly puts firms at odds with client expectations."

He returned to the center of the lectern. "Here's the irony: reluctance to embrace business principles doesn't strengthen lawyers' professionalism. It weakens it. A truly client-focused profession would prioritize value over billable hours, invest in systematic quality improvement, and ensure legal services reach a broader swath of the market and society who need them."

The Cravath System: One Firm's Model Becomes an Industry Standard

Rover's next slide showed a black-and-white photograph of Paul Cravath.

"To understand modern law firm structure, you need to understand this man. Paul Cravath took over leadership of what would become Cravath, Swaine & Moore in 1899, and over the course of the next three decades, he revolutionized legal practice by creating the first modern law firm."

He clicked through a series of points:

"Before Cravath, most law firms were loose confederations of individual practitioners. Cravath changed everything by introducing systematic recruiting from elite law schools, intentional apprenticeship-style approaches to developing talent, clear advancement paths, lockstep compensation, and institutional client relationships."

Dwarkesh Jones was taking notes. He'd heard of the Cravath System but never understood its origins.

"These innovations gave Cravath enormous competitive advantages," Rover explained. "The firm could deliver higher-quality service while developing institutional knowledge that transcended any individual lawyer's expertise. The model was so successful that virtually every major law firm adopted some version of it."

He paused, his expression shifting. "But here's the problem: the Cravath System was designed for a very different legal market. And many of its core assumptions now conflict with modern realities."

A new slide appeared: **The Cravath Legacy: Unintended Consequences**.

"First, there's the partnership tournament. The system treats partnership as the natural culmination of legal career development, creating competition among associates for limited partnership positions. This worked when most lawyers stayed at their first firm for entire careers. But in today's lateral movement environment?"

Several heads nodded around the room. The days of people starting with their firm and staying through partnership are rarer and rarer.

"Second, the pyramid problem. The system assumes each partner can manage multiple associates, creating structures that depend on physical proximity, strong mentorship, and relatively leisurely formation timelines for new lawyers. In the modern firm, and especially in hybrid practice and the post-2008 more-for-less environment, partners lack the time and training to mentor well, and associates are rarely physically near senior attorneys and cannot justify billing for work they need to develop skills that lead to partner-level competencies."

Jessica Park felt this viscerally. She loved the firm's culture, especially as compared to tales she heard from peers, but she'd been stunned at the limited feedback and elusive in-person time with partners and even senior associates she had craved when she was a new lawyer. She had friends who had graduated from business school and went through robust training academies in their corporate settings and spent a great deal of time on collaborative learning in B-school where law school and practice frequently felt very isolating and competitive.

"And finally," Rover said, "premium positioning. The system positions law firms as premium service providers for sophisticated clients, creating cultural resistance to serving smaller clients or using technology for routine services. As Tom noted, that 90+% of American civil legal needs that are unmet? That includes many businesses firms are well-positioned to serve. But the elitism baked into law firm culture has become an actual barrier to expanding lines of revenue for firms."

Maggie McNamee raised her hand. "But firms have modified these structures. We have different partnership tiers, alternative career tracks. Isn't that addressing these problems?"

"You're right that firms have adapted," Rover acknowledged. "But ask yourself: do those modifications feel like fundamental reimagining, or like patches on an increasingly outdated foundation?"

The room was quiet. Several people glanced at each other, recognizing the truth of his observation.

The Billable Hour: From Friend to Foe

"Now let's talk about the most consequential innovation in modern legal practice," Rover said, his tone becoming more pointed. "The billable hour."

A collective groan went through the room, followed by nervous laughter.

"I know, I know," Rover smiled. "Nobody likes talking about the billable hour. But understanding how it evolved from a client service improvement to its own clip on the straitjacket is crucial for imagining alternatives."

He displayed a timeline showing the spread of hourly billing from the 1960s through the 1990s.

"Before widespread hourly billing, law firms typically charged through retainers, contingency fees, or fixed fees. Clients were often uncertain about costs, and these arrangements created potential conflicts of interest. Hourly billing emerged as a solution promising greater transparency—clients would pay for exactly the lawyer time their matters required.

"For several decades," he continued, "this worked reasonably well. Corporate clients appreciated transparency. Law firms enjoyed predictable revenue. Lawyers could see direct connections between effort and compensation.

"But," and here his voice hardened slightly, "what began as one billing option among many gradually became the dominant, nearly exclusive, approach to pricing."

Alex Rivera raised his hand. "Why did that happen? If it was just one option, why did it take over?"

"Great question. Several converging factors." Rover clicked through a list:

- **Measurement Convenience**: Hours billed provided simple metrics for evaluating lawyer productivity
- **Revenue Predictability**: Enabled financial planning based on headcount and utilization targets
- **Risk Transfer**: Shifted financial risk from firms to clients
- **Professional Validation**: Reinforced lawyers' self-perception that their time was inherently valuable

"As hourly billing became orthodoxy," Rover explained, "law firms developed increasingly sophisticated systems to support it. Time tracking software, billable hour targets, and productivity metrics. Eventually, the entire infrastructure of legal practice shaped itself around hourly billing."

He paused, looking around the room. "And that's when the problems started."

A new slide appeared: **The Billable Hour's Distortion Effects**.

"First, the efficiency penalty. Hourly billing creates perverse incentives for inefficiency. Lawyers who complete work quickly earn less than those who work slowly. Technology that reduces time required for tasks directly threatens revenue."

Priya Patel shifted uncomfortably. She'd experienced this firsthand. Partners praised her for thorough work even as she wondered if she was being too slow.

"Second, the innovation barrier. R&D activities don't generate billable hours, making it difficult to justify investments in new service delivery methods. Partners who spend time on innovation reduce their personal compensation."

Lisa Martinez caught Lucy's eye across the room. This was exactly the dynamic she fought against constantly.

"Third, client misalignment. While hourly billing initially improved transparency, it now creates fundamental misalignment. Clients want problems solved efficiently and cost-effectively. Firms maximize revenue by maximizing time spent.

"Fourth, talent drain. Billable hour requirements contribute significantly to lawyer dissatisfaction and attrition. Time tracking and hour pressure reduce job satisfaction and contribute to mental health challenges."

Several of the younger attorneys nodded. This was a conversation they'd had privately many times. And all of the working parents with young kids still left at the firm felt this on a cellular level. It was exhausting and unsustainable for many of their peers who had moved on. Indeed, those in the room had developed a "one day at a time" approach to managing the stress or had switched to alternative career paths as the only lifeline.

"And finally, market restriction. Hourly billing makes legal services prohibitively expensive for most individuals and small businesses, artificially limiting the market and creating the civil justice crisis, which began to expand in the 1970s, tracking the rise of the billable hour."

Robert Kim found himself troubled by this analysis. He'd built a successful career around the billable hour. But hearing it described this way made the problems undeniable and made him feel slightly guilty about his leadership in a profession he was proud to be part of.

"So why does it persist?" Rover asked rhetorically. "Because it's become deeply embedded in law firm economics, culture, and identity. Partners who built careers maximizing billable hours naturally resist models that might reduce earning potential. Financial systems, compensation structures, and performance evaluation all assume hourly billing. And almost no lawyers have known another model and therefore have no reason to question it. They've inherited it, so it's become like fluoride in the water. It's omnipresent, pervasive, and now essential to the health of the business. What would happen if we removed it? It could be catastrophic, so we don't dare try."

He looked directly at the audience. "This is what economists call a coordination problem. Everyone would benefit from moving to better systems, but no single actor has sufficient incentive to bear the costs and risks of transition."

Regulatory Frameworks: The Moat Around Innovation

Rover's tone shifted again, becoming more technical. "Now let's talk about why innovation is so difficult even when firms want to change. The regulatory frameworks governing legal practice."

He displayed Model Rule 5.4 on the screen.

"This rule prohibits non-lawyers from owning equity in law firms or sharing legal fees. It reflects legitimate concerns about maintaining lawyer independence and protecting clients. But it also creates systematic barriers to innovation."

He clicked through the implications:

"Law firms can't access external investment capital to fund technology development or rapid expansion. They can't incorporate business expertise or technology knowledge at the ownership level. They can't partner with technology companies or process improvement specialists through ownership structures."

Michael Solomon raised his hand. "But other countries have different rules, right? What happened there?"

"Excellent question," Rover replied. "The UK's Legal Services Act of 2007 created Alternative Business Structures allowing non-lawyer investment. Since then, the UK legal market has seen significant innovation, in the form of technology-enabled service delivery, process standardization, new pricing approaches."

He pulled up a comparison chart showing innovation rates in the UK versus the US.

"The contrast is instructive. Not saying we should simply copy the UK model, as their regulatory approach has its own challenges. But it demonstrates how regulatory frameworks shape what's possible. It's also worth noting that private equity has recently become actively interested in purchasing the back offices of law firms through structures called Managed Services Organizations (MSOs). As commentator Jordan Furlong has noted, private equity raises its own concerns, so outside investments should be carefully scrutinized.

But Arizona is the first state to allow for limited Alternative Business Structures (ABSs) that permit non-lawyer ownership of legal services organizations, so we are seeing a natural experiment begin to play out in that jurisdiction.

The Path Forward

Rover's final slide was simple: **Understanding Enables Choice**.

"Here's why I wanted to share this history with you," he said, his tone shifting to something more personal. "The patterns I've described, from professional identity tensions to the Cravath legacy to the billable hour dominance to regulatory constraints, aren't accidental or easily modified. They reflect more than a century of a profession that was designed well for its day, but which is now under incredible stress."

He walked to the front of the stage, closer to the audience.

"But understanding these constraints also reveals opportunities. The same forces that create resistance to change also create competitive advantages for firms that successfully navigate transformation."

He counted on his fingers: "Cultural differentiation in firms that balance professional values with business innovation can stand out. Talent attraction and recruiting lawyers who increasingly seek firms offering modern approaches. And client value as corporate clients reward firms demonstrating business sophistication alongside legal expertise."

Rover paused, making eye contact around the room.

"I firmly believe that law firm DNA can be modified to meet the accelerating forces facing firms like yours. The question you face is whether you'll take responsibility for driving that evolution or wait for competitive pressures to force change upon you."

He smiled slightly. "Julian brought you here to design your firm's future. I've just explained why that's going to be hard. But hard doesn't mean impossible. It just means you need to be intentional, strategic, and honest about the constraints you're working within."

Lucy returned to the front. "Thank you, Professor Rover. That gives us crucial context for what comes next, an important part of the A in our ADKAR framework."

She looked at the group. "Let's take a fifteen-minute break. When we come back, we're going to examine the five forces converging on our profession right now. These are the forces that make this moment different from every other 'crisis' law firms have faced."

As people stood and stretched, conversations erupted throughout the room. Robert Kim found himself in discussion with Dwarkesh Jones and Tom Brennan about regulatory constraints. Jessica Park and Priya Patel were talking about the billable hour's impact on their careers. Maggie McNamee stood quietly, thinking about her grandfather's legacy and how he might have responded to this analysis.

The history lesson had landed. Now they needed to understand the present forces and imagine a different future.

Chapter 8

The Five Forces of Convergence

After the break, Lucy stood at the front of the room with a different energy than she'd had during the ADKAR session. Professor Rover had provided the historical context. Now it was time to examine the present forces creating urgency for change.

"Professor Rover explained how we got here," Lucy began. "Now we need to understand why this moment is different. Why Julian brought you here now, not five years ago or five years from now."

She clicked to a slide showing five overlapping circles, each labeled with a force: **2008 Financial Crisis**, **Intergenerational Workforce**, **COVID-19 Pandemic**, **Regulatory Change**, and **Generative AI**.

"These are more than random headlines floating through the ether. Each force connects with the others in ways that are fundamentally reshaping the modern law firm. And the fact that they're all colliding simultaneously is what makes this moment unprecedented."

Force One: The 2008 Reset That Never Reset

Lucy's first slide showed a stark graph: legal demand growth before and after 2008.

"The 2008 financial crisis was supposed to be a temporary disruption. A recession we'd bounce back from, like we always had. But something fundamental shifted in the relationship between law firms and their clients."

She walked to the center of the room. "Before 2008, corporate clients generally accepted our pricing, and large annual rate increases with little resistance were normal. Clients trusted us to staff matters as we saw fit. The billable hour was unquestioned."

Robert Kim nodded and smiled, remembering those days. The good old days.

"After 2008, everything changed. Corporate legal departments got more sophisticated. As firms de-equitized in an effort to survive and seasoned partners found themselves in the newly attractive General Counsel's role, they took the opportunity to reshape the way their enterprise used their outside counsel dollars. Having spent their careers sending out the bills, they knew there were savings to be had and hired legal operations professionals, bringing in leaders with MBAs who brought procurement expertise to legal spending. They started tracking metrics, issuing more rigorous RFPs, demanding alternative fee arrangements."

Tom Brennan spoke up. "I remember when we got our first client RFP that asked us to detail our technology stack and efficiency measures. We barely knew how to answer it."

"Exactly," Lucy said. "The client-firm power dynamic permanently shifted. What we call the 'new normal,' where clients have real leverage to demand more for less. This became our reality for most of the 2010s. It's also when firms created positions like mine and Lisa's that focus on innovation and legal ops so the firm ensures we are responding to the client's growing demand for efficiency and better service."

She clicked through data showing flat demand growth through most of that decade. "For years after 2008, demand was essentially flat. We couldn't count on growth through volume. We had to compete on efficiency, value, and differentiation."

"Now, it's true that 2021–2024 saw strong growth again," Lucy acknowledged, showing more recent data. "Demand exploded as we emerged from COVID and remains high. We had record profits in 2024 and even more growth in 2025."

Robert Kim perked up at this. Those recent years *had* been good.

"But," Lucy said, her tone shifting, "that success masks underlying vulnerabilities. We raised our rates an average of 6.5% last year, the fastest pace since 2008. Clients largely accepted it with some grumbling. But realization is headed down, so the 'math is not mathing,' as the kids say. Especially as economic uncertainty returns. And data from Thomson Reuters shows that, actually, the billable hour in the aggregate across most law firms has been on the decline since even before 2008. In fact, the high-water mark for the billable was all the way back in 2003. But rising rates over time has masked that underlying trendline for most lawyers for nearly thirty years. So, when will the dam finally break?"

She let the question hang. "The 2008 crisis taught clients they could demand more from us. The recent boom let us forget that lesson temporarily. But the fundamental shift in client expectations never went away. My guess is that the next major economic downturn is the nail in the coffin for this business model."

Force Two: Four Generations, One Firm

Lucy's next slide showed a timeline of the four generations working in law firms today: Baby Boomers, Gen X, Millennials, and Gen Z.

"This is new in our profession's history. We've always had age diversity, but never this much generational diversity with such different expectations about work."

She clicked to a demographic chart. "Baby Boomers, who built and led most of our firms, are retiring. They're taking with them not just expertise and client relationships, but also their willingness to work within the existing model."

Though he was older than the Boomers, Maggie McNamee thought about her grandfather and his generation of partners.

"Gen Xers in their late forties to mid-fifties are now in leadership roles. But here's the problem: there aren't enough of them. Gen X is roughly half the size of the Boomer generation. We literally don't have enough Gen X lawyers to fill all the leadership and rainmaker roles that Boomers are vacating."

Several newly gray Gen X heads around the room nodded. They'd felt this gap as they rapidly adapted to leadership responsibilities while many also balanced caregiving for kids and aging parents and serving demanding clients. No longer the "sandwich generation," they can better be described as the "panini generation," crushed with the weight of so many pressures.

"So we have to accelerate development of even younger leaders. Which brings us to Millennials, now the largest cohort in our workforce. They're in their thirties and early forties, and some want different things than previous generations."

Lucy pulled up survey data. "Millennials were known as they entered the workforce for prioritizing flexibility, work-life balance, mentorship, and meaning. As new members in the profession, they were notorious for being less willing to grind through 2,000 billable hours for eight to ten years on the mere promise of partnership. In fact, through most of the 2010s, only a minority of millennial associates even wanted to make partner."

Jessica Park bristled. A smart grinder who cared for her elderly mother and her young family, she had always hated being painted with this broad "Millennial" brush. As though she wanted to be off on a beach somewhere, doing yoga after a leisurely lunch. In reality, she and her friends had a harder time paying off student loans, buying a home, and faced diminishing chances of making partnership. She generally hated these broad stereotypes about generations. Individuals were individuals, as far as she was concerned. She'd met plenty of lazy Boomers and plenty of super hardworking Gen Zs.

Lucy's presentation continued, "That's changed a bit as Millennials have matured. By 2023, about 45% expressed interest in partnership, up from much lower numbers earlier. But the message is clear: we can't assume talented young lawyers will stick around using the old playbook.

"And then there's Gen Z," Lucy continued, showing images of young lawyers. "The oldest are just hitting their late twenties. They're true digital natives, the most diverse generation in history, and early indicators suggest they value work-life balance even more intensely than Millennials."

Alex Rivera shifted in his seat, recognizing himself and his peers in this description. He definitely loved technology and really wished the firm would embrace it more. Many days, he truly could not believe what passed for cutting-edge technology in law firms. He had more advanced technology in his backpack most days.

She clicked to data about career trajectories. "And they're moving on faster than ever, making it difficult to develop new leaders, maintain client service, and sustain the business model over time. But what gives us an edge is the reason associates say they stay with their firms."

She paused. "People aren't leaving for better pay necessarily. They're leaving because the work and the workplace don't align with their values. This means we have opportunity. We may not pay New York rates, but that's not necessarily what makes for sticky lawyers."

Force Three: The Pandemic Disruption That Upended Our Bedrock Work Environment

Lucy's slide showed a simple image: a laptop on a kitchen table.

"COVID-19 forced us to prove that remote legal work was possible. And you know what? It worked. Client service didn't suffer. In many cases, lawyer well-being improved."

She displayed survey data. "59% of lawyers reported that working from home had a positive impact on their well-being and job performance. 84% of legal decision-makers reported no frustration with lawyers being out of the office."

Michael Solomon thought about how much he'd appreciated not commuting during lockdown.

"But the legal profession was built on an apprenticeship model that assumed physical proximity," Lucy said. "Junior lawyers learning by osmosis, by walking by a partner's office, sitting in on client calls, absorbing firm culture through daily interaction.

"COVID proved we could work remotely. But it also revealed the costs. Mentorship suffered. Spontaneous collaboration decreased. Some junior lawyers felt isolated, disconnected from the firm's culture."

She clicked to current data. "It's hard to get solid numbers as policies fluctuate and reporting is scant, but some estimates suggest that as many as 83% of law firms have formal hybrid work policies. We're not going back to five days in the office, but we're also not staying fully remote. We're in this middle space, trying to figure out how to maintain culture, mentor effectively, and collaborate meaningfully when people are distributed.

"And this ties directly to generational dynamics," Lucy added. "Because younger lawyers view flexibility as non-negotiable. They've never known anything else and don't want to. If we mandate full-time office presence, we'll lose people to more flexible competitors. But if we're fully remote, we risk losing the very thing that makes us a firm rather than a collection of individual practitioners."

Lisa Martinez spoke up. "We've been struggling with this. How do you build firm culture and train associates when everyone's on different schedules?"

"Exactly the right question," Lucy said. "And we don't have perfect answers yet, even all these years later. But we know the old model of everyone in the office, 8 a.m. to 7 p.m., five days a week isn't coming back. We have to intentionally design new ways to build culture, mentor, and collaborate in a hybrid world."

Force Four: Regulatory Liberalization and New Competition

"For over a century, professional ethics rules have strictly prohibited non-lawyer ownership. Non-lawyers couldn't own equity, couldn't share in legal fees. This core tenet traces back to the ABA's original Canons of Professional Ethics in 1908 and was codified in ABA Model Rule 5.4, adopted by virtually every state.

Lucy's next slide showed a map with Arizona highlighted.

"That's starting to change," she continued. "In 2020–2021, Arizona broke with tradition. They created Alternative Business Structure programs allowing non-lawyer ownership of law firms."

Robert Kim frowned slightly. He'd heard about this but hadn't paid much attention.

"Now, over 100 alternative business structures have launched there. Estate planning companies backed by venture capital. Litigation finance firms employing lawyers. Legal tech startups with lawyer and non-lawyer co-founders."

Lucy clicked through examples. "And here's what's interesting: there's been no spike in consumer complaints. In a regulatory sandbox the state of Utah established to test similar structures, there was less than one complaint per 3,400 services provided. Compare that to traditional lawyers, who see a higher complaint rate.

"So what does this mean for us?" Lucy asked rhetorically. "It means new kinds of competitors. Accounting firms partnering with lawyers to offer integrated services. Tech companies employing lawyers to deliver automated legal solutions. Well-capitalized entities that can invest in technology and scale in ways traditional partnerships can't."

Tom Brennan was taking this all in for the first time. This had business model implications he hadn't fully considered.

"It also means opportunities," Lucy said. "If North Carolina and other jurisdictions where we practice (or where we might consider opening offices to create new models) were to adopt similar rules, we could potentially bring in non-lawyer partners with technology expertise, access external capital to fund innovation, or create multidisciplinary teams that serve clients more holistically.

"But even without regulatory change here, we're competing in a changed market," she continued. "57% of corporate legal departments now use Alternative Legal Service Providers for at least some work. The ALSP sector grew 18% annually from 2021–2023, reaching nearly $30 billion in global revenue."

She let that number sink in. "That's $30 billion in legal work going to entities that aren't traditional law firms. Document review, contract management, compliance, legal research, all work that used to be done by junior associates is increasingly done by specialized providers using technology and process efficiency.

"Some firms are responding by launching their own ALSPs or partnering with them," Lucy noted. "Many large firms now use independent ALSPs to deliver services to clients. Because either way, clients are using them, so some firms want to capture that usage in-house.

"And Professor Rover mentioned the emergence of private equity investment in MSOs as a novel financial force in legal services, a dynamic we're just starting to understand," Lucy said. "Lawyers created a regulatory moat that enriched them for decades. But those days are coming to an end. And we need to build new muscles while finding the opportunities that exist to apply those muscles to and build our future revenue streams."

Force Five: The AI Catalyst

Lucy's final slide was simple: the Open AI logo.

"And then there's artificial intelligence. Specifically, generative AI, which emerged in late 2022 and has been developing at exponential speed since."

She looked around the room. "We're going to spend significant time this afternoon diving deeper into AI. We'll hear from an outside expert about what it can do, what it means for legal practice, and how we need to respond. So I won't detail it all now.

"But here's why AI is the fifth force, and why it's the catalyst that makes the other four forces so urgent: AI threatens to fundamentally reshape the economics of legal practice."

Lucy clicked to a striking statistic. "One of our major clients told Julian that they believe 60% of their routine legal work could be handled by AI within five years. Not assisted by AI and not augmented or refined by AI, but "handled" primarily by AI with lawyer oversight."

The room was completely quiet.

"A Harvard Law study found that AI-assisted drafting cut the time to draft a litigation answer from sixteen hours to three to four minutes. That's not a 10% improvement or even a 50% improvement. That's a 100-fold productivity gain.

"Now, that's a best-case example," Lucy acknowledged. "Not every task will see gains like that. But even if AI makes us 30–40% more efficient on routine work, what does that mean for a business model built on billing hours?"

"It means we can't keep billing the same way we have. It means we need fewer junior associates doing routine work. It means clients will demand fee arrangements that reflect AI-driven efficiency."

Priya Patel felt both excited and anxious. AI could make her work more interesting, but what did it mean for her career trajectory?

"But AI isn't all doom and gloom," Lucy said. "Yes, it is a threat, but it also means new opportunities. AI can analyze millions of documents to find patterns humans would miss. It can predict case outcomes based on historical data. It can help us spot legal risks in contracts faster and more comprehensively than manual review.

"So the firms that embrace AI thoughtfully will be able to deliver better, faster, cheaper legal services. And the firms that resist it, or use it poorly, will fall behind."

The Convergence

Lucy returned to her original slide showing all five forces overlapping.

"Here's why Julian brought you here this week. Any one of these forces would be manageable. We've dealt with economic downturns before. We've adapted to generational change. We've navigated technology shifts.

"But all five at once? This is unprecedented. And they don't just add to each other; they multiply. They interact and amplify each other's effects."

She pointed at the diagram. "Client pressure from 2008 makes us vulnerable to ALSP competition. Generational expectations for flexibility contribute to remote work challenges. Regulatory changes enable business-savvy competitors. AI makes our traditional leverage model unsustainable right when we're facing a talent shortage fueled by relative generational sizes and changing career preferences.

"This is what epochal change looks like," Lucy said quietly. "Not one big change, but multiple forces converging to make the status quo untenable."

She clicked to a new slide: **What Got Us Here Won't Get Us There**.

"Everything Professor Rover described this morning, from the Cravath System to the billable hour to our professional identity to our regulatory framework, were innovations that served us well for decades. But they were designed for a different world.

"A world where clients had limited bargaining power. Where all lawyers wanted partnership and would wait patiently for it. Where everyone worked in the office five days a week. Where law firms had a monopoly on legal services. Where human time was the primary input to legal work.

"That world is gone," Lucy said simply. "And we can't pretend it's coming back."

Small Group Activity

Lucy distributed a worksheet to each table.

"Before we break for the afternoon AI session, I want you to spend fifteen minutes at your tables discussing these questions. Not developing solutions yet but making sure we're clear-eyed about what we're facing."

Five Forces Discussion Questions

For each force, discuss:

- Which aspects of this force do you see affecting our firm most directly?
- How is our current structure/culture helping or hindering our response to this force?
- What assumptions are we making that might not hold true going forward?

Cross-Force Questions:

1. Where do you see these forces amplifying each other for our firm?
2. If we do nothing, what's the most likely outcome in three to five years?
3. What's one thing we definitely need to stop doing, and one thing we definitely need to start doing?

The room broke into animated discussion. Robert Kim found himself acknowledging to Dwarkesh Jones that the ALSP competition was growing as he'd lost a piece of work to a specialized provider just last month.

At Table 5, Jessica Park and Sarah Williams discussed how the partnership model needed to adapt to retain talent who brought value and didn't want to pursue the traditional path but who didn't want to be treated as "not making it," either.

At Table 7, the younger attorneys debated which force worried them most. Priya argued it was AI. To her, it improves too quickly and she knows she needs to adapt or risk obsolescence. Alex added that regulatory change could enable new competitors to undercut them on price while they were still figuring out AI.

After fifteen minutes, Lucy called for attention. "One insight from each table."

The responses came quickly:

"We're still structured like it's 2005. The world changed, but we didn't."

"Client expectations have shifted permanently. We can't wait for them to come back to accepting our old model and they shouldn't have to demand change. We should present it *to* them."

"The generational divide might be real, but it's also both an opportunity and somewhat overstated. We could learn from each other instead of just accommodating differences or overgeneralizing about one another."

"Alternative providers aren't going away. We need to decide if we compete with them, partner with them, or become one ourselves."

"AI is here whether we're ready or not. The question is whether we lead the change or let it happen to us."

"If we do nothing, we'll slowly bleed talent and clients until we're forced to merge or dissolve."

Lucy nodded, taking in each comment. "I hear a common thread: We understand the urgency. We see the forces. What we need now is a path forward."

She glanced at her watch. "We're going to take a break. When we come back, we'll do a deep dive on the force that's moving fastest and has the most transformative potential: artificial intelligence.

"Julian and I have asked an expert to join us. She has been studying AI's impact on legal practice and can help us understand not just what AI is, but what it means for how we work, how we serve clients, and how we build careers."

As people stood and stretched, conversations continued. The day so far had built awareness of the problem, both historically and presently. Now they needed to understand the most urgent threat and opportunity: the technology that could make them either obsolete or extraordinary.

The choice, as Julian had said that morning, was theirs to make.

Chapter 9

Generative AI—The Catalyst Force

After the break, people returned to find the conference room transformed. Three large monitors had been wheeled in, and a woman in her early forties was setting up her laptop at the front. She wore dark jeans and a blazer, the uniform of someone who moved between academic and corporate worlds.

Lucy stood to introduce her. "Thank you all for that excellent discussion about the Five Forces. Now we're going to dive deep into the force that's accelerating everything else, and the one that makes this moment genuinely different from past disruptions."

She gestured to the woman at the front. "Dr. Sarah Conforti is a professor of computer science at Penn State University and the founder of LegalTech Futures, a consulting firm that helps law firms navigate AI adoption. She's advised some of the largest firms in the country and has been studying how generative AI specifically impacts legal practice. Sarah?"

Dr. Conforti smiled warmly. "Thanks, Lucy. And thank you all for having me. I know you've had an intense morning, so I promise to make this as practical and relevant as possible."

She clicked to her first slide, which simply asked: **What's your biggest hope—or biggest fear—about how generative AI could affect the way we do our work?**

"Before we jump in, I'd like to hear from you. For a suite of technologies, AI evokes a lot of emotion. So before we dive into the tech and what it means for your business and practices, I want to know more about how it makes you feel as humans. What's keeping you up at night, or what possibilities excite you. Who wants to start?"

The room was quiet for a moment. Then Alex Rivera raised his hand. "My biggest hope? That it frees us from the drudgery so we can do actual legal thinking. My biggest fear? That firms won't adapt fast enough and we'll lose ground to competitors who do."

"Good," Dr. Conforti said, writing "Drudgery → Thinking" and "Speed of adaptation" on a flip chart. "Who else?"

Jessica Park spoke up. "My hope is that it might make legal services more accessible and that we could serve clients we currently can't afford to serve. My fear is that it eliminates the entry-level work that helps junior lawyers learn the fundamentals."

"Excellent pair of hope and fear," Dr. Conforti noted as she wrote quickly in the practiced way of a seasoned professor. "Expanded access versus negative impact on formation. More?"

Robert Kim shifted in his seat. "My fear is that we sacrifice quality for speed. That we become so focused on efficiency that we lose the judgment and craftsmanship that makes legal work valuable."

"That's a common concern, especially among experienced practitioners," Dr. Conforti acknowledged. "And it's not invalid. Though I'd suggest the question isn't quality *or* speed, but how we maintain quality while gaining speed. Anyone else?"

Priya Patel raised her hand tentatively. "My hope is that it levels the playing field a bit. That someone like me, who's earlier in my career, might be able to produce work that's closer in quality to what a senior associate produces. My fear is that . . . I guess that I won't learn as much if the AI is doing too much of the thinking for me."

Dr. Conforti smiled. "That's incredibly self-aware. Hold onto that thought because we're going to talk a lot about the formation question." She looked around. "One more?"

Tom Brennan spoke from the back. "My fear, frankly, is the business model disruption. If AI makes us dramatically more efficient, how do we maintain revenue when our pricing is built on hours?"

"There it is," Dr. Conforti said. "The question that's making every managing partner and CFO nervous. We're definitely going to address that."

She clicked to her next slide: **On November 30, 2022, OpenAI CEO Sam Altman hovered over his laptop and hit post . . .**

"Let me start with a quick origin story, because understanding where we are helps explain why this is moving so fast . . ."

The Technology Overview

Dr. Conforti moved through the basics efficiently, from GPT architecture to the explosion of adoption to the exponential improvements in capability. She showed the comparison between GPT-3.5 and GPT-4 performance on legal exams, the leap from 40% to 90% proficiency on the LSAT exams in just five months in the dawning days of most lawyers' awareness of GPT technology.

"The legal profession's rapid response is unprecedented," she said, showing the ABA guidance timeline. "Within two years of ChatGPT's launch, we went from 11% of attorneys using generative AI to 30%. And that's just what people admit to."

She let that hang in the air for a moment. "Speaking of which . . . let's address the elephant in the room. How many people in this room regularly use ChatGPT or another generative AI tool for work-related tasks?"

While the firm had piloted several AI platforms for specific legal use cases in certain practice groups, it had a rather prohibitive policy and hadn't yet secured firmwide licenses for all attorneys.

Nonetheless, a few hands went up immediately. Alex, Priya, a couple of other younger associates. Lucy and Lisa knew that Priya was part of the AI testing group at the firm, but Alex was not. While they'd considered Alex because of his enthusiasm for technology, they weren't sure he was the best fit for the pilot because he was *so* eager to use AI in legal work. Then, more slowly, a few mid-level associates raised their hands. Sarah Williams raised hers. Even Dwarkesh Jones, somewhat sheepishly, raised his.

"And how many of you told anyone you were using it?" Dr. Conforti asked.

Most of the hands went down.

"This is what Professor Ethan Mollick from Wharton calls the 'secret cyborg' problem," Dr. Conforti explained. "People are using AI to enhance their productivity, but they're not telling anyone because they're worried about the perception. They're concerned that they'll seem less capable, or that they're cheating somehow."

She pulled up a slide showing research data. "When we ask people to self-report their AI usage versus when others report on their usage, there's a massive gap. People systematically underreport their own use of AI in professional settings."

Robert Kim looked troubled. He glanced at the younger associates, then back at Dr. Conforti. "So some of the work we're reviewing might have been AI-assisted without our knowledge?"

"Almost certainly," Dr. Conforti said. "And that's not necessarily a problem, as long as the quality is there and someone with actual intelligence is checking the artificial intelligence output. But it becomes a problem when it's happening in secret, because then we can't have honest conversations about best practices, quality control, or skill development."

Alex Rivera spoke up, his voice a bit defensive. "We're not using it to cheat. We're using it because it makes us better at our jobs. It's like . . . ," and he tried to come up with an analogy to persuade the partners, suddenly feeling like a teenager whose parents had caught him doing something he wasn't supposed to, "if someone figured out a better research method, wouldn't you want them to use it to understand issues more deeply so we can better advise our clients?"

"Absolutely," Dr. Conforti said. "And that's exactly the mindset shift we need to make as a field, especially since it will allow us to achieve previously unattainable outcomes for our clients, which should always be our focus. But we have to learn to use it responsibly, as a co-intelligence that augments rather than replaces our judgment, expertise, and critical thought, and that requires transparency and training."

Julian could sense a few of the partners bristle at Dr. Conforti's boldness in suggesting approaches to AI they hadn't approved and stepped in. "This is precisely why we're here this week. We need to understand that AI is the most powerful of the five forces and the one that accelerates and mixes with the others to demand of us new approaches to our work and business."

Impact on the Law Firm Business Model

Dr. Conforti's tone shifted as she moved to the next section. "Which brings us to the part that makes managing partners . . . and all of us, really . . . nervous. Let's talk about what AI means for how law firms actually make money."

She pulled up a slide with two images: 1) the traditional law firm pyramid, with partners at the top, senior associates in the middle, junior associates forming the broad base, and 2) a clock.

"The modern law firm has been built on two foundational pillars," she said. "Leveraged labor and the billable hour. Junior lawyers do high-volume work at lower rates, generating profit that partners capture. Everyone bills by the hour, creating predictable revenue streams. This model has worked for decades."

She clicked to the next slide, which showed the same pyramid with cracks running through it and a broken clock.

"AI is applying pressure to both pillars simultaneously."

Tom Brennan was leaning forward now, completely focused and slightly sick to his stomach.

"First, the leverage model. Traditionally, you might staff a matter with one partner, two senior associates, and four junior associates. The junior associates do document review, preliminary research, first drafts, due diligence, etc. The seniors refine and supervise. The partner provides strategy and client counseling, engaging with co-counsel, judges, that kind of thing."

She clicked again. "But what happens when AI can do in minutes what used to take a junior associate hours or days? When document review that required six associates for two weeks can be done by one associate with AI support in three days?"

The room was completely silent.

"Let me give you a real example. A major litigation firm recently had a case requiring standard staffing for a major litigation. Traditional approach: twelve junior associates, eight weeks, approximately $400,000 in associate time. With AI assistance: three associates using AI review tools, two weeks, approximately $80,000 in associate time."

"That's an 80% reduction in labor costs," Tom said quietly.

"Correct. And a corresponding reduction in billable hours if you're charging by time." Dr. Conforti let that sink in. "Now, you might think, okay, great, we'll just pass those savings to the client and everyone's happy. And initially, some firms tried that. But here's what actually happens . . ."

She showed a new slide: a quote from a corporate legal department head.

"'I'm not only your firm's client. I'm your firm's competitor. I think every day about how I can disrupt your work and bring it in-house.'"

The room was stunned into silence now. Dwarkesh Jones was offended, "That's pretty aggressive."

Marcus Reed, a regulatory partner, nodded grimly. "I've heard almost exactly those words from one of my clients. They've built their own AI capabilities internally and they're constantly evaluating what they can handle themselves versus what they need us for."

"Exactly," Dr. Conforti said. "This is the new reality. One of the things that makes this technology different from online research, e-discovery, and prior waves of technology in legal is its sheer democratization. Law firms had to invest in tech before because of client pressures. But now your clients are using AI themselves. In some cases, they're actually *prohibiting you* from using it in their outside counsel guidelines but feeding your work product through their own AI and critiquing it. And they're increasingly asking why they should pay you for work they could do internally."

Robert Kim spoke up, his voice tight. "So what are you saying? That firms should just accept lower revenue? How do we maintain quality, invest in our people, and stay competitive if our revenue is cut in half?"

"That's the wrong question," Dr. Conforti said, not unkindly. "The right question is: what value can we provide that AI can't, and how do we price that value appropriately?"

She advanced to a new slide: **Lawyer Formation in Transition**.

"Which brings us to the second major impact and the one that keeps me up at night much more than the business model question: how we develop lawyers. The traditional model was apprenticeship through doing. Junior associates learned by doing document review, drafting routine motions, conducting preliminary research. It was inefficient, but it was how you built skills."

Jessica Park remembered the many hours she spent on tasks that felt like drudgery at the time but conceded that she grew her skills over time through pattern recognition and intuition development as a result of those years of what felt at the time like grunt work.

"But if AI is doing that work, where do junior lawyers learn?" Dr. Conforti continued. "We're risking what I call an experience gap, a generation of lawyers who feel confident in their ability to supervise AI but who never developed the foundational skills a lawyer needs to understand context and legal judgment themselves."

"That's exactly my concern," Robert said. "How do you develop judgment if you've never done the basic work?"

"It's a legitimate concern," Dr. Conforti acknowledged. "But I'd argue the solution isn't to prevent AI adoption. I mean, let's not pretend the old way was ideal. I was a litigation associate long ago and don't remember relishing the experience. So, how can we completely reimagine how we develop lawyers into something both different and better?"

She clicked to a new slide: **The New Lawyer Formation Imperative**.

"Instead of formation through repetitive tasks, we need formation through intentional training. That means:

- **Quality control skills:** learning to evaluate AI output critically
- **Strategic thinking:** moving from rote task execution to solution architecture earlier in a lawyer's career
- **Technical fluency:** understanding AI capabilities and limitations
- **Client communication:** explaining AI use confidently and maintaining trust
- **Contextual conversations with AI:** learning to craft effective prompts and instructions to guide AI"

Priya was listening intently.

"I know this is overwhelming, but here's what's exciting," Dr. Conforti said, her energy lifting. "This could actually be better for lawyer development. Instead of spending three years doing rote tasks that have no real connection to a larger goal and that increasingly drive new lawyers from the profession, junior lawyers could spend that time on:

- Simulation-based training with realistic scenarios
- Earlier client contact and business development exposure

- Cross-functional experience with different practice areas
- Continuous learning as technology evolves
- Working with AI coaches that provide customized feedback"

Alex blurted out, "That sounds way better than what I've *been* doing!"

He blushed when he realized what he'd said out loud in front of the partners. The other associates agreed and smiled at him furtively. One gave him a low thumbs up of solidarity.

"It could be," Dr. Conforti said. "But only if firms invest in it intentionally. And that's hard when you're also dealing with revenue pressure from the efficiency gains."

She pulled up a slide showing a stark timeline:

2026: "Nice to have" AI capabilities

2027: Clients asking direct questions about AI use

2028–2030: AI proficiency becomes table stakes for major clients

"Here's the market pressure timeline. AI capabilities have gone in a very short time from being a nice differentiator to being the bare minimum expectation. Within eighteen to twenty-four months, firms without clear AI strategies will no longer have a seat at the table."

Tom Brennan was doing mental math, looking increasingly troubled. Marcus Reed had his arms crossed, staring at the screen.

"I know this is a lot," Dr. Conforti said. "So let's take a break here. When we come back, I want to talk about something more positive. I want to consider the opportunities this creates and what the law firm of the future might look like."

As people stood and headed for coffee, the energy in the room had shifted. The morning's theoretical discussions about change had become viscerally real.

Tom immediately pulled Julian aside. "We need to talk about the numbers. If we're looking at 30–40% efficiency gains on routine work, and clients are demanding lower fees . . ."

Marcus joined them. "It's not theoretical anymore. I had a client tell me last month they're setting matter budgets based on AI benchmarks. When I pushed back on a fee estimate, they showed me what their internal AI suggested the work should cost."

Robert Kim stood by the windows, looking out at the mountains. Dwarkesh Jones approached him cautiously.

"You okay?" Dwarkesh asked.

"I'm thinking about all the associates I trained over the years," Robert said. "The hours we spent together, me teaching them how to spot issues, how to think like a lawyer. If that's not how it works anymore . . ."

"Maybe it's not that it doesn't work that way anymore," Dwarkesh offered. "Maybe it's that we need to teach them different things? Or the same things, but differently?"

Near the coffee station, the younger associates were clustered together.

"Did you see their faces when Dr. Conforti talked about the 80% reduction in billable work?" Priya said quietly.

"I know we're supposed to be worried about our jobs," Alex said. "But honestly? I'm excited. If I never have to spend another sixty hours reviewing merger documents manually, I'll be thrilled."

Jessica was more thoughtful. "But will the firm actually invest in the new training she talked about, or will they just expect us to figure it out on our own while also being more profitable?"

Sarah Williams startled them. "That's exactly what we need to figure out this week. How to make the transition benefit everyone; the clients, the firm, and you all."

Lucy moved through the room, listening to conversations, taking mental notes. This was the moment the retreat needed, when the discussions shift from abstract to concrete, from understanding to urgency.

When people began filtering back to their seats, the mood was noticeably different. More sober, more focused. Dr. Conforti waited until everyone settled before continuing.

"I know that was heavy," she said. "But I promise the second half is more hopeful. Because while AI is disrupting the old model, it's also creating opportunities that weren't possible before. Let's talk about what those look like."

Opportunities Generative AI Creates

Dr. Conforti clicked to a new slide showing five interconnected circles: **Scale Expertise**, **Tackle Novel Questions**, **Innovate Client Engagement**, **Strategic Talent Deployment**, and **Enhanced Decision-Making**.

"Here's what I want you to understand," she began, her voice warming. "Major technological shifts destroy old business models. But they also create new possibilities that weren't feasible before. All law firms are facing the pressures I've described and your spreadsheets and conversations are suggestions. The question you're spending a week trying to answer is how to position *your* firm to capture those opportunities."

She walked to the center of the room, away from the screen.

"Let's start with something that should resonate with everyone here: the knowledge retention problem. Robert, you mentioned earlier that you've spent years training associates. What happens when you retire?"

Robert looked up, surprised to be called on and feeling suddenly disoriented at the thought of retiring. Recovering and hoping no one noticed his reaction, he responded, "We lose institutional knowledge. Client relationships. Expertise that took decades to build."

"Exactly. And traditionally, you tried to capture some of that through mentorship, shadowing, and your document management system. But how much actually got transferred?"

"If I had to guess? Maybe 30%," Robert admitted. "Optimistically."

Looking around again, Robert suddenly realized he was the oldest attorney in attendance at the retreat. Once he'd been a summer associate about to embark on an exciting career and here he was, the "dinosaur" at the firm. He blinked repeatedly and quickly in disbelief at how quickly time had passed when he wasn't watching.

"Now imagine this," Dr. Conforti said. "You spend six months working with your associates *and* AI to encode your expertise. And not just what they know, but how you think. The questions you ask when analyzing a deal. The red flags you've learned to spot. The creative approaches that have worked in tough situations."

She clicked to show a conceptual diagram. "You create what's essentially an AI reasoning model trained on your firm's collective expertise. Your junior lawyers can interact with it and ask it questions, test hypotheses, understand why an experienced lawyer might approach a problem a certain way. It's not a replacement for human mentorship, but it complements and scales it. A partner can mentor three people directly and three hundred people through AI augmentation."

Maggie McNamee looked intrigued. "I'm not *totally* sure how I feel about this yet, but in a weird way, it could actually honor my grandfather's legacy if we executed it thoughtfully. It would have made his approach to legal problem-solving available to people who never got to work with him."

"Precisely. And it solves your succession planning challenge while also accelerating the development of junior lawyers." Dr. Conforti moved to her next point.

"Second opportunity: tackling questions you currently can't handle economically. How many times have clients come to you with interesting legal questions that would require extensive research, but the fee would be disproportionate to the value?"

Several hands went up.

"AI changes that calculus completely. What used to require twenty hours of associate time to research thoroughly might now take two hours of AI-assisted research with one hour of partner review. Suddenly, you can say yes to matters you previously had to decline. You can explore novel legal theories. You can take on cases for clients who couldn't traditionally afford your expertise."

Jessica Park sat up straighter. This was exactly what she'd hoped for.

"Third, and this is where it gets exciting for business development because you can completely reimagine how you engage with clients. Most firms still operate on a reactive model: client has problem, client calls firm, firm produces legal advice, firm sends bill. Of course, there have been huge adaptations in marketing and business development, but in many cases the lawyers themselves are not always adept at this part of the role, which is obviously essential to the firm's health. But what if the relationship was continuous?"

Dr. Conforti pulled up a new slide. "Some firms are experimenting with subscription models where clients have ongoing access to AI-powered legal guidance for routine questions, with humans handling the complex issues. Others are embedding AI tools directly in client workflows. For example, you can imagine a contract management system that flags issues in real-time and automatically loops in the appropriate attorney when needed."

Marcus Reed was nodding. "One of my clients asked about something like that in the regulatory context. I honestly didn't know what they meant."

"That's the bleeding edge in legal right now," Dr. Conforti acknowledged. "The pricing models haven't been figured out yet, which means there's opportunity for firms that can innovate. Some are moving to value-based pricing based on outcomes. Others are doing fixed-fee arrangements enabled by predictable AI-assisted workflows. A few are experimenting with gain-sharing where they get compensated based on value created rather than time spent. But you still can't persuade me that a field accustomed to keeping scrupulous records in six-minute increments, capable of negotiating agreements that balance risk and cost, and required to uphold ethics cannot learn a better way to price."

Tom Brennan felt validated *again* and it was only Monday! He had thought the same thing forever, but the lawyers had always insisted there was no other way to price.

"Fourth opportunity: talent deployment. Right now, you're probably assigning work based on who has capacity and appropriate experience level. If you're being honest, you might pull in someone who happens to walk by your office. But what if AI could help you deploy talent based purely on strategic fit and utilization?"

She painted a scenario. "A major merger comes in. Instead of staffing it with whoever's available, you assemble a team based on who has the most relevant industry expertise, the best client relationship skills, and the strongest strategic thinking for this particular deal. The AI handles document review, due diligence coordination, initial drafting. Your lawyers focus entirely on judgment, strategy, and client service."

Sarah Williams was thinking about how this might affect work-life balance. If you weren't spending hours on routine tasks, maybe you could actually be strategic about when and how you worked.

"And finally," Dr. Conforti said, "enhanced decision-making. This is where AI becomes not just a tool but a thought partner."

She pulled up a quote from Ethan Mollick, the Wharton Professor she'd mentioned before, on the screen: *"For many people at work, the importance and stress of open-ended problems to which the answers are non-deterministic outweigh the importance and stress of closed-answer problems that require deterministic answers. LLMs are a useful co-intelligence for the former, even if they are still limited in the latter."*

"Most of the complex business questions you face at the firm, like questions about staffing, business development, succession planning, and talent recruitment and lawyer formation, isn't about finding the single right answer," Dr. Conforti explained. "It's about navigating ambiguity, weighing multiple factors, crafting strategies that balance competing interests. AI can help with that kind of thinking by serving as a devil's advocate, generating alternative approaches, and identifying blind spots in your reasoning."

Alex raised his hand, still feeling the need to justify his use of AI. "And that's actually how I've been using it most effectively. Not to give me answers, but to help me think through problems more thoroughly."

"That's exactly right. And that approach works whether you're a first-year associate or a partner with thirty years of experience." Dr. Conforti smiled. "The technology doesn't care about your seniority. It augments thinking at every level."

She moved to the next slide: **Building the Law Firm of the Future**.

"Here's what I want you to take away from this session. AI is already transforming legal practice and the business of law firms. So how does your firm respond from a place of strategic strength?"

She counted on her fingers. "Reactive looks like: resist until clients demand it, adopt tools piecemeal, worry about efficiency without reimagining the business model, let people figure it out individually, hope it doesn't disrupt too much.

"A strong strategy includes developing firm-wide fluency, experimenting thoughtfully, redesigning service delivery and pricing, and investing in new forms of training, so you can lead the transformation rather than being shaped by it."

Dr. Conforti looked around the room. "You have an opportunity that most firms don't because you're taking a week to think this through together, to build a strategy collaboratively, to make intentional choices about what kind of firm you want to be. That's valuable."

She clicked to her final slide: **Human First, AI Forward**.

"One last thing. The firms that will thrive aren't the ones that become AI companies that happen to practice law. They're the firms that stay deeply committed to the human elements of judgment, relationships, ethics, and creativity while they embrace AI to enhance all the valuable work they do. You stay anchored in what makes you valuable as humans while using technology to become better versions of yourselves."

She paused. "Questions?"

The room was quiet for a long moment as people processed their thoughts.

Finally, Dwarkesh Jones raised his hand. "How do we actually start? Like, tomorrow morning, what's the first thing we should do?"

"Start using it," Dr. Conforti said simply. "Pick a task you're doing this week, whether it's research, drafting, or analysis, and try it with AI assistance. Pay attention to what works and what doesn't. Share what you learn with colleagues. Build fluency through practice, not just sharing theory.

"But do it thoughtfully," she added. "Never trust AI output without verification. Always maintain human judgment as the final check. And be transparent about when you're using it."

Robert Kim spoke up, his voice measured. "I've been resistant to this, I'll admit. But listening to you . . . I think my resistance was partly fear that it would devalue what I've spent my career building. But what you're describing is augmentation and . . . this sounds like sci-fi and I feel embarrassed to say it, but potentially a way for my work at the firm to outlive me."

Dr. Conforti smiled, "That's exactly right. Look, I'm not here to hypnotize you or persuade you that AI is some benevolent force for good. AI is a general purpose technology, and it will cause unknown havoc, as well. But I'm here to help you understand that it is not going anywhere. Your clients and your competitors are using it to their advantage, and your imperative as business leaders is to learn how to leverage it for *yours*. Your expertise becomes more valuable, not less, because now it can be scaled and deployed more strategically. The judgment you've developed over thirty years of practice? That's irreplaceable. AI gives you more leverage to apply it."

She looked at Julian. "I think that's a good place to pause. You have a lot to discuss."

Julian stood and moved to the front. "Thank you, Sarah. That was exactly what we needed. You gave us both the sobering reality check and the hopeful vision."

He turned to the group. "We're going to break for the evening. I know this is a lot to process and we're only at the end of day one. Tomorrow we'll start learning the frameworks that can help us design our response to all of this. But tonight, I'd encourage you to sit with what you've heard. Talk to each other. Think about what it means for your practice, your career, our firm."

As people filed out toward dinner, the conversations were markedly different from the morning. Less philosophical, more urgent.

Lucy stood with Julian and Dr. Conforti, watching people leave in small clusters.

"How did it feel?" Lucy asked Dr. Conforti.

Dr. Conforti inhaled deeply. She always felt conflicted after these presentations. "Like I told them their house was on fire but also handed them the start of a blueprint for a better house . . . I hope," Dr. Conforti said wryly. "Which is about right. They're in that uncomfortable space between the old model dying and the new model not yet being clear."

"That's exactly where we need them to be," Julian said quietly. "Uncomfortable enough to change, hopeful enough to try."

Lucy nodded. Tomorrow they would start giving people tools to work with. But tonight, they needed to sit with the reality of what was coming.

Through the windows, she could see people gathering in small groups on the terrace under heat lamps, glasses of wine and beer in their hands, the Blue Ridge Mountains purple in the gathering dusk. The conversations looked intense, hands gesturing, faces serious and animated.

The retreat had shifted from awareness to urgency. Now they needed to build the desire and knowledge to actually do something about it.

Reader Reflection

The AI Catalyst

Dr. Conforti moved the conversation from "AI as overhyped magic trick" to business model disruption.

1. **The "Secret Cyborg" Audit:** Are you or your team members using AI tools in the shadows? What would happen if you brought that usage into the light to establish quality control and shared learning?

2. **The 60% Reality:** If a client told you tomorrow that they expect AI to handle 60% of your routine work, what higher-value work would you fill that time with?

3. **The Training Gap:** Dr. Conforti highlighted the danger of an "experience gap" where junior associates stop learning the basics because AI does them. Does your firm have a plan for "formation through intentional training" rather than just "learning by billing"?

Chapter 10

Moving to Client-Centricity Through Design Thinking

The Tuesday morning sun streamed through the floor-to-ceiling windows as people entered the breakfast area. People had spent the night processing, and it showed in the intensity of the conversations already happening over coffee.

Lucy had arranged the breakfast tables in groups of six, with small placards at each seat posing a single question: **What surprised you most yesterday?**

At Table 3, Robert Kim settled in with his coffee and found himself seated with Priya Patel, Sarah Williams, Michael Solomon, one of the tax partners, and a litigation associate. He read the question and smiled slightly.

"I suppose we're meant to discuss this," he said.

"Might as well," Sarah said. "I'll start. What surprised me was the secret cyborg thing. Not that people were using AI, but the gap between how much people use it and how much they admit to using it. That seemed like a cultural problem we need to fix. Maybe it's a cultural problem society is grappling with everywhere . . . ."

Priya nodded. "I was one of those secret cyborgs. Even though I'm in the firm's pilot program, I sometimes also move into using publicly available tools, too, for drafting suggestions and brainstorming ideas. And honestly, I felt a little defensive when Dr. Conforti called it out. I mean, I have good judgment. I know how to review AI outputs carefully at this point. Should I just be ignoring the ability I have to make everything I do better because of others' fear or ignorance or whatever is holding them back? But she was right, too. If we're all doing it in isolation, we're not learning from each other or developing best practices."

"What surprised me," Michael said carefully, "was how quickly the conversation shifted from 'should we use AI' to 'how do we use AI strategically.' We skipped the debate about whether we *should* be using AI and went straight to figuring out how to lead it. I guess that's because so many of us *are* already using it . . . secretly, like she said."

Robert considered this. "What surprised me," he said slowly, "was that I came in thinking AI was primarily a threat to quality and left thinking it might be an opportunity to actually improve how we serve clients. I'm not saying I'm convinced yet, but I'm . . . open to being convinced."

The table was quiet for a moment, recognizing this as significant.

"That's huge," Priya said softly.

"Don't get too excited," Robert said with a slight smile. "I said open, not sold."

At Table 1, Jessica Park sat with Dwarkesh Jones, Tom Brennan, Marcus Reed, and two associates from different offices. The conversation had already started when she sat down.

". . . the business model disruption," Tom was saying. "I knew AI would create efficiency gains, but I hadn't really thought through the downstream effects on pricing, staffing, everything. It's more comprehensive than I realized."

Dwarkesh nodded. "What surprised me was the timeline. Not that long until it's table stakes? We have basically no time at all to figure this out."

"What surprised me," Jessica said, "was the lawyer formation piece. Dr. Conforti acknowledged the problem about losing the apprenticeship model, but she also painted a picture of something potentially better. As a junior associate, I was so frustrated with how much time I spent on work that didn't feel like learning. The idea that we could be more intentional about development actually made me feel more hopeful for future lawyers and for the work they do for our clients."

Marcus Reed had been quiet, but now he spoke up. "I was surprised by my own reaction, honestly. I went in thinking this was Lucy's innovation project that Julian was indulging. I left realizing these are the most important strategic questions the firm is facing. The client who said they're our competitor? That was a wake-up call."

One of the junior associates, Maya Davis, added, "What surprised me was how much the partners don't know about AI. I don't mean that as criticism; I just assumed leadership was way ahead of this and we were catching up. Turns out we're all kind of figuring it out together."

"Which is good, I think," Dwarkesh said. "Better that we acknowledge where we actually are than pretend we have it figured out."

At the front of the room, Lucy watched the conversations with satisfaction. This was exactly the kind of reflective processing they needed before diving into design thinking work.

Julian joined her, carrying two coffees. He handed her one. "They're engaged."

"They are. And they're being honest with each other, which is what we need."

At Table 5, Alex Rivera was holding court with a mixed group that included Maggie McNamee, Lisa Martinez, and several associates.

"What surprised me," Alex said, "was that the AI discussion wasn't just a technology conversation. I came in thinking we'd talk about tools and implementation. But it was about business strategy, talent development, and client relationships. AI was the catalyst but not the whole story. It's actually a human story, which is way more interesting."

Maggie smiled. "That's Lucy's influence. She's always understood that innovation isn't about technology, it's about how we work together as complicated humans."

"What surprised me," Lisa said, "was the level of client sophistication. I knew they were getting more demanding, but the idea that they're building their own AI capabilities and actively thinking about how to disrupt our work because they are so frustrated with the way we serve them; that was sobering."

"It changes the relationship," Maggie agreed. "From service provider to something more like . . . competitive partner? I'm not sure what to call it."

"Mutual transformation," one of the associates suggested. "We're helping them transform their legal function while they're pushing us to transform how we deliver services."

After about twenty minutes, Lucy moved to the front and called for attention.

"Good morning. I hope everyone slept well; or at least, slept enough to be functional today."

A ripple of laughter.

"I've been listening to your conversations, and I'm hearing exactly what we need to hear. Remember Jeffrey Hiatt's ADKAR framework for change. Yesterday we built awareness of why transformation is necessary. Today we're going to continue building that awareness as we also start building the knowledge and ability to actually design transformation to respond to the changes we learned about yesterday."

She clicked to her first slide: **Design Thinking: From Lawyer-Centric to Client-Centric**.

"Here's the thing about the legal profession," Lucy began. "We're very good at thinking about legal problems. We have been indoctrinated from our first days in law school to 'think like a lawyer.' We learn by exploring case law, learning how judges think. We're less good at thinking about problems from a client's point of view. There's a difference."

She walked to the center of the room. "A client comes to you and says they need help with a merger. What's the legal problem?"

"Due diligence, transaction structure, regulatory compliance, documentation," Dwarkesh Jones said.

"Exactly. And we're excellent at solving those problems. But what's the client's actual problem?"

The room was quiet.

"The client's problem might be: 'I'm trying to grow my business and this acquisition seems like the path, but I'm terrified of making a mistake that costs me everything I've built, and I need someone to help me navigate not just the legal complexity but the strategic uncertainty.'"

Jessica Park was nodding.

"Design thinking," Lucy continued, "is a methodology for understanding and solving problems from the user's perspective. In the case of the legal services we provide, it's the client's perspective. It forces us to start with empathy rather than expertise. To understand what the client actually needs rather than assuming we know."

She clicked to a new slide showing five connected phases:

Empathize → Define → Ideate → Prototype → Test

"Over the next two days, we're going to learn this methodology by applying it to real challenges our firm faces. But first, I need to explain why this matters and why the legal profession has historically resisted it.

"Innovation requires creativity, but we are not taught how to be creative as lawyers," Lucy said.

"Now, I know what you might be thinking. We *are* creative. We find creative ways to structure deals, construct persuasive arguments, solve our client's legal problems. And that's absolutely true. But where do we get those solutions?"

"Precedent and legal reasoning," Dwarkesh said.

"Exactly," said Lucy. "We look at what's been done before. How other deals were structured. How other cases were argued. What other firms do. And then we build from there. We're very good at incremental innovation, and taking what exists and making it slightly better. We're terrible at imagining something fundamentally different. Because we've never been taught frameworks, methodologies, and mindsets for bold reimagination of what could be. We've been taught to build on what has come before, and the best of us are creative within the constraints of a very constrained industry.

"We talked yesterday about the industry's *structural* impediments to change. But we human lawyers also make change uniquely challenging. As I noted already, there's our training."

Lucy clicked to the next slide: **Lawyer Personality Research—Larry Richard**.

"And then there are our personalities. Dr. Larry Richard, a lawyer and psychologist who studies lawyers, has spent decades researching how lawyers as a group differ from the general population. The news isn't great when it comes to innovation and creativity."

She walked through the chart on screen:
"Compared to the general population, lawyers are:

- Lower in resilience—we struggle to bounce back from setbacks
- Higher in urgency—we want results now, not through patient testing and iterative improvement
- Higher in skepticism—we look for what's wrong rather than what's possible
- Lower in sociability—we prefer working alone to collaborative creativity
- Higher in autonomy—we resist interdependence

Now, compare that to what innovation actually requires:

- Viewing failure as learning, not defeat
- Patience through experimentation and iteration
- Optimism about possibilities
- Collaboration and building on others' ideas
- Interdependence and co-creation"

Robert Kim shifted in his seat. "So you're saying we're fundamentally unsuited to what you're about to ask us to do?"

"I'm saying," Lucy replied carefully, "that we need to consciously work against our natural tendencies. That innovation for lawyers requires deliberate mindset shifts and frameworks to guide us, because left to our own devices, we'll default to what's comfortable, which is incremental adjustment that builds on precedent."

She clicked to her next slide: **The Shift We Need to Make**.

"The most important mindset shift, and the one the entire legal profession has avoided, is moving from lawyer-centered to human-centered design. Or what's commonly called design thinking."

She walked to the center of the room, away from the screen.

"Right now, when a client comes to us with a problem, where do we start?"

"With our expertise," Sarah Williams said. "What do we know about this kind of problem?"

"Exactly. We start with us. We are the experts as lawyers. We analyze the issues through our framework, apply our knowledge, and deliver our solutions. It's very lawyer-centric."

Tom Brennan smiled inside, having felt this very deeply in every conversation he'd ever had at the firm, including and especially the ones in which *he* was the subject matter expert, not the lawyers.

Lucy pulled up a simple diagram showing a traditional legal service model:

Lawyer → Analysis → Solution → Client

"Design thinking flips this completely. Instead of starting with the expert, you start with the human experiencing the problem. You seek to deeply understand their experience. We don't jump to conclusions about what we think they need, but we remain curious about what they *actually* need. Not the problem they articulate, but the underlying need driving that problem."

She clicked to show the design thinking process again:

Empathize → Define → Ideate → Prototype → Test

"This is a five-stage iterative process popularized at Stanford d.school, the design thinking firm IDEO, and other leading thinkers and institutions in the design thinking space. Let me walk you through what each stage means, and why it's so different from how we're trained to think."

Empathize: Understanding the Human Experience

"The first stage is empathy or deeply understanding the person or group experiencing the problem. This means interviewing them, observing them in context, asking questions without immediately jumping to solutions."

Lucy pulled up examples. "In other fields, this looks like hospital designers watching how nurses actually move through a ward, not just asking them what they need. Or bank innovators observing how people interact with ATMs in real environments, not in focus groups.

"For us, it might mean watching how clients actually use the documents we produce. Sitting in on their internal meetings to understand the business context around legal decisions. Talking to associates about what they actually experience in their development, not what the partnership says they should experience."

Michael Solomon raised his hand. "But we do talk to clients. We have regular check-ins, satisfaction surveys."

"Do you?" Lucy asked gently. "Or do you ask them how satisfied they are with your work? Those are different questions. One is asking them to evaluate you. The other is trying to understand their experience and needs without reference to you at all."

Michael sat back, considering this.

"The empathy stage requires genuine curiosity," Lucy continued. "It requires setting aside your expertise temporarily and becoming a learner. For lawyers who are trained to be experts who have answers, this is more uncomfortable than we may want to admit."

Define: Framing the Problem Generatively

"Stage two is defining the problem by taking what you learned and articulating the core problem you're trying to solve. But not as a problem statement in the traditional sense. Design thinkers frame their questions in a very specific and intentional way. As a 'How Might We' question."

She wrote an example on the whiteboard: **How might we help junior associates develop practical skills in a world where AI handles routine work?**

"Notice the structure. 'How might we' does several things simultaneously:

- It's **optimistic**—it assumes solutions exist
- It invites **collaboration**—'we,' not 'I'
- It's broad enough to **allow for many ideas**—'might' suggests multiple possibilities
- But concrete enough to **channel action**—it's about a specific challenge
- 'Might' builds in the **likelihood of early attempts not working**
- And it frames the entire exercise as **exploration, not evaluation**"

She looked at Robert. "Compare that to how a lawyer might frame the same problem: 'Associates need more training opportunities given reduced billable work available due to AI efficiencies.'

"That's a statement of constraint," Lucy said. "It shuts down creativity before it starts. It assumes we already know the answer. The 'How Might We' opens up possibility."

Tom Brennan took a picture of the "How Might We" slide with his phone. This was the kind of reframing he could work with. It immediately struck him as a very different set of words than his lawyer colleagues would normally use, and he thought to himself with a smile, "How might we get the lawyers to use 'How Might We' questions more?"

Ideate: Quantity Over Quality

"Stage three is ideation. The goal in this stage is to generate as many possible solutions as you can without judgment. The aim is quantity. Wild ideas. Bad ideas. Impossible ideas. Incremental ideas. All of it."

Lucy smiled. "This is where lawyers really struggle. We're trained to evaluate. To find flaws. To be skeptical and critical. In ideation, you have to suspend all of that and just generate."

She pulled up research data on ideation and innovation. "Ideas are the fuel for innovation, so we need lots of them or we'll stall out before we get started. Studies show that truly innovative ideas rarely come first. They come after you've exhausted the obvious solutions and your brain starts reaching for something different. But you can't get to idea number twenty-seven if you're judging and discarding ideas one through five.

"We'll practice this today," she said. "And I promise you, it will feel uncomfortable. You'll want to critique ideas as they emerge. You'll want to explain why something won't work. Your job is to resist that impulse and keep generating. Your brains should feel tired at the end of the day. If they don't, you haven't pushed them to find non-obvious solutions."

Prototype: Making Ideas Tangible

"Stage four is prototyping. In prototyping, we create rough versions of promising ideas so we can test them. In product design, this might be a cardboard mock-up. In legal services, it might be a new process, a service offering, a communication approach.

"The key word is 'rough,'" Lucy emphasized. "You're not building the finished product. You're building something testable. Something you can put in front of users to see if you're on the right track."

Robert raised his hand. "In law, the stakes are too high for rough prototypes. We can't just test unproven approaches on client matters."

"I'm glad you brought that up," Lucy said, "because this is a common objection lawyers have to this process. But let me offer some perspective."

She clicked to a new slide showing examples from heavily regulated industries: **Medicine, Finance, Travel**.

"These industries have life-or-death stakes, massive regulatory constraints, and huge liability concerns. And yet they've all used design thinking to drive innovation."

She walked through examples:

"Mobile banking that allows people to access their money from phones when security and fraud were massive concerns. That required prototyping and testing.

"Ride-sharing apps that involve people getting into strangers' cars carries massive insurance and safety implications. Who would have thought fifteen years ago that we would willingly get into a stranger's car to drive us anywhere? Now we can't imagine the alternative. And these apps started as experiments.

"ApplePay on wearables so you can pay for things by waving your watch? This raises huge financial security questions, but financial services institutions partnered with tech companies to prototype and test new concepts before deploying them safely.

"Patient portals give patients direct access to their medical records. That access raises major privacy and liability concerns, but healthcare stakeholders worked together to pilot programs that balanced risk with progress through design thinking.

"All of these were prototyped and tested before they were fully deployed. The prototyping didn't mean abandoning professional standards. To the contrary, testing new approaches allowed for the application of appropriate safeguards.

"But none of these started as fully finished designs. They all started as prototypes. Companies, banks, and healthcare systems could test and pilot before deploying and refining more."

She pulled up more examples. "And sometimes the innovations are smaller but meaningful":

"Think of those superhero window washers in pediatric hospitals. Kids were scared during medical procedures and someone asked, 'How might we bring joy into frightening moments?' Superheroes at their windows was one idea that emerged."

"Or in-flight entertainment. People get bored and anxious during flights, so airlines asked, 'How might we provide a helpful distraction that reduces boredom and anxiety for passengers?'"

"Or blanket warmers in oncology departments, which became a new way to serve cancer patients who are frequently cold during treatment. That innovation was the result of a competition among healthcare workers at the University of Pennsylvania who asked, 'How might we improve patient outcomes?'"

"These didn't require abandoning medical standards or safety regulations. They required observing human needs and experimenting with solutions."

Robert was listening carefully. "But how do we experiment with legal work that carries real consequences and reputational risk to the firm if something goes wrong?"

The room was very quiet.

"I'm not suggesting we prototype on live client matters without permission," Lucy clarified. "I'm suggesting we stop using 'the stakes are too high' as a blanket excuse not to innovate. Objections like that are part of the reason we haven't been able to innovate as an industry and face so many competing threats at once. In the case of design thinking, we can prototype internally. We can pilot with willing clients. We can test with smaller matters before scaling. Other industries with high stakes figure this out. We can, too."

Test: Learning Through Feedback

Lucy moved into explaining the final stage of design thinking, "Stage five is testing. This is where you put your prototype in front of actual users, gather feedback, and iterate. Not once, but repeatedly and constantly. This is where the magic happens, because real users will always surprise you."

Lucy pulled up an image of ChatGPT's early interface.

"Remember when ChatGPT first launched? We all played with it, thought it was amusing but not particularly useful. Many of us dismissed it. But OpenAI kept testing, iterating, improving based on how people actually used it. They released new versions every few months, each dramatically better than the last."

She paused. "Nobody's laughing now. Indeed, it's a major part of the reason we're all gathered here trying to reimagine a century-old business model. That's the power of iterative testing and improvement."

She clicked to her summary slide: **Hallmarks of Design Thinking**.

- **Curiosity**—asking questions instead of providing answers
- **Co-design**—solving with people, not for them
- **Iteration**—refining through cycles of testing and feedback
- **Bias to action**—experimenting instead of analyzing to paralysis

"I want you to remember these essential ingredients for design thinking, and especially that last one," Lucy said, pointing to "Bias to action," "that one is especially important for lawyers. We suffer from what's called analysis paralysis. Because we are such skilled critical thinkers, we want to think through every scenario, anticipate every problem, before we act. Design thinking says: act small, learn fast, adjust quickly."

Lucy took a breath and looked around the room.

"So here's what I'm asking you to do today and for the rest of this week. First, start the process of unlearning the framing that puts lawyers at the center of the universe. Start to see yourselves as providers of solutions with *clients* at the center, not with you as the experts who know best."

"Second, practice design thinking as a new way to organize your approach to everything from practice group organization to go-to-market strategy, from associate development to succession planning, from conversations with law schools to how we price our services."

"Third, recognize that our culture and its focus on collaboration, innovation, and people, is our greatest asset for this journey. If you want to preserve what makes this firm special and avoid the alternative of being acquired and absorbed into someone else's culture, you need to change course. And design thinking is the bold change that will differentiate you."

"I won't pretend this will be easy. Everything about our training and temperament works against this approach. But the five forces aren't giving us a choice between change and no change. Our only remaining choice is between reactive change imposed by market forces *upon* us and proactive change that we design together."

Julian stood and moved to the front beside Lucy. "Questions? Reactions? Pushback?"

For a moment, nobody spoke. Then Robert Kim raised his hand.

"This all sounds good in theory. But I still say legal work is different. The stakes are too high. A badly designed change might annoy clients. Worse, it could cost a client their company, a huge deal, substantial sums of money, or something else significant. The PR fallout alone could take the firm we've built and even torpedo our chance to be acquired. How do we reconcile that with experimentation?"

Others around the room began nodding and murmuring in agreement. They leaned in to hear Lucy respond.

"I'm going to push back on your premise," Lucy said respectfully. "Again, other industries have higher stakes than we do in many cases. Medicine deals with life and death, airlines carry hundreds of people tens of thousands of feet in the air, financial services companies are tasked with safeguarding peoples' life savings while hackers everywhere attempt to infiltrate their systems constantly, and they've figured out how to innovate responsibly. The question is how to build the safeguards that let us experiment responsibly."

"Give me an example of what 'design thinking' in a law firm looks like then," Robert pressed.

"Alright. Let's say we want to redesign our associate training program. Traditional approach: partnership committee discusses, makes a decision, implements it, hopes it works. Design thinking approach: we interview associates about their actual learning needs, we prototype a new training module with a small group, we gather feedback, we iterate, we expand. At no point are we putting client work at risk.

We're just being more intentional and user-centered about our internal process."

Robert nodded slowly. "That I can see."

Marcus Reed raised his hand. "I hear what you're saying about being client-centered. But at the end of the day, we're the experts. Clients don't know what they don't know. Sometimes we need to tell them what they need, not just respond to what they ask for."

"Absolutely," Lucy agreed. "Design thinking doesn't mean abdicating expertise. It means understanding the context in which your expertise needs to be applied. When you empathize deeply with clients, you often discover that the legal question they're asking is actually a symptom of a deeper business challenge. Your expertise becomes more valuable because you're applying it to the real problem, not just the surface question. You're not just responding in the abstract. You're providing contextual intelligence that actually responds to their problem because you took the time to understand and define it first."

She clicked to preview the day's agenda. "Actually, that's part of why we have general counsel joining us for lunch. You'll have a chance to practice empathy interviewing by asking questions to understand their experience without immediately jumping to legal solutions. It's harder than it sounds."

Tom Brennan spoke up. "I like the framework. But I'm worried about the bias to action piece. Moving fast and experimenting sounds great, but doesn't that increase risk? We're in a profession where careful analysis is valued precisely because it prevents costly mistakes."

"This is the analysis paralysis trap," Lucy said with a smile. "You're right that careful analysis prevents some mistakes. But it also prevents innovation, slows response time, and often leads to overthinking simple problems. Design thinking says: analyze enough to reduce catastrophic risk, then move to small experiments that let you learn what you couldn't have predicted through analysis alone."

She pulled up a comparison: "Here's the traditional approach to, say, redesigning our client intake process: form a committee, study it for six months, draft a comprehensive plan, implement firm-wide, discover problems. Design thinking approach: observe actual intake experiences for two weeks, identify pain points, prototype a new approach with three clients, learn what works, iterate, expand. Which actually reduces risk?"

Tom was nodding. "The second one. Because you're learning with real feedback before scaling."

"Exactly. Bias to action doesn't mean reckless action. It means right-sized action appropriate to what you're trying to learn."

Priya raised her hand tentatively. "This makes sense for how we serve clients. But I'm wondering if it also applies to how we work together internally? Like, could we use design thinking to figure out how to develop associates better in an AI world?"

"Not only could you," Lucy said warmly, "that's exactly what we're going to practice this week. We're going to take real challenges facing this firm and use design thinking to reimagine solutions. Associate development is definitely on the list."

Alex jumped in. "And I'm guessing the client-centricity piece applies to us in that scenario? Like, thinking about associates as the users experiencing the development system?"

"Now you're getting it," Lucy said. "Design thinking works for any situation where humans are trying to solve problems for other humans. External clients, internal colleagues, even yourselves. You can use this framework anywhere."

Sarah Williams raised her hand. "I love this framework. But I'm worried about whether we can sustain it. We're all going to leave here energized and then get back to the office and immediately get pulled into client emergencies and billable hour pressure. How do we make this stick?"

"That," Lucy said, "is exactly why we're spending a week on this and why we're building implementation plans. This isn't a one-time workshop. It's the beginning of a cultural shift. And Julian has committed to building the structures that support it. We are committed to protected time for innovation, rewards for collaborative work, metrics beyond billable hours."

Julian nodded. "Sarah's question is a good one. We're not just training you in a methodology and hoping you use it. We're redesigning how the firm operates to make this the new normal. We're not sugarcoating this and we don't expect to leave here ready to transform everything Monday. This will take time. But learning and practicing together from the same playbook is how we start."

Lucy looked at her watch. "Okay, we're falling into the analysis paralysis trap already and we haven't even started!"

The room laughed.

"We're going to take a break. When we come back, we're diving into the first stage: empathy. We're going to practice deeply understanding different stakeholder perspectives on the transformation this firm needs. And I promise you, it's going to feel uncomfortable and unnatural. But that's exactly why we need to practice."

As people stood, Lucy saw some faces that looked excited, mostly the younger lawyers. The pragmatists looked skeptical but intrigued. And the traditionalists looked resistant, still processing whether this was serious or just another initiative that would fade.

Julian pulled her aside as people filed out. "Nice work. You built the case without making it feel like an attack on how they currently work."

"We'll see if it holds," Lucy said. "The real test is when they have to actually do it. Talking about empathy is easy. Practicing it is a little different."

"Then let's give them the chance to struggle in a safe environment," Julian said. "Before they have to do it for real."

Reader Reflection

The Design Thinking Shift

Lucy challenged the group to move from "Lawyer-Centric" to "Client-Centric."

1. **The Empathy Test:** When was the last time you asked a client how they *experienced* your service, rather than just delivering the legal answer?
2. **Analysis Paralysis:** Lawyers are trained to spot risks and find flaws. How does this "issue-spotting" mindset hinder innovation in your firm? Can you identify a recent idea that was killed too early because of skepticism?
3. **Who is the User?** Lucy noted that associates and partners are also "users" of firm systems. If you treated your internal colleagues as clients you had to retain, what one internal process would you redesign first?

Chapter 11

Empathy Workshop

When people returned from break, they found their tables had been transformed. Each seat had a Sharpie, a stack of brightly colored Post-it notes, and at the center of each table sat a large poster board divided into four quadrants labeled:

1. Thinks/Feels
2. Sees
3. Hears
4. Says/Does

Lucy stood at the front with an energy that suggested they were about to do something different.

"Alright, we're going to practice empathy interviewing. But we're not starting with legal work or client service. Instead, we're starting with something everyone in this room has experienced: traveling through an airport."

A few attorneys exchanged puzzled looks.

The Airport Exercise

"Here's how this works. At each table, I want you to identify the person whose birthday is next on the calendar. That person is going to be interviewed about their most recent airport experience, from the moment they left their house to the moment they arrived at their destination."

People started looking at each other, some rolling their eyes and checking watches. Lucy let it pass.

"Everyone else at the table," Lucy continued, "you are the interviewers. But here are the rules."

She clicked to display the rules on screen:

Rules for Empathy Interviewing:

- You cannot speak except to ask questions
- You must suspend all judgment
- You can only exhibit curiosity
- Ask "Why?" until you exhaust an area of inquiry
- Using your Sharpie, write down one insight you learn from the interview
- Listen actively and dig past the surface answers
- Place your Post-its on the table in front of you as you finish writing each insight; use a fresh Post-it for each new insight

"The person being interviewed should talk through their entire experience in detail," Lucy explained. "Everyone else, as you hear something interesting, like an emotion, an observation, a pain point, something the interviewee did or saw, write it down. One insight per Post-it. Don't judge whether it's important. Just capture it. Then rip that Post-it off the stack and put it in on the table in front of you and wait for the next insight."

She held up a worksheet. "I'm giving each table this interview guide with sample questions. You don't have to follow it exactly, but it'll help you get started. The key is to dig deep. If someone says they were stressed, ask why. If they mention a long line, ask how that made them feel. Ask about what they saw, what they heard, what they were thinking."

At Table 3, they quickly determined that Priya Patel's birthday was next in early April.

"Oh no," Priya laughed. "I'm a terrible traveler! This is going to be so embarrassing."

"Perfect!" Lucy called out from the front when she overheard Priya's concern. "Empathy isn't about ideal experiences. It's about real ones. You have twenty minutes. Begin."

The Interviews

At Table 3, Robert Kim looked at the interview guide, then at Priya. This felt awkward, but he started with the first question.

"Can you walk us through your most recent experience at an airport, from arrival to boarding your flight?"

Priya took a breath. "Okay, so I was flying to Seattle for a conference last month. I took an Uber to the airport because parking is so expensive. I was running a little late because my Uber got stuck in traffic, so I was already anxious when I arrived."

Sarah Williams was writing on a Post-it: *Anxious before even entering airport—traffic stress*

"I had to drag my suitcase through the door," Priya continued, "and there was a family blocking the entrance trying to figure out where to go. I felt bad about being annoyed with them, but I was stressed about missing my flight."

Dwarkesh Jones wrote: *Conflicted emotions—stressed but guilty about being annoyed*

Robert asked: "What were you thinking as you entered the airport?"

"Honestly? I was calculating. How long would security take? Did I have time to check my bag or should I try to carry it on? Where was my gate? Should I get coffee now or after security? It was just this mental checklist of things I needed to optimize."

Michael Solomon wrote: *Mental load—constant calculation and optimization*

Sarah followed up: "What did you see around you?"

"Chaos," Priya said immediately. "Families with strollers, business travelers on their phones, people looking lost. The signage wasn't great. I had to ask someone where to check in even though I'd been to this airport before. And there was this overwhelming smell of Cinnabon mixed with cleaning products."

Post-its were appearing rapidly now as people captured sensory details.

"What was the most stressful part?" Robert asked, reading from the guide.

Priya didn't hesitate. "Security. I always get anxious about security. Did I remember to take my laptop out? Are my liquids in the right sized containers? Am I going to set off the metal detector? There was a really brusque TSA agent who snapped at the person in front of me for not having their boarding pass ready, and I immediately started triple-checking that I had everything right."

Michael wrote: *Fear of doing something wrong—authority figure stress*

Dwarkesh asked gently: "Why do you think security makes you so anxious?"

"Because . . ." Priya paused, thinking. "Because I feel like I'm being judged as incompetent if I mess up. And because the stakes feel high even though they're not . . . like, I'm not going to miss my flight because I forgot to take my shoes off, but in that moment it feels catastrophic. And everyone behind me is waiting, so there's this pressure to perform perfectly under observation."

Robert was writing that down, struck by how much emotional weight was attached to something he'd never given much thought to.

"Was there anything that pleasantly surprised you or made the experience smoother?" Sarah asked.

Priya brightened. "Actually, yes. After security, I was still frazzled, and I stopped at a coffee kiosk. The barista saw me looking stressed and said, 'Deep breath; you made it through the hard part. What can I get you?' It was such a small thing, but having someone acknowledge that I was stressed and be kind about it completely changed my mood. I actually teared up a little."

Multiple Post-its captured this: *Human kindness transformed experience, Acknowledgment of stress = relief, Small gesture, big impact*

"How did the airport experience affect your overall mood toward your trip?" Dwarkesh asked.

"It kind of set the tone," Priya admitted. "I was so wound up by the time I got to my gate that I couldn't even enjoy having made it. I just felt depleted. And I was traveling for something good. I was going to a conference I was excited about. But the airport experience took some of that excitement away."

As the twenty minutes concluded, their table was filled with colorful Post-its. Lucy called time.

At Table 1, Jessica Park had been interviewed about a very different experience. She had been traveling with her mother, who used a wheelchair. The table's Post-its were clustered around themes of invisibility, accessibility failures, and the exhausting labor of advocating.

At Table 5, Alex Rivera had described a business trip where everything went smoothly. He enjoyed an early flight, PreCheck, he worked the whole time in the airport lounge. His map had notably fewer Post-its, but they captured a different kind of stress: the pressure to be productive, the inability to just rest, the feeling that airports had become satellite offices.

At Table 7, Tom Brennan had recounted traveling with his two young children. His description of managing a stroller, car seats, snacks, bathroom trips, and meltdowns while navigating security had left the table somewhat traumatized on his behalf.

Organizing the Insights

"Alright," Lucy said. "Now comes the synthesis. Take your Post-its and organize them on the empathy map. Put observations about what they said or did in that quadrant. Things they saw go here. What they heard goes here. And thoughts and feelings, which might be the richest quadrant, go here."

The room filled with the rustling of Post-its being unstuck and restuck, voices debating which quadrant certain insights belonged in. After about ten minutes, the maps started taking shape.

"Now," Lucy said, "look at your map. What patterns do you see? What surprises you? Are there quadrants that are empty or sparse?"

At Table 3, Sarah spoke first. "Our 'Hears' quadrant is pretty empty. We didn't really ask about sounds."

"Interesting," Lucy said, walking over. "Does that mean the auditory experience doesn't matter? Or that you need different questions to uncover it?"

"Probably the second," Dwarkesh acknowledged. "We didn't probe on it."

Alex Rivera had a thought from another table, "I never hear anything at the airport now because I'm always wearing airpods. I only take them out at security."

"Hmmm, interesting," Lucy said, "How many people hear things at the airport these days? I hadn't thought about that before, but it probably is a modern phenomenon in public transportation. I wonder if that makes it challenging to disseminate information to the entire airport . . ."

Robert was studying their map. "What strikes me is how much of this is emotional. The 'Thinks/Feels' quadrant is overflowing. Anxiety, stress, guilt, fear of judgment, relief from kindness. I would have thought airport experience was mostly logistical. How do I get from point A to B? But it's actually deeply emotional."

"That," Lucy said, "is the power of empathy interviewing. You uncover layers that people don't lead with. Priya, if I'd asked you 'How was your last airport experience?' what would you have said?"

"Probably 'Fine, got there on time,'" Priya admitted. "I wouldn't have volunteered all the emotional stuff unless someone asked."

Lucy moved to the front and asked tables to share what they'd learned about their interviewee's experience. The responses varied widely:

Table 1 shared Jessica's mother's wheelchair experience. They talked about how many airport staff didn't make eye contact with her mother, how the "accessible" features often weren't actually functional, and how exhausting it was to constantly advocate for basic needs.

Table 7 shared Tom's experience traveling with kids and the lack of family-friendly spaces, the judgment from other travelers, the impossible logistics of managing children through a system designed for independent adults.

Table 5 shared Alex's smooth but somehow still stressful experience and the pressure to be constantly productive, the inability to disconnect even in transit.

As each table shared, Lucy captured themes on a whiteboard:

- Anxiety about doing something wrong
- Impact of human kindness (or lack thereof)

- Physical accessibility failures
- Emotional load of caregiving while traveling
- Pressure to optimize every moment
- Fear of judgment from staff or other travelers

"Now," Lucy said, "what did you learn from this exercise?"

Maggie McNamee raised her hand. "That I had no idea what traveling with a wheelchair would be like. I've been through airports hundreds of times and never noticed all the ways they fail people with disabilities."

"I learned that one kind person can transform an entire experience," Sarah said. "Priya's barista moment was more important than any of the logistics."

Dwarkesh spoke up. "I learned that people's experiences of the same space can be radically different. Alex had an easy time because he has PreCheck and travels light for business. Tom had a nightmare because he was managing kids. Same airport, completely different realities."

"And here's the key question," Lucy said. "If airports were designed only by frequent business travelers who thought everyone's experience was like theirs, what would get missed?"

"Everything we just heard," Robert said quietly. "People with disabilities, families with children, people who are anxious travelers. They'd design for themselves and assume that's universal."

"Exactly," Lucy said. "And now let's bring this back to law firms. When we design our systems, like client onboarding, matter management, associate development, and client communication, who are we designing for?"

The room was silent.

"We're designing for ourselves," Jessica said. "For firm lawyers who think like firm lawyers, who understand our jargon, who know how firms work."

"Right. And what might we be missing?"

"Everything our clients actually experience," Marcus said. "All the pain points, the stress, the confusion. Because we're not stopping to ask or experience what it's like from their perspective."

Lucy smiled. "That's why we're going to practice empathy interviewing with actual clients at lunch. We have three general counsel joining us. These are clients who've agreed to be vulnerable and honest about their experience working with outside counsel. You're going to interview them the way you just interviewed your colleagues about airports. And you're going to map what you hear."

She distributed new empathy map templates. "These will be at your tables during lunch. Everyone at the table should be listening actively and capturing insights. After lunch, we'll synthesize what we learned and use that to move into the Define stage, crafting 'How Might We' statements based on real client pain points."

She paused. "But here's what I want you to take from the airport exercise. Even for something as universal as airport travel, everyone's experience was different. Some of you had smooth trips, some had nightmares. Some faced accessibility barriers, some faced family logistics challenges. And until we really asked, with curiosity and without judgment, we didn't know."

"The same is true for our clients," Lucy continued. "We think we know what they need because we're experts. But until we truly understand their experience and not just the legal question they're asking, but the context, the stress, the constraints, the human reality of what they're navigating, we're designing for ourselves, not for them."

Robert was nodding slowly. This had been more revealing than he'd expected.

"You have thirty minutes before lunch," Lucy said. "Take a break, clear your heads. When you come back, you're going to do this for real."

As people stood and stretched, the conversations were more animated, warmer, and more personal than earlier breaks.

At the coffee station, Maggie pulled Jessica aside. "Thank you for sharing about your mom's experience. I had no idea."

"I don't talk about it much at work," Jessica said. "It feels too personal. But hearing everyone's airport stories made me realize how much we miss when we don't share those experiences."

Nearby, Robert was talking with Dwarkesh. "I've traveled constantly for thirty years. It never occurred to me that someone might find the experience as stressful as Priya described. I just . . . do it. I never thought about the emotional dimension."

"That's humans for you," Dwarkesh chuckled, amused by Robert's surprise at basic human emotion but somehow also touched by his amazement. "We assume our experience is universal. But this morning showed us it's not."

Lucy stood with Julian, watching people process.

"I have to admit, I was skeptical, but the airport exercise went better than I expected with a bunch of lawyers," Julian observed. "They seemed to get it."

"They got that empathy reveals things you wouldn't see otherwise," Lucy said. "Now we'll see if they can transfer that to clients. That's the real test."

Chapter 12

Empathy Interviews with General Counsel

The room had been rearranged for lunch. At the tables, chairs were now arranged theater-style facing a panel table at the front where three guests sat with Julian. At each of the participant tables, now positioned around the perimeter, new empathy maps had been placed. The new maps had four quadrants labeled:

1. Hears
2. Feels
3. Needs
4. Experiences

Lucy stood at the front as people placed their lunch plates on the tables and settled in for the session.

"Before we begin, I want to thank our three guests for being here and for their willingness to be extraordinarily candid with us. They know what we're doing this week and how we are learning to be more client-centric through design thinking, and they've agreed to help us practice."

She gestured to the empathy maps. "Just like this morning with the airport exercise, I want you to listen actively and capture insights on

Post-its. But this time, we're listening to understand our clients' actual experience working with us and with outside counsel generally."

She pointed to the quadrants. "Capture what you hear them say about communication, the good and bad. Note their emotional responses, their frustration, relief, anxiety, and when they feel confidence. Pay attention to what they actually need from outside counsel, which might be different from what they ask for. And observe what they experience in working with law firms. What is the journey, the pain points, and the moments that matter?"

Julian stood and moved to join the three guests at the panel table.

The Client Panel

"Let me introduce our guests. To my left is Rebecca Tisdale, General Counsel at Apex Manufacturing. Rebecca oversees all legal matters for a company with 12,000 employees across eight states, and she deals primarily with products liability litigation, employment disputes, and regulatory compliance."

"In the middle is Dr. James Wilson, Chief Legal Officer at Meridian Health Systems. James manages legal and compliance for a healthcare organization with twenty-three hospitals and extensive pharmaceutical partnerships. His work spans M&A, FDA regulatory matters, and IP licensing."

"And to my right is Maria Santos, General Counsel at Pinnacle Retail Group. Maria handles everything from commercial contracts and supply chain issues to consumer class actions and data privacy matters for a retail operation with over 800 stores."

"We're going to have a conversation," Julian said. "I'll start with some questions, but I encourage all of you to jump in. This is your chance to hear directly from clients about what we're doing well and where we can improve."

He turned to the panel. "Let's start with a broad question. What's the biggest frustration you experience working with outside counsel, not necessarily this firm, but law firms generally?"

Rebecca Tisdale didn't hesitate. "Communication. Or rather, the lack of it. I can't tell you how many times I've had to chase firms for status updates, only to learn about something important weeks after it happened."

She leaned forward. "Here's an example. We had a products liability case last year with a different firm. They had been advancing a series of conversations with opposing counsel about settlement I would have wanted regular updates about, then sent me an email a month after our last exchange saying we were on the verge of reaching terms and was I prepared to sign off? A month! I'm sitting there wondering why I haven't heard anything, and they'd already made moves toward a major strategic decision without my input."

Around the room, Post-its were appearing: *Delayed updates create anxiety, Major decisions without client input, Feels excluded from own case.*

James Wilson nodded. "I'll add that it's not just timing, but also clarity. I'll ask my firms a simple question like: 'Can we do this transaction this way?' And I'll get back a ten-page memo with citations and caveats when what I need is: 'Yes, with these three conditions,' or 'No, here's why, and here's an alternative.'"

More Post-its: *Wants concise answers, Legal memos when business needs clarity, Translation gap.*

"My CEO doesn't read legal memos," James continued. "He needs me to tell him yes or no and what the risks are. When outside counsel gives me a treatise, I have to translate it myself. That's time I don't have."

Maria Santos jumped in. "And what makes communication even harder is that I often don't hear anything until I get the bill. Then I'm learning about all this work that happened that I didn't know about or didn't approve. Nothing upsets me more than a surprise invoice that's double what I expected."

Bill surprises undermine trust, No warning about overages, Budget predictability critical.

Julian asked, "What would good communication look like?"

"Proactive," Rebecca said immediately. "Don't wait for me to ask. If something significant happens, tell me that day. If you're approaching the budget limit, warn me before you exceed it. If you're considering a strategic change, consult me before making it."

"Brief," James added. "Lead with the answer, then provide the reasoning if I need it. Think of it as an executive summary that actually summarizes."

"Frequent communications," Maria said. "Even if it's just 'no updates this week, everything's on track.' Radio silence makes me anxious. I start imagining problems."

Robert Kim was writing on his Post-its furiously: *Proactive, brief, frequent.*

Julian shifted topics. "Let's talk about efficiency and staffing. What frustrates you there?"

Maria laughed, but not with humor. "I'll be blunt. I feel like I'm constantly paying for law firms to train their junior associates on my dime. I'll get a bill with twenty hours of associate time on something that should have taken five, and when I look at the work product, it's clear someone was learning as they went."

Alex, usually confident and upbeat, looked stung, but kept writing: *Doesn't want to fund training, Over-lawyering costs add up.*

"And the staffing," Maria continued. "I've had firms put three partners on a matter that needed one. Or staff a team of six when three would do. I know the leverage model is how you make money, but from my perspective, I'm paying three times what I should be."

Rebecca nodded her agreement. "To build on Maria's good points, I'll give you a specific example. We had a patent matter. It was a routine office action response. The firm sent me a twelve-page letter. Twelve pages! The first ten pages were boilerplate that included background on patent law, an explanation of the filing system, that sort of thing . . . The actual analysis I needed was in the last two pages."

She looked around the room. "When you're filing fifty patents a year, and every response is twelve pages instead of two, that's thousands of dollars multiplied by fifty. It adds up. And honestly, I flip past the boilerplate anyway to get to the analysis. So you're billing me for content I don't read."

Priya was writing: *Less boilerplate, more analysis, Efficiency = value, Client skips unnecessary content.*

James added, "The other efficiency issue is decision-making speed. I'm under constant pressure from the business to move fast. When outside counsel takes weeks to get back to me because the matter has to go through internal review layers, conflicts checks, and partner approval, that's time we don't have. Our competitors are moving. We need answers quickly."

Tom Brennan captured: *Business moves faster than law firm bureaucracy, Speed matters as much as quality.*

"Let's shift to something deeper," Julian said. "Do you feel like outside counsel understand your business?"

All three panelists looked uncomfortable.

"Sometimes," James said diplomatically. "The firms we work with most closely, like yours, have taken time to learn our industry. But I've had plenty of experiences with lawyers who give me technically sound legal advice that completely misses the business reality."

"Can you give us an example?" Julian prompted.

"Sure. We were negotiating a licensing deal for a pharmaceutical compound. Our outside counsel, and it wasn't your firm, recommended terms that would have been legally bulletproof but commercially unacceptable to our partner. They were optimizing for legal protection without considering that we needed this deal to close, and that our partner relationship was more valuable than the specific terms."

He paused. "When I pushed back, the lawyer got defensive. 'This is the right legal structure,' he kept saying. But it wasn't the right business structure. Eventually I had to negotiate around the lawyer instead of with their help."

Jessica wrote: *Legal correctness ≠ business success, Need to balance protection with commercial reality.*

Rebecca added, "I think the biggest gap is understanding our risk tolerance. Lawyers are trained to identify every possible risk. But I can't avoid all risk; instead, I have to decide which risks are worth taking. What I need is help prioritizing and quantifying risks, not just a list of everything that could go wrong."

She looked at the group. "Here's what I mean: Last year, we had outside counsel tell us a litigation would cost $100,000 to defend. The maximum exposure if we lost? $75,000. That should give you pause, right? Winning can mean losing when the costs are excessive. But the lawyers were ready to fight to the death without considering proportionality."

Dwarkesh Jones wrote: *Cost-benefit analysis critical, Proportionality matters, Winning at excessive cost = losing.*

Maria brought it to pricing. "And here's where business understanding really matters. You all know that I have a budget. It's not unlimited. When a firm treats my legal budget like it's elastic, or when they raise rates every year without question and without any value add, it shows they don't understand the pressure I'm under to control costs."

She leaned forward, her voice firm. "I'm going to be really candid here. I feel like we're all being grossly overcharged right now, and we all know it. All three of us worked in law firms before we were in-house. We know firsthand that the billable hour model incentivizes you to be inefficient. Every hour you spend makes you more money, so where's your motivation to be faster?"

The room was silent. Tom Brennan wrote: *Feels overcharged, Billable hour = wrong incentives, Model misaligns interests.*

"I know that's uncomfortable to hear," Maria said. "But it's true. And the firms that acknowledge it and work with me on alternative fee arrangements, fixed fees, and value-based pricing are the ones I trust. Because they're showing me they care about my success, not just their billables."

Julian, to his credit, didn't flinch. "That's exactly the kind of honesty we need. Let me ask about something else. What delights you? When does working with outside counsel actually feel good?"

The energy in the room shifted slightly.

Rebecca smiled. "When someone makes me look good to my CEO. We had a situation last year where we needed to present a complex employment law situation to our board. I can say this without blowing smoke because it was your firm that helped me create a board-ready presentation. Not a legal memo, a presentation. With clear recommendations, risk quantification, and suggested actions."

She looked at Sarah Williams. "Sarah, you did that for us. And my CEO came up to me afterward and said, 'That was exactly what we needed.' That's when I love working with outside counsel. It's when you make me shine internally."

Sarah looked both proud and slightly embarrassed as people at her table wrote: *Help client succeed internally, Board-ready work adds value, Make GC look good.*

James nodded. "For me, it's the human moments. I had a really stressful deal negotiation. It was late, I was exhausted, nothing was going right. The partner handling it called me and said, 'This is hard. You're doing great. We're going to figure it out.' Just acknowledging the stress and being encouraging completely changed my mindset." Robert

Kim was surprised to find himself thinking back to Priya's story about the kind barista at the airport.

James looked around. "You're not just legal technicians. You're partners in high-stakes, stressful work. It might sound like touchy-feely nonsense or standard language firms use on their website, but when you remember that I'm a human being who's stressed and worried and trying to do my best, it matters enormously."

Michael Solomon was writing: *Acknowledgment of stress = huge, Human kindness transforms relationship, Partner not just vendor.*

Maria added, "And I love when outside counsel are proactive. Not waiting for me to call with a problem, but calling me to say, 'Hey, there's a new regulation you should know about,' or 'I saw this news about your competitor and thought of a risk you might want to consider.'"

She smiled. "That's when I feel like you're really on my team. You're thinking about my business even when I'm not actively engaging you. That's partnership."

Post-its multiplied: *Proactive counsel valued highly, Thinking ahead = partnership, Don't wait to be asked.*

"Let me ask about innovation," Julian said. "What do you need from law firms that you're not getting?"

James leaned back. "Honestly? I need you to evolve your business model. The billable hour is dying and good riddance. We all know it. But most firms are clinging to it because it's comfortable and profitable."

He gestured around the room. "This? What you're doing this week? This is what I want to see from all my outside counsel. Actively rethinking how you work, how you price, how you staff matters. Most firms talk about innovation and they have fancy branded technology initiatives, but I don't feel any different in how they serve me. They're optimizing an ancient model, not reimagining a better one."

Rebecca agreed. "I'll add to that. I need firms to use technology to actually make my life easier, not just to make your work faster while charging me the same. If AI lets you do research in one hour instead of ten, I expect my bill to reflect that."

She looked serious. "And I need more flexible service delivery. Sometimes I need a full litigation team. Sometimes I just need one smart lawyer for a quick consult. Sometimes I need a fixed-fee arrangement for routine work. The firms that can flex to meet my different needs are the ones I keep calling."

Maria jumped in. "And please, please stop assuming your way is the only way. I've started mandating certain AI tools because firms were using old, expensive methods. When I said 'use this tool,' some firms pushed back. Why? Because they weren't used to it."

She shook her head. "My response is: when you pay the bill, you pick the tool. I'm the client. If I want you to use specific software because it's more efficient and gives me better data, that shouldn't be a battle."

Around the room, Sharpies flew across Post-its: *Tech should benefit client, not just firm, Flexible service delivery critical, Client has right to dictate tools.*

Julian looked at his colleagues. "Questions from the group?"

Dwarkesh Jones raised his hand. "Rebecca, you mentioned the surprise settlement discussions. How do your outside litigators handle ongoing communications in an ideal scenario?"

Rebecca didn't pause. "In that specific case, they should have known from the outset when I wanted updates and provided those along the way. They should update me. 'Rebecca, opposing counsel is open to settlement. Here are the terms they're proposing. Here's what I think the pros and cons are. What do you want to do?' Then we decide together. I'm the one who has to live with the outcome. I should be driving the conversations. I don't have to be on the *phone* with opposing counsel; that's why I hired a firm. But we should be aligned and connected around strategy."

Tom Brennan asked, "Maria, you mentioned feeling overcharged. If we moved to a fixed-fee model, would you accept that we might have to price conservatively to protect ourselves? Meaning it might not always be cheaper than hourly?"

Maria considered this. "If the fee is predictable and fair, yes. What I can't have is surprises. If you tell me upfront, 'this matter will cost $50,000' and it costs $50,000, I can budget for that. If you tell me it'll be $20,000 and it turns out to be $80,000, you've undermined my credibility with my CFO. I'd rather have certainty than the possibility of it being cheaper."

She added, "And honestly, if you price it right, you should make good money on fixed fees. When you work efficiently, you make more per hour. That aligns our interests. I want you to be efficient, and you benefit from being efficient. That's way better than the billable hour where efficiency hurts you."

Jessica Park asked, "Dr. Wilson, you mentioned needing things translated from legal to business language. Do you ever feel like that means we're not giving you the full picture?"

James smiled. "Great question. No, I trust that you're giving me the full picture. I just need the executive summary first. Think of it as layered communication. Lead with the business layer, the recommendation and key risks. Then provide the legal analysis for me to review if I need to dig deeper. But don't make me dig through ten pages to find the answer."

As the panel wound down, Julian asked one final question. "What made you willing to be so candid with us today?"

Rebecca answered first. "Because you asked. Do you know how rare that is? Most firms never ask for real feedback. They send satisfaction surveys with softball questions, but they don't create space for honest conversation."

She looked at Lucy. "When Lucy reached out and explained what you're doing this week and that you want to understand our experience, I was thrilled. I want you to do this. I need you to do this. And I'll be brutally honest if it helps because I want you to succeed."

James nodded. "Same here. I don't want to find new outside counsel. I want the firms I already trust to get even better. Taking a whole week to rethink how you work gives me confidence that you're serious about evolving."

Maria added, "And frankly, I wish more of my outside counsel would do things like this. Most firms don't seek out active feedback. They just keep doing what they've always done until clients leave. You're being proactive about improving, and that makes me want to invest in this relationship."

She looked around the room at all the lawyers taking notes. "Also, I can see you're actually listening. You're not just being polite; you're capturing what we're saying. That suggests this isn't theater. You're going to actually do something with this feedback."

Julian stood. "Thank you. Truly. This has been uncomfortable in the best possible way. You've given us exactly what we needed to hear."

As the three guests left to warm applause, Lucy moved to the front.

"Alright, you have fifteen minutes. At your tables, organize your Post-its on the empathy maps. Look for patterns. Identify surprises. Note what's missing. Then we're going to debrief together."

Synthesis and Debrief

The room erupted in activity. At Table 3, Robert, Sarah, Dwarkesh, Priya, and Michael clustered around their empathy map, sorting through dozens of colorful Post-its.

"Look at the 'Feels' quadrant," Sarah said. "It's overwhelmingly about frustration. Frustration about costs, about being surprised, about not knowing what's happening."

Dwarkesh nodded, placing several Post-its in the NEEDS quadrant. "And what they need: predictability, partnership, proactive communication. Those aren't complicated things, but we're not consistently delivering them."

Robert was studying the EXPERIENCES quadrant. "I'm struck by how often they feel excluded from their own matters. Rebecca's settlement discussions story, James's lawyer insisting his legal approach was best. We're making decisions for them instead of with them."

Priya pointed to a cluster of Post-its. "And the communication gap is huge. They want brief, frequent, proactive updates. We tend to give detailed, infrequent, reactive reports. We're solving for what we think they need instead of what they actually need."

At Table 1, Jessica, Marcus, Tom, and two associates were having a similar realization.

"The billing stuff is brutal," Tom said, looking at their FEELS quadrant filled with words like "frustrated," "surprised," "overcharged." "They fundamentally don't trust that our interests are aligned with theirs."

Jessica was arranging NEEDS Post-its. "But look at what they actually need: certainty, partnership, efficiency, recognition of their internal pressures. Those are all things we could deliver if we structured our relationships differently."

Marcus pointed to the HEARS quadrant. "And when they hear things from trusted voices, like Sarah, such as in the case of Rebecca's board presentation, it's when we helped them succeed internally, not just delivered legal work."

At Table 5, Alex, Maggie, Lisa, and several others were focused on the innovation theme.

"They're clearly telling us our business model is broken," Alex said bluntly. "Maria said we're all being overcharged. James said the billable hour is dying. They want something different and most firms aren't giving it to them."

Maggie was more measured. "But they also said they want us to succeed. They don't want to replace us; they want us to evolve. That should give us hope."

Lisa nodded. "And they're willing to work with us on it. Maria said she'd accept fixed fees even if they're not always cheaper, just for predictability. That's a real opening."

After fifteen minutes, Lucy called the group together. "What did you learn?"

Hands shot up around the room.

Sarah spoke first. "I learned that communication isn't just about frequency, but also about *what* we communicate. Clients want to be consulted on big decisions, warned about budget issues, and kept in the loop even when there's nothing new. We're thinking about communication as information transfer. They're thinking about it as partnership."

Marcus added, "I heard loud and clear that our billing model actively works against their interests. Every hour we bill makes us more money but costs them more money. That's not alignment and it breeds mistrust. We need to find pricing that aligns our incentives."

Jessica said quietly, "I learned that we make decisions for clients instead of with them. Even when we think we're acting in their best interest or taking something off their plate, if we don't involve them in the decision, we're undermining the relationship."

Alex raised his hand. "I learned that they're desperate for real innovation, but most firms aren't delivering it. We have a huge opportunity here if we're actually willing to change how we work."

Robert spoke, his voice thoughtful. "I learned that what delights them isn't perfection but humanity. James's story about the partner who acknowledged his stress. Rebecca looking good to her CEO because of Sarah. Maria feeling like we're thinking about her even when she's not asking. Those aren't legal skills. Those are relationship skills."

Lucy nodded, capturing themes on the whiteboard:

- **Communication** = Partnership, not just information
- **Pricing** = Alignment, not extraction
- **Staffing** = Efficiency, not leverage
- **Business understanding** = Essential, not optional
- **Innovation** = Opportunity, not threat
- **Humanity** = Connection, not transaction

"Now," Lucy said, "here's the design-thinking question. Based on what you heard today, what problems should we be trying to solve?"

She pulled up a blank slide. "We're moving into the Define stage. That means taking all this rich empathy work, from the airport exercise this morning to the client panel just now, and articulating the core problems we're trying to solve."

She pulled a new slide up: **How Might We . . .?**

"This is where we'll pick up after lunch. We're going to practice crafting 'How Might We' statements based on what you learned today. Each table will identify a problem area and frame it as a possibility, not a constraint."

Julian stood. "Take a break. But as you do, think about what you heard. Because this afternoon, we're going to start crafting problem statements. And the solutions will only be as good as our understanding of the real problems."

As people filed out for the break, several people approached the three clients, who had lingered, to thank them directly.

Lucy stood with Julian, looking at the empathy maps scattered around the room, now covered with colorful Post-its organized into patterns.

"They got it," Julian said quietly.

"They did," Lucy agreed. "They heard things they didn't want to hear. But they heard them."

She looked at the themes on her whiteboard. "The question now is whether they can move from understanding to action. From 'this is what I heard' to 'this is what the problems are.'"

"That's what this afternoon is about," Julian said.

Chapter 13

Defining Client Problems

After the break, people returned to find the room rearranged again. The empathy maps had been moved to the walls, creating a gallery of colorful Post-its organized into patterns. The tables remained in their small groups, but now each had new materials: large sheets of paper, fresh markers, and a handout titled "Crafting 'How Might We' Statements."

Lucy stood at the front, visibly energized. "Alright, you've started some of the hardest work by truly listening to understand our clients' experiences. It's not always easy to hear how we fail and frustrate clients, but we really need to understand their perspective to begin defining problems we can work *with* them to solve. You captured what they said, how they felt, what they need, and what they experience. Now we move into the Define stage of design thinking."

She clicked to a new slide: **From Insights to Opportunities**.

"In traditional legal problem-solving, we move quickly from problem to solution. A client says they have an issue, we immediately start thinking about how to fix it. But design thinking inserts a critical step between understanding and solving. We stop to define the problem in a way that opens up possibilities rather than constraining them."

She advanced to the next slide showing the How Might We (HMW) template:

How might we [action verb] [user or stakeholder] [achieve a desired outcome] in order to [address key insight or overcome barrier]?

"This is the 'How Might We' framework, and it's deliberately optimistic and open-ended. Everything about it is designed to invite creativity rather than shut it down."

In spite of himself, Robert Kim was taking notes.

"Let's break down why this structure works," Lucy continued, walking through each component:

"**Action verb**—we start with momentum. Words like help, enable, redesign, reduce, support, reimagine. Not 'should we' or 'could we,' but 'how might we.' It assumes solutions exist and invites us to find them.

"**User or stakeholder**—this keeps empathy at the center. We're not solving for ourselves, we're solving for someone else, someone specific.

"**Desired outcome**—this clarifies what success looks like from the user's perspective, not ours.

"**Key insight or barrier**—this ties back to what we learned during empathy work. It keeps us grounded in real needs, not imagined ones."

She clicked to show an example:

Weak HMW: How might we automate client onboarding?

Strong HMW: How might we help new clients feel confident during onboarding to reduce their anxiety about whether they chose the right firm?

"See the difference?" Lucy asked. "The weak version jumps to a solution: automation. Automation might be a good solution, but by embedding it in the problem statement, we've eliminated all other possibilities. The strong version stays focused on the human need for confidence and reduced anxiety, which leaves the solution space wide open."

Alex Rivera raised his hand. "So we're trying to name the problem, not solve it yet?"

"Exactly. And that can sometimes be hard for lawyers because you're trained to move quickly from problem to solution. Design thinking says: slow down, make sure you're solving the right problem first."

Lucy moved to a flip chart and wrote three headers across separate sheets:

COMMUNICATION

PRICING

COLLABORATION

"Based on what we heard from our client panel and what you captured on your empathy maps, these are three major challenge areas that emerged. I'm going to divide the room into three sections. Each section will work on crafting HMW statements for one of these challenges."

She pointed to different areas of the room. "Tables 1 and 2, you're focusing on communication. Tables 3 and 4 on pricing. Tables 5, 6, and 7 on collaboration, particularly around how we work with clients during intake and throughout engagements."

People shifted to look at their table partners, already starting to think about the problems they'd tackle.

"Before you start," Lucy said, "let me give you some tips for crafting strong HMW statements."

She clicked through guidance points:

"**Start from a pain point or observation, not a solution.** If you catch yourself embedding a solution in your HMW, like 'How might we build an app that . . . ,' catch yourself, stop and reframe. What's the underlying need the app would address?

"**Check your scope.** If it's too broad, you'll generate chaos. 'How might we make clients happier?' If it's too narrow, you'll limit creativity. 'How might we send status emails on Fridays?' You want the Goldilocks zone so that you're focused enough to guide ideation but open enough to invite creativity.

"**Test for neutrality.** Your HMW shouldn't imply a specific solution path. If someone could look at your statement and immediately know what you're planning to do, it's too prescriptive.

"**Expect to generate many before you land on the right one.** In design sprints, teams often generate twenty to thirty HMWs, then cluster them into themes before choosing the strongest ones. So don't fall in love with your first attempt."

She set a timer on the screen. "You have twenty minutes. Each table should generate at least five different HMW statements for your assigned challenge area. Use your empathy maps, think about what you heard from our panelists, and remember that we're naming problems, not solving them yet. Go."

Workshopping at the Tables

The room erupted into activity. At Table 1, Dwarkesh Jones was already writing on the large paper.

"Okay, communication," he said. "What did we hear from the clients about communication problems?"

Jessica Park consulted her notes. "Rebecca's annoyance about ongoing settlement discussions story . . . she wasn't consulted. James wanting concise answers instead of ten-page memos. Maria being surprised by bills because she didn't know work was happening."

Tom Brennan added, "And all of them wanted proactive updates, even when there was nothing new to report. Radio silence created uncertainty."

"So what's the underlying need?" Dwarkesh asked. "Not 'they want more emails' but what do they actually need?"

Jessica thought for a moment. "They need to feel like partners in their own matters. Like they have visibility and control."

"Okay, so . . ." Dwarkesh started writing: "How might we communicate with clients so they feel like active partners in their matters?"

Tom looked at it critically. "That's pretty broad. 'Active partners' could mean lots of things."

"Fair," Dwarkesh said. "What specifically about partnership?"

Jessica pulled up the empathy map. "Look at the 'Feels' section. They have anxiety about not knowing what's happening, anxiety about costs, anxiety about being excluded from decisions."

"So maybe it's about confidence?" Dwarkesh suggested. "How might we communicate with clients so they feel confident about . . ."

He paused, thinking. "About what? The work we're doing? The value they're getting?"

Tom jumped in. "I think it's simpler than that. They need confidence that we understand their need for clarity. Especially once a matter is ongoing and they have less visibility."

Dwarkesh started writing a new version: "How might we communicate with our clients so they feel confident that the firm understands their need for clarity once a matter is ongoing and they have less visibility into its status?"

The table studied it for a moment.

"That's really specific," Jessica said. "Is it too narrow?"

"I don't think so," Tom replied. "It captures the exact moment when things break down—once a matter moves past intake, when they're not seeing day-to-day activity, when we assume no news is good news but they're assuming we forgot about them."

"It doesn't prescribe a solution," Dwarkesh noted. "We could solve this with better reporting, with client portals, with different staffing models, with clearer scoping at the beginning. The statement stays open."

They decided to keep it and started considering other angles of the communication problem.

At Table 3, the pricing discussion was more heated.

"The problem is obvious," Robert Kim said. "They think we're overcharging them."

"But that's a conclusion, not an insight," Sarah Williams countered gently. "Why do they think that? What's the underlying issue?"

Priya Patel looked at their empathy map. "Maria said the billable hour incentivizes inefficiency. Every hour we spend makes us more money, so where's our motivation to be faster?"

"Right, it's a misalignment of incentives," Michael Solomon added. "They want efficiency, and we profit from inefficiency. Or at least that's how they perceive it."

Robert frowned. "We're not deliberately inefficient. We do thorough work."

"I know," Michael said carefully, sensing Robert's defensiveness. "But the perception is real. And when clients feel like our incentives conflict with theirs, trust breaks down."

Sarah started writing: "How might we price our services so clients don't feel like we're incentivized to be inefficient?"

The table looked at it skeptically.

"That's defensive," Priya said. "It's focused on what we're not when we say 'don't feel like we're incentivized.' What if we flip it to what we want them to feel?"

Sarah tried again: "How might we price our services so clients feel our incentives align with theirs?"

"Better," Michael said. "But what incentives specifically? Clients have lots of incentives."

Robert thought about Maria's comment. "She said she'd rather have certainty than the possibility of it being cheaper. And she said when we work efficiently under a fixed fee, we make more per hour, which aligns our interests."

"So it's about aligned incentives leading to their success," Priya said. "Not just aligned generally but specifically aligned with their success and whatever that means for each client."

Sarah wrote a new version: "How might we reimagine our pricing models so clients feel our incentives are aligned with their success, not our time?"

The table went quiet, considering it.

"'Reimagine' is good," Michael said. "It signals we're not just tweaking rates, we're rethinking the whole approach."

"And the contrast is clear when we compare their success to our time," Robert added, somewhat reluctantly. "That's the fundamental tension."

"Does it leave room for different solutions?" Priya asked. "Fixed fees, value-based pricing, subscription models?"

"I think so," Sarah said. "It doesn't prescribe the mechanism, just the outcome; they should feel the alignment."

They kept that one and started generating others to explore different aspects of the pricing challenge.

At Table 5, the collaboration discussion was producing multiple directions.

"What did the clients say about collaboration?" Alex Rivera asked, reviewing notes.

"Maria loved when firms were proactive, calling her about new regulations before she asked," one associate offered. "That felt like partnership."

"Rebecca wanted to be consulted on major decisions, not told after the fact," Maggie McNamee added. "The settlement discussion story was brutal. She found out a month later about major ongoing discussions that were happening without her input."

Lisa Martinez pointed to the empathy map. "Look at this cluster in the 'Experiences' section: they feel excluded from their own matters. Decisions get made without them, work happens without their knowledge, then they get a bill."

"So when does that feeling start?" Alex wondered. "I bet it begins at intake."

Maggie nodded slowly. "You're right. If the first interaction is transactional because they send us information, we quote a fee, we start work, then the pattern is set. They're the client who sends questions, we're the firm that sends deliverables back over the wall with an invoice attached, and round and round it goes."

"But if intake felt collaborative from the start," Lisa said, thinking aloud, "if they felt like we were designing the engagement together rather than proposing terms . . ."

Alex started writing: "How might we reimagine the client intake process so that in-house counsel feel collaboration begins before engagement?"

The table considered it carefully.

"I like 'before engagement,'" Maggie said. "That captures the timing so that we're not focused on that part after we're already working together, but from the very first conversation."

"And 'feel collaboration begins' is good because it's about their perception and experience," one of the associates added. "Not just that we think we're being collaborative, but that they feel it."

"Does it leave room for different approaches?" Lisa asked, testing the neutrality tip Lucy had listed. "We could solve this through better scoping conversations, through co-design workshops, through different onboarding processes, through technology that lets them see our thinking . . ."

"Yeah, it's open," Alex confirmed. "It's about the feeling of collaboration starting early, not about how we create that feeling."

They decided it was a strong enough problem statement to get started.

Sharing and Refinement

As the twenty minutes concluded, Lucy called for attention. "I've been listening to your discussions, and I'm hearing really thoughtful work. Let's share what you've developed."

She turned to Tables 1 and 2. "Communication groups, what's your strongest HMW statement?"

Dwarkesh Jones stood. "We generated several, but the one we kept coming back to is: 'How might we communicate with our clients so they feel confident that the firm understands their need for clarity once a matter is ongoing and they have less visibility into its status?'"

Lucy wrote it on the flip chart under COMMUNICATION. "Tell me why this one feels strong."

Jessica Park answered. "It captures the specific moment when communication tends to break down. We think that is right after initial engagement, when the client has less day-to-day visibility. And it focuses on their need for confidence, not just information."

"And it doesn't prescribe how we communicate," Tom added. "It could be reports, calls, portals, different staffing, so the solution space stays open."

Lucy nodded. "Great work. I particularly like that you identified the specific timing as 'once a matter is ongoing' because that's where the breakdown typically happens. Intake gets lots of attention, but ongoing communication is where relationships fray."

She turned to Tables 3 and 4. "Pricing groups?"

Sarah Williams stood. "Our strongest statement is: 'How might we reimagine our pricing models so clients feel our incentives are aligned with their success, not our time?'"

Lucy wrote it on the PRICING flip chart. "Walk me through your thinking."

Everyone at the table was surprised when Robert Kim spoke up. "We started more defensively. We were focused on proving we're not inefficient. But we realized the real issue is perceived misalignment of incentives. When clients believe we profit from spending more time, trust breaks down regardless of whether it's true."

Priya added, "And 'their success' is deliberately broad because success looks different for each client. For some it's winning a case, for others it's efficient resolution, for others it's risk mitigation."

"The contrast of 'their success, not our time' makes the problem crystal clear," Michael Solomon said.

Lucy smiled. "This is exactly right. You've named the fundamental tension in billable hour pricing without embedding a specific solution. Fixed fees, value-based pricing, subscriptions, or something we haven't even thought of yet, all of those remain possible responses to this HMW."

She turned to Tables 5, 6, and 7. "Collaboration groups?"

Alex Rivera stood, energized. "We have: 'How might we reimagine the client intake process so that in-house counsel feel collaboration begins before engagement?'"

Lucy wrote it on the COLLABORATION chart. "I love this. Tell me why 'before engagement' matters."

Maggie McNamee explained. "Because if collaboration starts after we've already scoped the work, set the fee, and begun working, we've already established a vendor-client dynamic. But if collaboration begins during intake as we scope, define the problem, and discuss fees, we establish a partnership dynamic from day one."

"And it shifts the question from 'what will you do for us' to 'what will we accomplish together,'" Lisa Martinez added.

Lucy stepped back and looked at the three statements on the flip charts:

> **COMMUNICATION:** How might we communicate with our clients so they feel confident that the firm understands their need for clarity once a matter is ongoing and they have less visibility into its status?
>
> **PRICING:** How might we reimagine our pricing models so clients feel our incentives are aligned with their success, not our time?
>
> **COLLABORATION:** How might we reimagine the client intake process so that in-house counsel feel collaboration begins before engagement?

"These are excellent," Lucy said. "Do you see what you've done? You've taken extensive conversations with clients, dozens of Post-it notes, and distilled them into three focused problem statements that are clear enough to guide action but open enough to invite creativity."

She walked along the flip charts. "Each one focuses on the client's experience and what they feel, what they need, what they perceive. Each one identifies a specific leverage point, whether that's ongoing communication, pricing models, or the intake process. And none of them prescribe solutions."

Robert Kim found himself nodding. The process had been uncomfortable. There was so much focus on feelings and perceptions rather than technical legal solutions, but he couldn't deny the resulting problem statements. These were real problems, clearly articulated.

Julian stood. "Fifteen-minute break, then we have one more session before dinner. But I want to note what just happened here. We moved from complaints and feeling defensive, for example, 'our clients don't like our billing,' to insights like 'clients need to feel our incentives align with theirs.' That's a fundamentally different starting point for innovation."

As people filed out for the break, people's attention shifted to how they might tackle the new problems they'd articulated.

At the coffee station, Jessica Park found herself talking with Robert Kim, an unlikely pairing.

"I have to admit," Robert said carefully, "that was more useful than I expected. We've talked about pricing problems for years, but I've never heard anyone frame it quite that way, as 'aligned with their success, not our time.'"

"It names what we all know but don't say," Jessica replied. "The billable hour creates real conflicts between what's good for clients and what's good for our revenue."

Robert was quiet for a moment. "The question is whether we can actually solve it. Lots of firms have tried alternative fee arrangements. Most still default primarily back to hourly billing."

"Maybe because they were trying to solve the wrong problem," Jessica suggested. "They were trying to solve 'how do we price differently' instead of 'how do we align incentives.' That's a different question."

Robert raised an eyebrow, skeptically, "I hope you're right."

Near the windows, Alex and Priya were enthusiastically discussing the intake HMW with Lisa Martinez.

"This could completely change how we start client relationships," Alex was saying. "I mean, granted, I've never actually *been* in one of these conversations, but it sounds like they're structured all wrong to me. Imagine if the first conversation wasn't all about the firm's individual lawyer capabilities and credentials, but about telling a story about how the firm could solve problems for the client by co-designing the engagement around the client's specific needs?"

"It would require a different skillset," Lisa noted. "Less pitch, more facilitation. More questions, fewer answers up front. More listening and more demonstration of curiosity and understanding. Frankly, less showing off."

"But that's what clients are asking for," Priya said, referencing the panel. "They want partnership, not just star lawyers. This could be how we signal that from the start."

Across the room, Sarah Williams and Tom Brennan were having a quieter conversation about implementation.

"These are great problem statements," Tom said. "But solving them and actually changing our pricing models, redesigning intake, and transforming how we communicate is a million times harder, if not altogether impossible."

"Totally," Sarah agreed. "But at least now we know what we're trying to accomplish. That's better than just trying things randomly and hoping something sticks."

Lucy stood with Julian, watching the conversations intently.

"Well, we're moving from philosophy to practice," Lucy said. "This morning was about understanding, which is important but somewhat abstract. This afternoon was about defining problems. They're putting shape around issues they can actually work with. Eventually we'll move into generating solutions and that's when the lawyer rubber meets the creative road and things get exciting."

"Or contentious," Julian said with a slight smile, putting his hand to his temple, anticipating the headaches to come.

"Or both," Lucy agreed. "But that's what transformation looks like. If everyone's comfortable, we're not pushing hard enough."

Reader Reflection

Reframing the Problem

The firm moved from complaining about clients to defining opportunities using "How Might We" statements.

1. **The Complaint Audit:** Think of the last time you vented about a client. If you stripped away the emotion, what was the underlying unmet need (for you or the client)?
2. **The "Goldilocks" Zone:** Look at a problem your firm is currently trying to solve. Is it framed too broadly ("How might we fix our culture?") or too narrowly ("How might we get associates to enter time by Friday?")? Try rewriting it to find the middle ground.
3. **Solution Bias:** Are you trying to solve a problem before you've defined it? (e.g., deciding to buy new software before understanding why the old process failed).

Chapter 14

Turning the Lens Inward: Design Thinking for Internal Transformation

When people returned from the break, Lucy changed the slide to show a simple Venn diagram with two overlapping circles: **External Clients** and **Internal Stakeholders**. In the middle, where the circles overlapped, the diagram stated "Design Thinking to Solve End User Needs."

"I know it's been a long day, but before we break for dinner, I want to expand your thinking about who benefits from design thinking," she began. "This morning and afternoon, we've focused on external clients, like general counsel, in-house legal departments, the people who hire us and pay our bills. And obviously that's critical. We wouldn't exist without them. But there's another group of users whose experience determines whether this firm succeeds or fails."

She clicked to reveal photos of associates at desks, partners in meetings, staff members working.

"Your colleagues. Your future lateral recruits. Law students deciding where to start their legal careers. Business development teams trying to coordinate across practice groups and support our lawyers in going to market with their services. These are all users experiencing systems you've designed, often unintentionally."

Jessica Park sat up straighter. This was suddenly very relevant to her own experience.

"Think about it," Lucy continued. "Associates are users of your training and development system. What's their experience? Do they feel supported in building skills, or do they feel like they're just billing time on client matters without any context or connection to a broader purpose or goal? Do they understand their career trajectory, or are they confused about what partnership really requires or what alternatives exist to that path as their own preferences change?"

She walked to the whiteboard. "Law students are users of your recruitment process. What do they experience? Do they feel like the firm genuinely wants to understand their goals and fit, or do they feel processed through a standardized interview machine where they try to differentiate us from other firms through our website and opaque rankings lists?

"Partners trying to develop business are users of your go-to-market systems," she continued. "What's their experience? Do they feel like the firm makes it easy to collaborate across practice groups, or are they essentially running solo practices with a shared letterhead?"

Robert Kim found this framing oddly compelling. He'd never thought of associates as "users" of a system before. He'd always thought they should experience the same system he had—after all, it had produced him! He took deep pride in his talent in mentoring new lawyers. But in some ways, he treated his talent as a rare gem and guarded it jealously. But the lens Lucy was applying also made sense to him. Maybe strong systems should be an asset that benefited the entire firm.

"The same empathy work we did today with clients, including the listening, the observation, the understanding of needs and pain points, can all apply internally, too," Lucy said. "And frankly, it might be even more important, because these are the people who have to implement whatever changes we design this week."

She clicked to a new slide: **Wednesday's Focus**.

"Tomorrow, we're going to apply design thinking to two critical internal challenges that came up repeatedly in Julian's keynote and in Professor Rover's historical overview:

"First, associate development in an AI-augmented world. How do we train lawyers when the traditional apprenticeship model of learning through high-volume routine work is being disrupted? What does formation look like when AI handles document review, preliminary research, and first drafts?"

"**Second, business development transformation.** How do we move from autonomous rainmakers operating independently to coordinated teams that deliver integrated client solutions? How do we create go-to-market strategies that reward collaboration instead of solo performance?"

She waited a minute to let the group absorb that for a minute before moving on.

"These are hard problems. But they're also design problems. They require us to deeply understand the users, who in this case are associates and partners, and then build systems that serve their needs while advancing the firm's strategic goals."

Dwarkesh Jones raised his hand. "But aren't these fundamentally different from client service problems? With clients, we're trying to deliver value they'll pay for. With associates, we're trying to . . . what, exactly?"

"Great question," Lucy said. "What are you trying to do with associates?"

Sarah Williams answered. "Develop them into excellent lawyers who want to stay at the firm, serve clients well, and eventually become leaders here."

"Exactly," Lucy said. "So associates are users of a development system, and the outcome you want is their growth, satisfaction, and retention. That's absolutely a design challenge. You need to understand what they need to thrive, identify barriers to their success, and create systems that serve them better."

She turned to address Dwarkesh's implicit skepticism directly. "You're right that it's different from client service in one key way because you actually have more control over the system. With clients, you're trying to influence their experience within constraints they set from an external place. With internal systems, you have the power to fundamentally redesign them."

"Which makes it both easier and harder," Maggie McNamee observed. "Easier because we control the variables, but also harder because we have to acknowledge our current systems aren't working and because we might have less incentive to change our own systems when change isn't being forced upon us by those that pay the bills."

"Precisely," Lucy said. "But while we might not feel the pressure in the same way, we feel it in another way through the talent that walks out the door or doesn't come here in the first place. And that's talent we don't get to deploy for our clients' benefit to help retain and grow our ability to solve their problems well. And that's what tomorrow is about. We need to honestly assess what's not working and collaborate to redesign what could work better."

She clicked to show a modified empathy map template labeled **Internal Stakeholder Empathy Map** with the same four quadrants: HEARS, FEELS, NEEDS, EXPERIENCES.

"Before dinner, I want to give you a preview exercise. At your tables, I want you to spend just ten minutes doing empathy mapping for one internal stakeholder group. Tables 1 and 2, focus on first-year associates. Tables 3 and 4, focus on mid-level associates, people in years three to five. Tables 5, 6, and 7, focus on partners trying to develop business."

She distributed fresh Post-its. "You're not interviewing these people because we'll do that tomorrow. But based on your own experiences, your observations, and your conversations, what do you think these stakeholders hear, feel, need, and experience?"

"And be honest," she added with a slight smile. "This only works if we're willing to acknowledge uncomfortable truths. Don't tell me what you wish associates experienced. Tell me what they actually experience."

Everyone was exhausted. People stood and stretched their arms skyward, audibly exhaling. Many checked their phones, responding to the many unanswered client emails that were piling up in their absence. Some filtered out to use the restrooms. Lucy knew they needed a break, but she also needed their precious time for their collective focus. This whole week was such a delicate balance; everything could go south at any minute!

Preview Exercise: Internal Empathy

At Table 1, Dwarkesh Jones and Jessica Park found themselves working on first-year associate experience with Tom Brennan and two others.

"What do first-years hear?" Dwarkesh prompted.

"'Bill more hours,'" Jessica said immediately. "That's the constant refrain."

"'You should be learning,'" Tom added. "Though I'm not sure we always provide the structure for that to happen."

"'This is how we've always done it,'" one of the associates at the table said quietly. "Not explicitly, but implicitly and especially if you dare to ask why something works a certain way, that's the answer you get."

They started adding Post-its to the HEARS quadrant.

"What do they feel?" Dwarkesh asked.

There was a pause. Jessica finally spoke. "Overwhelmed. Uncertain about whether they're doing well. Afraid to admit when they don't understand something."

"Isolated," the associate added. "Especially in hybrid work. You're home working on a project and you're not sure if you're doing it right but you don't want to bother the partner too many times."

"Anxious about hours," Tom said, writing it down. "Are they billing enough? Too much to the wrong matters? Will they make the utilization targets?"

The FEELS quadrant was filling with words that were increasingly uncomfortable: overwhelmed, uncertain, isolated, anxious, inadequate.

At Table 3, Robert Kim found himself working on mid-level associate experience with Priya Patel, Sarah Williams, and Michael Solomon.

"By years three to five, they hear different messages," Robert said. "More about quality of work, taking initiative, developing specialization."

"Also 'partnership track,'" Priya added. "There's this constant evaluation happening of whether they are partner material or not, but it's not always transparent what that actually means."

"And they hear mixed messages," Sarah observed. "Be entrepreneurial but don't take risks. Be efficient but bill enough hours. Be specialized but be flexible when we need you on other matters."

"What do they feel?" Robert asked.

"Frustrated," Michael said immediately. "They're good at what they do, they've proven themselves, but they still don't have much autonomy or control over their work."

Priya hesitated, then spoke honestly. "I feel like I'm on a treadmill. I keep working harder, producing more, getting better feedback, but the partnership goalpost keeps moving. Like, what exactly do I need to do to prove I belong here long-term?"

The table was quiet for a moment. Robert found himself reflexively defending the model but also knew from his own experience years before how accurately that seemed to capture the mid-level experience.

"And there's the fear that we're not developing the right skills," Priya continued. "If AI is going to handle routine work, am I learning what I need to be learning to be valuable five years from now?"

At Table 5, Alex Rivera and Maggie McNamee were working on partner business development experience with Lisa Martinez and several others.

"What do partners hear about business development?" Alex asked.

"'It's your responsibility,'" Maggie said. "Individual partners own relationships, generate work, protect their books of business."

"'Cross-selling is important,'" Lisa added. "But there's no real structure or incentive for it. We say we want collaboration, but compensation is based on individual origination."

"'The firm brand helps you,'" one of the corporate partners said, "but then when you need firm resources for a pitch or proposal, you're competing with everyone else for those same resources."

They moved to FEELS.

"Alone," Maggie said simply. "Even in a firm with so many lawyers, business development often feels like a solo sport."

"It sounds like you're conflicted," Alex offered after listening to a few partners share. "Between wanting to collaborate with colleagues and feeling like you're in competition for the same clients and origination credit."

"Uncertain about how to scale," Maggie said. "You can only do so many client dinners, attend so many conferences, maintain so many relationships personally. There's no system for team-based BD."

The empathy maps were filling quickly with observations that felt simultaneously obvious and novel. Obvious because every partner in the room had experienced or observed these patterns. Novel because they'd rarely articulated them quite this way, as user experience problems right out in the open like this as part of a design activity rather than just venting about "how things are as a partner in a law firm."

After ten minutes, Lucy called time. "I know that was brief, and we'll go much deeper tomorrow. But I want you to notice what just happened."

She gestured to the empathy maps around the room. "You identified pain points, emotional experiences, unmet needs, just like you did with external clients. The difference is these are your colleagues. Your future recruits. In some cases, you."

She walked among the tables, scanning the Post-its. "I see a lot of anxiety, uncertainty, frustration, and isolation. I see needs for clarity, support, structure, and autonomy. I see experiences of mixed messages, competition, and systems that don't quite work."

Julian had been watching quietly. Now he spoke up. "This is why I brought you here. Not just to improve client service, though that's obviously critical, but to redesign how we work internally. Because if we can't create systems where our own people thrive, we won't survive as a firm, no matter how well we intend to serve clients."

Lucy nodded. "Tomorrow morning, we're going to do this empathy work more rigorously. We'll talk to actual associates, review data on satisfaction and retention, and really understand the experience of being developed as a lawyer in this firm right now. Then we'll define the problems by crafting HMW statements and break into teams to design solutions to internal and external stakeholder problems."

She clicked to her final slide of the day: **Design Thinking Applies Everywhere**.

"The framework is the same whether you're designing for external clients or internal colleagues:

Empathize with their actual experience, not what you assume

Define problems in ways that open up possibilities

Ideate lots of potential solutions without judgment

Prototype rough versions to test quickly

Test with real users and iterate based on feedback"

She looked around the room. "Client service, associate development, business development, pricing models, and communication strategies are all design challenges. And all of them require the same fundamental shift in mindset: from expert who knows the answers to learner who seeks to understand users' needs."

Julian stood. "That's a lot to process for one day. Let's break for dinner. But tonight, I'd encourage you to reflect on what you heard, both from our client panel and from your own observations about internal stakeholders. Because tomorrow we're going to use those insights to start thinking about how this firm develops talent and builds business."

"And," Lucy added with a smile, "tomorrow afternoon we'll practice developing HMW statements for these internal challenges, just like we did today for client service. So you'll get better at this framework before we move into ideation on Thursday."

Dinner Conversations: Shifting Inward

The dining room that evening had a noticeably different energy than the night before. Monday's dinner had been dominated by conversations about AI, client pressure, and business model disruption, all external forces acting on the firm. Tuesday's dinner turned inward, with people discussing their own experiences and observations more personally.

At a table near the windows, Jessica Park was having an unexpectedly candid conversation with Sarah Williams and two senior associates about what it actually felt like to be a mid-level associate right now.

"That empathy mapping exercise was uncomfortable," Jessica admitted. "Seeing 'uncertain,' 'isolated,' 'anxious' up on the board? Those are exactly the words I would use to describe my experience some weeks, but I've never said that out loud to partners before."

Sarah nodded sympathetically. "I remember that stage. You're good at what you do, you're getting positive feedback, but you have no idea if you're actually on track for partnership or just . . . existing."

"And the AI conversation makes it worse," one of the senior associates added. "Like, I'm working hard to develop skills that might not even be relevant in five years. Am I learning the right things?"

"That's exactly what we need to address tomorrow," Sarah said. "Not just telling people what to learn but actually designing a development system that makes sense for the future we're heading into, not the past we came from."

Across the room, Robert Kim was having a surprisingly engaging conversation with Alex Rivera and Priya Patel about business development.

"I've been doing BD the same way for thirty years," Robert said. "Client dinners, conferences, speaking engagements, personal relationships. It works, but you're right in that it doesn't scale. And it doesn't really leverage the firm's capabilities. I'm selling Robert Kim, who happens to work at this firm, but not the full resources of the firm."

"But the compensation system rewards that, doesn't it?" Priya asked carefully, surprised at how open Robert was being with them and afraid he would shut the door just as they were peering inside. "You get credit for originating work. Why would you share that credit or collaborate if it reduces your individual compensation?"

Robert was quiet for a moment. "You're not wrong. The system incentivizes exactly the behavior we say we want to change."

"So what would a team-based BD system look like?" Alex asked, less cautious than Priya. "How do you reward collaboration without letting people freeload on others' work?"

"That," Robert said, "is the question we need to craft tomorrow."

At the leadership table, Julian was debriefing the day with Lucy, Tom Brennan, and Lisa Martinez.

"The empathy mapping for internal stakeholders hit differently than the client work," Tom observed. "With clients, we could maintain some emotional distance; they're external, we're analyzing their needs. But when we're empathizing with associates, that's us examining our own systems and acknowledging they're not working."

"That's why it's so important," Lucy said. "External client focus is necessary, but not sufficient. If we improve client service while our people are miserable and leaving, we haven't actually solved anything. In some ways, we've made it worse because we're trying to build solutions but we won't have the talent to execute on them."

"The question is whether we can be honest enough about our internal dysfunction to actually fix it," Lisa added. "It's one thing to admit our pricing model frustrates clients. It's another to admit our development system is failing associates."

Julian nodded slowly. "Tomorrow will be the test. If people can show up with the same honesty we saw in that brief empathy exercise and actually acknowledge what's not working instead of defending the status quo, could we design something genuinely better?"

"Perhaps . . . and if they can't?" Tom asked.

"Then we'll know that too," Julian said, thinking of Sandy and the merger offer, "And we'll make decisions accordingly."

Nearby, Maggie McNamee sat with several mid-level partners discussing the challenges of balancing practice development, client service, and firm leadership.

"I'm at the point where I need to decide what kind of partner I want to be," one corporate partner was saying. "Do I focus on becoming a rainmaker? A practice group leader? A technical expert? Because the firm seems to reward rainmaking above everything else, but that's not where my strengths are."

"And the firm says it values all three," Maggie replied, "but the compensation system and partnership advancement criteria tell a different story. We need to decide if we genuinely want multiple paths to success, or if that's just something we say in recruiting materials."

"That's a design problem," another partner observed, already using Lucy's framework. "We need to empathize with different partner types, like rainmakers, service partners, and leaders, and design systems that allow all of them to thrive."

Throughout the dining room, variations of these conversations played out. The day's work had created a shared vocabulary of concepts like empathy, user experience, and design thinking, and maybe even a shared willingness to examine uncomfortable truths about how the firm actually functioned versus how they claimed it functioned.

As dinner wound down and people began drifting toward their rooms, Lucy found herself standing with Julian on the terrace overlooking the mountains. The sun had set, leaving the Blue Ridge Mountains silhouetted against a deepening purple sky.

"You know what surprised me today?" Julian said. "How emotional the empathy work was. When we were mapping the associate experience and I saw 'isolated,' 'uncertain,' 'anxious,' I felt that. These are people I'm responsible for, and we're not serving them well."

"That's empathy working," Lucy said quietly. "That discomfort you're feeling? That's what drives real change. Not data, not strategic imperatives, but genuine understanding of what people experience in the systems we've created."

Julian nodded. "Then tomorrow we lean into the discomfort."

"Tomorrow we lean into the discomfort," Lucy agreed.

Chapter 15

Reimagining Associate Development

The Wednesday morning sun broke through scattered clouds as people filed into the breakfast area.

At the coffee station, Jessica Park found herself in conversation with several other mid-level associates about last night's dinner discussions.

"Did you notice how many partners actually acknowledged the development system isn't working?" one litigation associate said quietly. "Robert Kim came *this* close to admitting the apprenticeship model is broken."

"Acknowledging it is one thing," Jessica replied. "The question is whether they'll actually redesign it, or just make small tweaks and hope it's enough."

Priya Patel joined them, plate in hand. "Lucy said this morning is about associate development. I'm curious if they'll actually involve us in the design, or if it'll be partners talking about what they think we need and design it *for* us."

"I guess we'll find out," Jessica said.

Near the windows, Robert Kim was having coffee with Dwarkesh Jones and Tom Brennan, discussing the same topic from a different perspective.

"The problem is we know the old model is breaking down," Robert said, "but we don't have a clear picture of what should replace it. How do you develop judgment without doing the foundational work?"

"That's the question," Dwarkesh agreed. "Though I wonder if we're too attached to how we were trained. Maybe there *are* better ways to develop lawyers that we haven't imagined because we keep trying to replicate our own experience."

Tom was reviewing his notes. "The financial piece terrifies me. It's existential. It's great to say, 'let's build a better system.' But If corporate clients stop paying for junior associate time because AI is more efficient, where does funding for training come from? Do we eat those costs? Pass them to clients differently? Build them into pricing models?"

"I honestly have no idea, and it doesn't seem like anyone else does, either. All questions for today, I suppose," Robert said.

At 9:00 a.m., people settled into the conference room. Lucy stood at the front with someone new, a woman in her late fifties with silver-streaked hair, wearing jeans and a blazer, radiating a kind of rugged confidence that seemed a bit unexpected for a legal audience.

"Good morning," Lucy began. "I hope you're all processing yesterday's work. We shifted from understanding external client needs to recognizing that design thinking applies just as powerfully to our internal systems. Today we're going to examine two of those internal systems in depth, starting this morning with associate development and our relationship with legal education."

She gestured to the woman beside her. "Professor Katherine Morrison teaches at Duke Law, here in North Carolina. She's spent her career studying how law schools prepare—or fail to prepare—lawyers for actual practice. She's also the author of *The Theory-Practice Divide: How Law Schools Lost Their Way and How We Fix Them,* which I strongly recommend all of you read after this retreat."

Professor Morrison smiled warmly at the group. "Thank you, Lucy. And thank you all for letting me crash your retreat. When Lucy described what you're doing this week and how you're taking five days to fundamentally reimagine how your firm operates, I knew I wanted to be part of it. Because the challenges you're facing as a firm are intimately connected and are a mirror in many ways to the challenges law schools face as institutions."

She clicked to her first slide, which showed two portraits side by side: Christopher Columbus Langdell and Paul Cravath.

"To understand how we got to our current crisis in lawyer development, we need to understand these two men and the systems they created in the late nineteenth and twentieth centuries because they are systems we're still operating within today, despite the fact that the world has changed dramatically."

The Langdell Method Meets Cravath Apprenticeship

Professor Morrison walked to the center of the room, away from the screen.

"Christopher Columbus Langdell became dean of Harvard Law School in 1870 and revolutionized legal education by introducing the case method. Instead of practitioners teaching new lawyers the law, professors would teach students to think like lawyers by analyzing judicial opinions and extracting legal principles."

She clicked to show a late-nineteenth-century law school classroom, students with casebooks open.

"This was genuinely innovative for its time. It moved legal education from rote memorization to analytical reasoning. It created a scientific approach to law that asked students to examine cases as a scientist might examine specimens, looking for patterns and principles."

"But," and here her tone shifted slightly, "Langdell made a critical assumption that shaped legal education for the next 150 years. He believed that 'law is a science' and that everything students needed to know could be found in appellate court opinions. Practical skills like client counseling, negotiation, drafting documents, and trial advocacy were mere technical skills that could be picked up through practice."

Alex Rivera was listening carefully. This was starting to explain a lot about his law school experience and why he felt so unprepared to actually *do* anything practical when he became a lawyer, especially when it came to leveraging technology.

"This created what we call the theory-practice divide," Professor Morrison continued. "Law schools became focused on teaching legal doctrine and analytical reasoning, the '*thinking* like a lawyer' part.

The assumption was that law firms would teach the practical skills, the '*practicing* like a lawyer' part."

She clicked to show Paul Cravath's photograph again. "And for a while, this division of labor worked reasonably well. Paul Cravath's system, which I know you discussed Monday with Professor Rover, created structured apprenticeship programs at law firms. Firms hired the best law school graduates produced through Langdell's program and trained them systematically in practical skills while giving them increasingly complex work."

"Law schools did theory, firms did practice, and everyone was more or less satisfied with the arrangement."

She paused, looking around the room. "But that system depended on several assumptions that no longer hold true. And understanding why those assumptions have broken down is crucial to designing something better."

Why Theory Remains Divorced from Practice

Professor Morrison's next slide showed a statement that surprised some in the room: **Very few tenured law professors have practiced law for more than five years before entering academia**.

"Here's the first problem," she said. "The incentive structure in law schools actively selects against practice experience. To get a tenure-track position at most law schools, you need elite credentials from schools like Harvard, Yale, and Stanford, plus a prestigious clerkship, maybe a fellowship. What you don't need is significant practice experience."

She clicked through a career trajectory diagram. "The typical path to legal academia is: law school → law review → clerkship → teaching fellowship → tenure-track position. Maybe you practiced for a year or two, maybe you didn't. Either way, you're hired primarily based on scholarly potential, not practice wisdom."

Sarah Williams raised her hand. "But surely the scholarship informs practice? Understanding legal theory helps lawyers practice better?"

"Sometimes, yes," Professor Morrison acknowledged. "But let me show you something." She pulled up research data. "Scholars are rarely cited by courts and therefore don't have much impact on the actual substantive law. The vast majority of law review articles are read by other legal scholars and nobody else. They're written to advance academic careers by getting tenure, to get cited by other scholars, to establish expertise in narrow doctrinal areas."

She let that sink in. "Meanwhile, the American Bar Association's own surveys show that new lawyers feel deeply unprepared for practice. They don't know how to manage a case, conduct client interviews, negotiate settlements, or draft contracts. Law schools taught them to analyze appellate opinions brilliantly, but not to do the daily work of lawyering. The divide between what happens in law schools and what happens in the legal world outside its walls continues to grow even as the world of legal practice becomes more complex and demands a faster evolution of skills from new lawyers."

Robert Kim spoke up. "But we've always known this. Law schools teach theory, firms teach practice. That's how it's always worked."

"Right," Professor Morrison said. "Which brings us to the second major assumption that's breaking down."

Corporate Subsidization of Professional Development

Her next slide showed a financial flow diagram:

Corporate Clients → Firms (paying for junior associate time) → Associate Development

"For decades, the Langdell-Cravath bargain worked because corporate clients were willing to subsidize associate training. They paid for junior associates to do document review, preliminary research, routine drafting, due diligence. This work was revenue generating for the firm and also educational (if mind-numbing!) for the associates. Associates learned while doing billable work, and clients accepted paying for that learning curve."

Tom Brennan was nodding. This was his world. He knew that associate work fueled the firm's financial success while developing its new lawyers. He also knew clients hated paying for it and pushed back against it all the time. An increasing number refused to pay for first- and second-year work at all.

"This subsidy model made financial sense for firms," Professor Morrison continued. "You hired smart law school graduates, paid them healthy salaries to compete with peer firms for top talent, billed their time at increasingly higher rates as they developed skills, and eventually, if they were good, they became profitable associates and then partners who generated significant revenue."

She clicked to a new slide showing the model breaking down. "But four things have undermined this bargain:

"**First, client sophistication.** General counsel have gotten much better at scrutinizing bills and pushing back on paying for junior associate training time. As one GC told me, 'I'm happy to invest in your associates' development, but not at hundreds of dollars an hour for low value-add work.'"

Several people glanced at each other, remembering yesterday's panel conversation and countless client conversations.

"**Second, alternative legal service providers (ALSPs), off-shoring, and legal ops.** Why pay law firm rates for document review when specialized companies and international operations can do it faster and cheaper? Why pay billed rates for junior associates to do preliminary research when the GC's legal ops team can optimize across available intelligence to push back and lower rates, decreasing firm realization rates across the sector?"

"**Third, associate salaries and billable rates for their time** have skyrocketed. Rather than modest salaries, the largest firms in the world now pay their new lawyers $250,000 a year and up and bill their time at $500 an hour and more, not exactly a bargain for anyone. And with associates moving on from their firms by paying down their student loans with those big salaries, firms are no longer recouping their investment in recruiting and training them, and the churn results in significant costs to the firms, in both dollars and friction in client service as new lawyers are brought on board."

"**And finally, artificial intelligence.** This is the big one. AI can now do in minutes what used to take junior associates hours or days. Document review, legal research, first-draft memos, due diligence analysis. This is all the work that used to be both billable and formative."

She pulled up a chart showing associate utilization rates declining over the past few years. "Corporate clients are asking: why should we pay for human associates to do work that AI can do better, faster, and cheaper? And firms are struggling to answer that question."

Julian felt this viscerally. This was why they were sitting in this room.

"So the financial model that supported associate development, with corporate clients paying for junior lawyers to learn through doing and clients footing the tab while law schools teach theory and collect massive amounts of tuition for the promise of well-paying jobs where the practical training will happen, is collapsing," Professor Morrison said. "Which means firms need to find new ways to fund and structure professional development."

Physical Proximity Assumptions in a Hybrid World

Professor Morrison's next slide showed two images side by side: a crowded law firm office from the 1990s and a laptop on a kitchen table.

"The Cravath apprenticeship model assumed something else too: physical proximity. Junior lawyers learned by being around senior lawyers, and sitting in on client meetings, overhearing phone calls, getting real-time feedback on work product, absorbing firm culture through daily interaction."

She walked among the tables. "How many of you learned crucial lessons just by being in the office? Someone stopping by your desk to explain something? Overhearing a negotiation? Watching a partner handle a difficult client call?"

Many hands went up, especially among the more senior attorneys.

"That's tacit knowledge transfer," Professor Morrison explained. "Knowledge that's hard to articulate explicitly but relatively easy to absorb through observation and participation. And it only works when people are physically together regularly."

She clicked to show data on remote work trends. "COVID-19 proved that legal work could happen remotely. But it had a cost. Junior lawyers working from home reported feeling isolated, uncertain about expectations, unable to learn from informal interactions. Skill development suffered when people weren't physically together."

Dwarkesh Jones raised his hand. "But we've developed hybrid models now. People are in the office some days."

"True," Professor Morrison said. "But hybrid work creates coordination challenges. If associates are in the office Tuesday and Thursday, but the partners they need to learn from are in Monday and Wednesday, proximity doesn't help. If client meetings happen virtually, associates can't just 'sit in' informally; they have to be specifically invited. And they can't just "listen in" on Zoom. If a client can see them, they will wonder if they're paying for them to be on the call, which is unfair to both the client and the associate.

She showed research findings. "Studies of hybrid work in professional services show that junior employees bear the highest costs. Senior people with established relationships and knowledge can work remotely effectively. But junior people trying to learn their profession struggle without consistent access to mentors and peers.

"So the physical proximity assumption that undergirded the Cravath system, where junior lawyers would learn by being around senior lawyers, has been disrupted by hybrid work," she concluded. "Which means firms need intentional development structures, not just osmotic learning."

The Question of Who Develops Lawyers

Professor Morrison's next slide showed a question: **If law schools don't teach practice skills, and firms can't rely on client-subsidized apprenticeship, who develops lawyers?**

"This is the crisis we're about to be facing," she said plainly. "We have a broken system where neither law schools nor law firms are effectively preparing lawyers for modern practice, and each passes the buck to the other, with the newest members of the profession caught in the gears of change, carrying the burden of student debt and with the reasonable but misplaced expectation of a well-designed system to develop them."

She clicked through disturbing statistics:

- 45% of associates report feeling unprepared for their jobs
- Only 23% of hiring partners believe new law school graduates are "practice ready"
- Lawyer well-being crisis strongly correlated with lack of mentorship and unclear career development

"The traditional answer of 'law schools teach thinking, firms teach doing' doesn't work anymore. Firms don't have the time, resources, or billable work to support multi-year apprenticeships. And law schools aren't changing fast enough to fill the gap."

The Leadership Imperative

Professor Morrison's tone shifted, becoming more optimistic. "But this crisis also creates opportunity. Scott Westfahl and David Wilkins wrote a *Stanford Law Review* article titled "The Leadership Imperative" that I think every law firm leader should read. Their core argument is that legal talent development needs to become a strategic priority and a shared responsibility among schools, firms, and clients, not an afterthought or a beneficiary of a commercial transaction."

She pulled up key concepts from the article:

"**Collaborative Ecosystem:** Moving away from the traditional, segregated model (where law schools teach theory, firms teach practice, and clients pay for it) toward a shared responsibility model where schools, firms, and clients actively collaborate to co-develop legal talent throughout a lawyer's career.

The "Three-Skill" Portfolio: Expanding lawyer training beyond just **technical legal skills** (knowledge of doctrine and analysis) to equally emphasize **professional skills** (teamwork, empathy, design thinking, leadership) and **network-building skills** (creating and managing professional relationships).

Competency-Based Development: Shifting away from time-based apprenticeship models (learning by "osmosis" or tenure) to intentional, structured development paths where lawyers must demonstrate specific competencies and behaviors at each career stage.

Lawyers as Leaders: Viewing leadership development not as a "soft skill" for senior partners, but as a core professional requirement for lawyers at all levels, necessitating early training in decision-making, resilience, and organizational dynamics.

She looked around the room. "This requires firms to think like professional development organizations, not just legal services businesses. It requires investment of time and money in systematic training that may not be billable."

Robert Kim looked skeptical. "With what budget? If clients won't pay for training time . . ."

"You build it into your business model differently," Professor Morrison said. "Maybe through premium pricing for experienced lawyers. Maybe through fixed-fee arrangements that let you invest efficiency gains in development. Maybe through lower associate compensation in exchange for better training. But you can't just hope it works itself out. I'm not suggesting there are easy answers. But I'm confident that the old model is breaking fast. If you want to produce new lawyers, you need to build something better to replace it."

Frameworks for the Future

Professor Morrison's final slides showed two reform efforts.

"**The MacCrate Report** in 1992 and the **IAALS Foundations for Practice** survey in 2016 both tried to answer the question: what should new lawyers actually know how to do?"

She displayed the list of fundamental lawyering skills:

1. **Problem Solving** (identifying and diagnosing problems, generating strategies)
2. **Legal Analysis and Reasoning** (analyzing case law, statutes, and legal theory)
3. **Legal Research** (identifying legal issues and finding governing authorities)
4. **Factual Investigation** (planning and conducting factual inquiries)
5. **Communication** (effectively writing and speaking in legal contexts)
6. **Counseling** (advising clients on their legal options and risks)
7. **Negotiation** (resolving disputes and structuring transactions)
8. **Litigation and ADR Procedures** (understanding trial, arbitration, and mediation)
9. **Organization and Management of Legal Work** (efficiency, systems, and time management)
10. **Recognizing and Resolving Ethical Dilemmas** (applying the rules of professional conduct)

"Notice what's on this list," she said. "Problem-solving. Communication. Counseling. Negotiation. Organization and management of work. These aren't just 'learn the law' skills. These are professional competencies that require deliberate development."

She clicked to the IAALS framework, which organized skills into five categories:

1. **Lawyer as Practitioner:** Mastering the core legal skills and functional competencies of the trade.
2. **Lawyer as Professional:** Acting with integrity, honesty, and adherence to ethical standards
3. **Lawyer as Communicator:** Communicating effectively with clients, colleagues, and the court
4. **Lawyer as Problem Solver:** Thinking critically to resolve client issues, not just identifying legal risks
5. **Lawyer as Self-Starter:** Demonstrating resilience, managing one's own workload, and taking ownership of professional development

"This is a much more comprehensive vision of what it means to be practice-ready. And the key insight is that neither law schools nor law firms can deliver this alone, especially as the corporate subsidization piece breaks down. It requires real partnership. Otherwise, I worry that the profession is not providing a return on investment to its newest members."

She looked directly at Julian. "Some progressive law schools are changing. Creating practice-based courses. Hiring more practitioners as faculty. Building experiential learning programs. But they can't replicate the real client work and firm culture that shapes professional development. That's your domain.

"Meanwhile, firms can't replicate the structured learning, dedicated time for skill development, and safe environment for experimentation that schools can provide. That's their domain."

She clicked to her final slide: **Collaborative Solutions Needed**.

"What we need is a new bargain. Law schools and law firms working together to develop lawyers. Schools focusing on foundational competencies and providing structured early training. Firms providing real-world experience, mentorship, and advanced skill development. Both institutions sharing responsibility and costs."

She paused, looking around the room. "But it requires law firms to see associate development as a strategic investment, not a cost to be minimized. And it requires law schools to see practice readiness as core to their mission, not peripheral, or even worse, beneath them."

Professor Morrison smiled slightly. "I understand you're spending this week reimagining your firm's future. I'd argue that reimagining how you develop lawyers needs to be central to that future. Because in an AI-augmented world, your competitive advantage isn't going to be efficiency. Technology can provide that. The competitive advantage is going to be the wisdom, judgment, and relationship skills of exceptionally well-developed lawyers."

She looked at Lucy. "That's my provocation for you. I'll stick around for questions, but I suspect you have work to do."

Discussion and Questions

Lucy moved to the front as Professor Morrison sat down. "Questions for Professor Morrison before we move into our workshop?"

The room was quiet for a moment, people processing. Then Priya Patel raised her hand.

"You talked about law schools and firms sharing responsibility for development. But practically, what would that look like? Do we fund law school programs? Do they provide post-graduate training?"

Professor Morrison nodded. "Great question. Some firms are already experimenting. Some fund summer programming at law schools that focuses on practical skills. Some create formal partnerships where law school clinical programs become training grounds for their future associates. Some hire recent graduates for year-long 'fellowship' programs that are explicitly developmental rather than billable.

"The key is getting away from the idea that development ends when someone graduates law school. In other professions, like medicine, accounting, and engineering, there are structured post-graduate training programs. Law has the bar exam, then . . . nothing systematic. We don't even have good metrics around employment outcomes after nine months post-graduation."

Tom Brennan spoke up. "This all costs money at a time when our revenue model is under pressure!"

"Yes," Professor Morrison said bluntly. "Which is why the business model question and the development question are inseparable. If you're still trying to maximize billable hours from day-one associates, you can't invest properly in their development. But if you move to different pricing models that include fixed fees, value pricing, and subscription services, you create room to invest in people."

Tom was drawing diagrams, seeing all the connections clearly and trying without success to imagine a solution.

Jessica Park raised her hand. "You mentioned individualized pathways. What does that mean for someone like me, who is a mid-level associate, good at what I do, but uncertain about whether partnership is even what I want?"

"First, thanks for the bold question in this venue!," Professor Morrison replied. Jessica blushed, immediately questioning the wisdom of what she'd just said.

"Seriously, though, that's exactly the question the profession needs to grapple with," Professor Morrison replied. "Traditional firms have one path: associate to partner, with departures or other roles framed as 'not making it.' We increasingly have non-equity partners, of counsel, business roles, but culturally it can still feel like you haven't achieved 'success.' But what if there were multiple *valuable* career paths? What if you could be a senior associate who specializes deeply? Or counsel who focuses on client service rather than business development? Or move in and out of practice and other roles?"

She looked around. "The profession needs to stop treating equity partnership as the only measure of success and start valuing different contributions differently. But that requires redesigning career structures, compensation systems, and status markers. It's a total redesign project, and it's really long overdue."

Sarah Williams raised her hand. "I'm interested in the hybrid work challenge you identified. How do we provide mentorship and culture-building when people aren't physically together consistently?"

"Intentionality," Professor Morrison said. "Can't rely on osmosis anymore. You need structured programs: regular mentorship meetings, skill-building sessions, feedback loops, cohort-based learning. Some firms are creating dedicated 'development weeks' where people come together intensively. Others are using technology better to record meetings for teaching purposes, creating knowledge bases, using AI to supplement human mentorship.

"First, we have to acknowledge that it won't just happen organically in hybrid work. And honestly, even in a fully physical world, it wasn't happening well. Because it wasn't designed for a modern era. You have to redesign it for the world as it actually exists."

Alex Rivera spoke up. He was always so frustrated that no one saw the possibilities technology offered. They only saw the risks. "What about the AI piece? You said AI is disrupting the training work. But couldn't AI also *enhance* training? Help people practice skills, provide feedback, create simulations?"

Professor Morrison's face lit up. "Absolutely! This is where I get optimistic. AI could be the best teaching tool we've ever had. Imagine associates practicing client interviews with AI clients, getting immediate feedback. Practicing negotiation with AI opposing counsel. Drafting documents and having AI identify weaknesses in their reasoning."

William Klept, one of the most skeptical partners in the room who had spent the first couple of days silently stewing about this entire retreat, immediately felt his muscles clench up at the idea of AI training new associates. He couldn't imagine Julian would entertain such a foolish notion. What did this associate know about anything? Hadn't he heard about hallucinations and all the dangers AI posed to the proper practice of law? And who was this outside "expert" they'd brought in who didn't have to bear any of the risk for a technology when it went haywire?

Professor Morrison continued, "AI doesn't replace human mentorship; the judgment, the wisdom, the relationship skills still need human teachers. But it can complement human mentorship by providing unlimited practice opportunities, immediate feedback, and personalized learning paths. Look, many lawyers talk about the world we've lost like it was ideal. I was a law firm associate once. I don't know about you, but I don't recall it being a perfectly designed developmental model for learning a very challenging craft.

"So now we have challenges, but also a chance to build something better. We can choose to invest in using AI for development or just use it to increase efficiency without reinvesting in people. But I think the latter is a very short-sighted strategy in a profession rooted in human problem-solving."

Lucy stood. "Thank you, Professor Morrison. I think we're well positioned for what we need to do next."

As the professor gathered her materials and people stood to stretch, Lucy clicked to the next slide: **Empathy Work: Understanding the Associate Experience**.

"We're going to take a fifteen-minute break, and then we're going to do something different from yesterday. Yesterday we empathized with clients through listening to a panel and analyzing their responses. This morning, we're going to empathize with associates by interviewing them directly."

She looked at the associates scattered throughout the room. "After the break, I want all associates, first-year through senior, to gather at the front of the room. Partners and of counsel, you're going to conduct structured empathy interviews. Not mentoring conversations, not performance reviews, but genuine inquiry to understand their experience of being developed as lawyers in this firm."

William Klept crossed his arms, looking over to his laptop to get an update on the client emails that were relentlessly piling up in his inbox. To him, this was a ridiculous waste of time. He had clients with plenty of law firms ready to serve them, waiting for him to respond and this "expert" was leading associates who should be working on matters and generating revenue down a rabbit hole. They did not belong in this conversation, which was an utter waste, in his opinion. The firm should have stuck with a standard retreat format, with a partners-only review of financials and advice from a pricing expert on how to remain profitable.

Meanwhile, there was a visible shift in the room. The associates looked both nervous and intrigued. The partners looked uncomfortable.

"This might feel awkward," Lucy acknowledged. "That's okay. Empathy work often does. But if we're going to redesign our development system, we need to understand the current experience with fresh eyes. Not what we assume associates experience or what you remember from when you were an associate, but what they actually experience."

Julian stood. "To be clear: this is a safe space. Associates, I want you to be honest about your experience, both the good and the frustrating. Partners, I want you to listen without defending, without explaining, without problem-solving yet. Just seek to understand. We've structured these interviews as much as possible to partner associates with lawyers they don't normally work with to maximize authentic answers."

Lucy clicked to show the interview framework they'd use. "After the break, we'll organize into pairs, with one associate and one partner or of counsel. Thirty minute interviews. Then we'll synthesize what we heard and craft HMW statements together."

As people filed out for the break, the conversations were noticeably anxious. Associates glommed together, comparing notes about what they should and shouldn't say. Partners looked wary and preemptively annoyed about what they were about to hear.

Near the coffee station, Robert Kim said to Tom Brennan, "This feels risky. Do we really want associates telling us everything that's wrong with how we develop them?"

"Only if we're serious about fixing it," Tom replied. "Otherwise, what's the point of this week?"

Jessica Park stood with Priya and Alex, also nervous. "How honest should we be?" Priya asked. "I mean, do they actually want to hear that I feel like I'm stumbling around figuring things out on my own?"

"I think that's exactly what they need to hear," Jessica said. "If we're not honest now, nothing changes."

Lucy stood with Julian, watching the anxious energy. "This is the moment," she said quietly. "Either they're willing to hear uncomfortable truths, or they're not. And if they're not, we'll know we're not ready for real transformation."

"Then let's find out," Julian said, nibbling on his cuticle, a nervous habit he'd developed while preparing for oral argument during his first year in law school. This week was beginning to feel more ambitious than he thought his partners were prepared for. What had he unleashed on them and how could he put the toothpaste back in the tube now?

The break stretched slightly longer than fifteen minutes; people needed the extra time to prepare for what was coming. But eventually, Lucy called them back. The associates gathered somewhat awkwardly at the front. The partners and senior lawyers spread out around the room, waiting for instructions.

It was time to stop theorizing about associate development and start understanding it from the people living through it.

Reader Reflection

The Talent Crisis

Professor Morrison argued that the "Langdell-Cravath" bargain is broken because clients will no longer pay for junior lawyers to learn by osmosis.

1. **The Funding Gap:** If clients refuse to pay for junior associate time (due to AI efficiency or billing guidelines), who pays for your lawyers' training? Is your firm absorbing that cost intentionally, or just watching margins erode?

2. **The "Osmosis" Myth:** In a hybrid world, do you have a structured plan for transferring "tacit knowledge" (judgment, soft skills, firm culture), or are you still relying on associates just "picking it up" by being near you?

3. **Competencies:** What would you list as the most important competencies for lawyers at your firm to master at each stage of their development? Does your firm currently structure its systems to incentivize these outcomes?

Chapter 16

Empathy Interviews: Understanding Associate Experience

Lucy distributed a one-page interview guide to each partner and of counsel.

"This is a structured empathy interview," she explained. "Not a conversation where you jump in with your own experiences or solutions. Your job is to ask questions, listen deeply, and understand. Take notes—not to evaluate, but to capture what you hear."

She displayed the interview framework on screen:

EMPATHY INTERVIEW GUIDE: ASSOCIATE DEVELOPMENT

Opening: "I want to understand your actual experience of being developed as a lawyer here. Not what the firm says it provides, but what you actually experience day-to-day."

Questions to explore:

- Walk me through a typical week. When do you feel like you're learning? When do you feel stuck?
- Tell me about a time you felt supported in your development. What made that work well?

- Tell me about a time you felt lost or uncertain. What was missing?
- How do you know if you're doing well? What signals tell you you're on track?
- What skills are you worried you're not developing? Why?
- What would you change about how you're being developed if you could change anything?

Throughout: Ask "Why?" and "Tell me more about that" to go deeper. *Resist the urge to explain or defend.*

Closing: "What else should I understand about your experience that I haven't asked about?"

"You have thirty minutes per interview," Lucy said. "Partners, pick an associate you don't work with regularly, as a fresh perspective is valuable here. Associates, be honest. This only works if you tell us what's real, not what you think we want to hear."

The room reorganized into pairs, spreading out to different corners, tables, even out onto the terrace for privacy. The nervous energy was palpable. It was like dozens of first dates, but with even higher stakes.

Interview One: First-Year Experience

Robert Kim found himself paired with Maya Davis, a junior associate in the litigation department. They settled at a corner table, and Robert opened his notebook with slightly awkward formality. Maya seemed so young. He couldn't believe he'd ever been such a junior lawyer. Could it really have been almost thirty years ago he'd been in her shoes? It seemed like just yesterday, but he also felt like he had virtually nothing in common with this new lawyer.

"So," he began, consulting the guide, "I want to understand your actual experience of being developed as a lawyer here. Not what the firm says it provides, but what you actually experience day-to-day."

Maya hesitated, choosing her words carefully. "Can I be really honest?"

"That's the point," Robert said, and was surprised to find he meant it.

"Okay. Most days, I feel like I'm guessing. I get assignments with directions like 'review these documents,' 'research this issue,' 'draft this memo,' but I rarely understand why. Like, what's the broader context? What's the strategy? What matters most to the client?"

She looked down at her hands. "So I do the work as best I can, send it back, and then . . . nothing. Maybe I get some edits in track changes, maybe I don't hear anything for days. And I'm left wondering: Did I do it right? Was it good enough? What should I do differently next time?"

Robert was writing, his pen moving quickly. "Tell me more about the feedback piece."

"It's not that I never get feedback," Maya clarified. "Sometimes someone will say 'good work' or 'this needs more depth.' But it's sparse. And it's rarely connected to bigger picture development, like, 'here's how this assignment fits into your skill-building' or 'here's what you should focus on improving.'"

"How do you know if you're doing well?" Robert asked.

Maya laughed. "I don't, really. I track my hours, so I know if I'm hitting my billable targets. But in terms of actual lawyering skills? I have no idea if I'm where I should be at month nine of practice."

"What skills are you worried you're not developing?"

"Client interaction," Maya said immediately. "I've barely spoken to a client. I remember during law school, everyone said I should choose a firm that would give me 'client contact.' But now? I see partners on calls when I walk by their offices, but I'm not included. Do they not want me on the calls because they're afraid I would say something stupid? Should I ask to be included? But I don't because I'm not sure what's going on and I assume there's a reason I'm not included. So I'm becoming good at research and document review, but I have no idea how to actually counsel someone, or explain complex issues clearly, or manage client expectations."

She paused. "And also, judgment. Everyone talks about developing judgment constantly, but what does that even mean? This comes up especially now when people talk about how AI will impact lawyers. We're all going to skip 'rote work' and have to develop 'judgment' faster, but how? I do tasks, but I'm not making strategic decisions. I'm executing someone else's strategy, which is fine, but when do I learn to think strategically myself?"

Robert and Maya talked for a while more, exploring why Maya had chosen the firm, the things that kept her up at night, and what her long-term goals were. Robert found himself remembering how disorienting that phase of his career was and how lost he felt, even though he was working so hard to prove himself. Most times, he, too, felt like he was just barely keeping his head above water.

Robert asked the closing question. "What else should I understand about your experience that I haven't asked about?"

Maya thought for a long moment. "I think . . . I came here because of the culture. Everyone said this was a place that cared about development, that invested in associates. And I believe people mean that. The people here are really nice. I hear horror stories from friends at other firms, and I'm truly grateful not to be there. But the reality is everyone's so busy that development happens—when it does at all—in the cracks between billable work. There's so little structure. Very few regular check-ins. No development plan. It's just . . . do assignments, hope you're learning, hope someone notices if you're struggling. And sometimes there are good programs the firm puts on that I really want to attend, but a partner will email me with something urgent, so I can't go. So I can see how the firm feels it *is* creating these opportunities for us and we're just not showing up, but it feels like we have no choice but to do billable work at the expense of everything else."

She looked up at Robert. "I don't think anyone's doing this on purpose. I think everyone's well-intentioned but overwhelmed. But the result is I feel like I'm on my own most of the time in figuring out how to become a lawyer."

Interview Two: Mid-Level Experience

Across the room, Maggie McNamee was interviewing John Forte, a fifth-year corporate associate. They'd moved to the terrace for privacy.

"Walk me through a typical week," Maggie said. "When do you feel like you're learning?"

John considered this. "To be honest, as strange as it might sound, I learn most when something goes wrong. When a deal gets complicated, when negotiations get tough, when a client pushes back or something like that. In those situations, I'm actually thinking hard and developing skills. The routine work doesn't teach me much anymore. I can draft a basic stock purchase agreement in my sleep."

"And when do you feel stuck?"

"When I'm doing work I've already mastered because we need to bill hours," John said bluntly. "Like, I'll spend twenty hours on due diligence that I could probably do in ten if we structured it differently or used better technology. But we need the billable time, so I do it the long way. And I'm not learning anything; I'm just billing."

Maggie wrote that down, trying not to react defensively.

"Tell me about a time you felt supported in your development."

John's expression softened. "Last year, Sarah Williams pulled me into a negotiation even though it wasn't my deal. She spent time beforehand explaining the dynamics, the client's priorities, what she was trying to accomplish. During the negotiation, she'd look to me for input. Afterward, we debriefed on what worked, what didn't, what I should watch for next time."

"That one experience taught me more than six months of routine drafting. Because it was intentional and she was deliberately developing me, not just using me for staffing."

"What made that different from other experiences?"

"She explained the 'why,' not just the 'what.' She gave me decision-making opportunities, even small ones. She debriefed so I could understand my own learning. And she made time for it even though she was busy."

Maggie asked, "What skills are you worried you're not developing?"

John didn't hesitate. "Business development. Client relationship management. How to actually originate work. I'm becoming a really good service lawyer. If you give me a deal structure, I'll execute it beautifully. But I have no idea how to generate work, how to build a client relationship from scratch, how to identify opportunities."

"And the partnership track conversation assumes I'll figure that out somehow, but nobody's teaching me. So either I'm naturally good at it, which I might not be, or I'm going to hit year seven and realize I don't have the origination credentials for partnership."

"How do you know if you're doing well?" Maggie asked.

"That's just the thing. I don't know what 'doing well' means anymore. I get good feedback on my work product. My hours are solid. But I don't know if I'm on a partnership track, or if I should be looking to lateral, or if there's some other path I should be considering. Nobody's told me, 'Here's where you are, here's what you need to develop, here's what the path looks like.'"

He looked frustrated. "I'm five years in. Shouldn't someone have had that conversation with me by now?"

"What would you change if you could change anything?"

"Structure," John said immediately. "Regular development check-ins, and not performance reviews, but actual conversations about what I'm learning and what I need to learn. Clear expectations for each year, like 'by year four, you should be able to do X, Y, Z.' Intentional assignments that build specific skills, not just whatever staffing needs exist. And honest conversations about partnership, like who's on track, who's not, what the criteria actually are."

He paused. "And I'd create time for development that's not billable. Because right now, everything that helps me grow long-term like training programs, shadowing, practice pitches, networking, all of that comes out of my personal time because it's not billable. That's not sustainable."

Interview Three: Senior Associate Experience

Near the windows, Dwarkesh Jones was interviewing Elena Rodriguez, a seventh-year litigation associate. Elena had a reputation as one of the firm's strongest associates, which made what she was about to say even more striking.

"I'll be direct," Elena said when Dwarkesh asked about her experience. "I'm probably leaving within the year."

Dwarkesh looked surprised. "You're one of our best associates! What's driving that?"

"That's actually part of the problem," Elena said. "I'm good at what I do. I get great feedback. My hours are always above target. But I've been having these conversations with partners about partnership, and the message I keep getting is, 'You're doing great, keep doing what you're doing, we'll see how things look in a year or two.'"

"That's not a path. That's a holding pattern."

She leaned forward. "I'm seven years in. I need to know: Am I on a partnership track or not? What specific things do I need to demonstrate?

What's the timeline? What do I need to develop that I haven't developed yet? And nobody will give me straight answers."

"Tell me more about that," Dwarkesh prompted.

"I think—and maybe I'm wrong—but I think the partnership isn't sure what they want from people like me. I'm a great service lawyer. Give me a case, I'll run it efficiently and effectively. But I'm not a natural rainmaker. I'm not out there generating work through my network.

"And I get the sense that the real metric is origination. But nobody will say that explicitly. So I'm in this limbo where I'm told I'm doing great, but I don't know if 'great' means I'm on a path to partnership or just a path to being a very senior associate forever."

"What skills are you worried you're not developing?" Dwarkesh asked.

Elena laughed. "At this point? None. I've developed the skills. I can handle complex litigation independently. I can manage client relationships on existing matters. I can mentor junior associates. What I can't do, and what nobody's taught me, is how to originate significant work. And I'm not even sure I want to, which is maybe the real issue."

"What do you mean?"

"I mean maybe partnership as currently structured isn't what I want. Maybe I want to be a really senior service partner who focuses on execution rather than business development. Or maybe I want to go in-house where I can do sophisticated work without the billing pressure. Or maybe there's some other model I haven't imagined."

She looked directly at Dwarkesh. "But the firm only really has one successful path that *feels* like success, which is equity partnership with origination. Everything else is treated as 'didn't make it.' And I'm not willing to spend two more years chasing an unclear partnership standard when I could be building a career that actually fits what I'm good at and want to do."

"What would you change if you could change anything?"

"Multiple paths to success," Elena said immediately. "Not everyone should have to become an originating partner. Some people should be able to be senior service lawyers at a high-level, high-compensation, high-*respect*, but focused on execution rather than business development. Some people should be able to move in and out of different roles that include practice, management, and teaching.

"And clear standards for whatever path you choose. Not 'we'll see how it goes,' but 'here are the specific criteria, here's the timeline, here's how you're tracking against those criteria.'"

She paused. "And honestly? Better use of AI and technology so we're not all grinding on routine work at year seven. I should be doing sophisticated strategic thinking by now, not document review because we need to staff the matter."

"What else should I understand?"

Elena was quiet for a moment. "I think the firm means well. I think people care about development. But the system is broken. And talented people like me are leaving not because the work is bad or the people are bad necessarily, but because we can't figure out how to build sustainable careers here. And that's a huge waste of the investment you made in developing us."

Synthesis: Patterns Emerge

After thirty minutes, Lucy called everyone back together. The energy in the room had shifted noticeably. The vibes were heavier, and more somber. Partners looked troubled. Associates looked relieved to have been heard, but also vulnerable, exhausted, and worried they'd said too much.

"That was uncomfortable," Lucy acknowledged. "Let's not pretend it wasn't. But discomfort is where learning happens." The group didn't look so sure.

She clicked to a blank empathy map on screen. "Let's synthesize what you heard. Not defending, not explaining—just acknowledging what associates experience. Partners and senior lawyers, what did you hear?"

Sarah Williams spoke first, her voice thoughtful. "I heard that feedback is sparse and disconnected from bigger picture development. Associates don't know if they're doing well or what they should be working on improving."

Tom Brennan added, "I heard that billable pressure and development needs are in direct tension. Everything that helps long-term growth, including training, shadowing, and practice development, comes out of personal time because it's not billable."

Maggie McNamee said quietly, "I heard that we say we value development but don't create structure for it. Good mentorship happens sporadically when someone makes time, not systematically."

Robert Kim, in spite of himself, spoke up. "I heard that junior associates feel isolated and uncertain. They're doing tasks without understanding context or strategy. And they're not developing client skills because we're not including them in client interactions."

Dwarkesh Jones added, "I heard that senior associates don't have clarity about partnership criteria or timelines. And that we only have the one valued path of originating equity partner even though really valued people might want or be suited for different kinds of success."

Marcus Reed said, "I heard that we're using associates for staffing needs rather than making intentional development assignments. The work they get is driven by what matters need coverage, not what skills they need to build."

Lucy was capturing themes on the whiteboard:

FEEDBACK—Sparse, not developmental, not connected to growth plans

STRUCTURE—Ad hoc mentorship, no systematic development

CONTEXT—Tasks without strategy, execution without understanding

CLIENT ACCESS—Limited interaction, no relationship

BUSINESS DEVELOPMENT—Not taught, assumed to figure out, but critical for partnership

CAREER CLARITY—Unclear paths, vague criteria, uncertain timelines

BILLABLE PRESSURE vs. DEVELOPMENT—Tension between short-term revenue and long-term growth

MULTIPLE PATHS—Only one valued trajectory (originating partner)

TECHNOLOGY—Could enable better learning, but not leveraged well

HYBRID WORK—Increases isolation, reduces informal learning

She stepped back from the board. "Do you see what you've identified? These go well beyond minor tweaks. These are fundamental system design problems."

Julian stood, his expression serious. "I'm hearing that we've created a system where well-intentioned people are failing to develop associates effectively, but not because they don't care; because the system doesn't support it. Is that fair?"

Heads nodded around the room. People seemed deflated.

"Then we need to design a different system," Julian said, feeling like there was *really* no way to shove that toothpaste back in the tube now. He had officially nibbled his cuticles to dangerous levels. A not small part of him started to think that merging with Wagner would be a much easier and certain path than the approach he'd started implementing this week.

Crafting HMW Statements: Associate Development

Lucy, undeterred by the challenges the group was surfacing, clicked to a new slide showing the HMW template again.

"Now we're going to do what we did yesterday afternoon by taking these insights and turning them into 'How Might We' statements. But this time, you'll work in mixed groups of partners and associates together."

She reorganized the room into four groups, deliberately mixing seniority levels.

"Each group is going to focus on one theme area from our synthesis. You have twenty minutes to generate HMW statements, at least three per group. Remember: start from pain points, not solutions. Keep it focused but open. Test for neutrality."

She assigned the themes:

Group 1: Feedback and development structure

Group 2: Context, strategy, and client access

Group 3: Career paths and partnership clarity

Group 4: Balancing billable work and development needs

The groups formed and immediately dove into animated discussion. The dynamic was different from yesterday because these problems felt more personal, more urgent, and more insurmountable. These weren't abstract client problems. These were *their* problems.

Group 1: Feedback and Development Structure

Robert Kim found himself working with Maya Davis, Jessica Park, and two other associates, along with Sarah Williams.

"The feedback issue feels fundamental," Jessica said. "We don't know if we're developing well because we don't get systematic feedback."

Maya added, "And when we do get feedback, it's usually about a specific work product, like 'this memo needs more detail,' but it's not about our overall development as lawyers."

Robert was taking notes. "So what's the underlying need? What do associates actually need that feedback would provide?"

"Confidence," Sarah suggested. "Confidence that they're on the right track. Confidence about what to work on improving."

"And direction," Jessica added. "What should I prioritize developing this year? What matters most?"

They started drafting: "How might we provide feedback to associates so they feel confident about their development progress and clear about what to prioritize?"

The group looked at it critically.

"It's pretty broad," Maya said. "Feedback could mean a lot of things."

"What if we focus on the systematic piece?" Robert suggested, surprising the group, given his reputation for valuing tradition. "The problem isn't that no feedback happens, but that it's not structured."

They revised: "How might we create structured feedback systems so associates receive regular developmental guidance that helps them understand their progress and priorities?"

"That's better," Sarah said. "It focuses on the structure problem without prescribing what kind of feedback."

They generated several others:

- "How might we help partners provide developmental feedback in ways that feel supportive rather than evaluative?"

- "How might we integrate feedback into regular workflow so it's not an additional burden on billable time?"
- "How might we create peer feedback mechanisms so associates learn from each other, not just from partners?"

Group 2: Context, Strategy, and Client Access

Maggie McNamee was working with John Forte, Alex Rivera, and several others on the context and client access challenges.

"The core problem," John said, "is that we're doing tasks without understanding the bigger picture. We're executing without understanding strategy."

"And we're not included in client interactions," Alex added, "so we're not learning client relationship skills."

"So what's the need?" Maggie asked. "What would make the difference?"

"Understanding the why, not just the what," Marcus said. "Why are we taking this approach? What's the client trying to accomplish? How does this fit into a broader strategy?"

They drafted: "How might we provide context with assignments so associates understand the strategic purpose of their work, not just the task itself?"

"That's good," Alex said. "But it doesn't address the client access piece."

"What if that's separate?" Maggie suggested. "Two related but distinct problems?"

They kept the first HMW and added: "How might we create opportunities for associates to develop client relationship skills earlier in their careers?"

One of the senior associates pushed further: "But it's not just about creating opportunities, but also about making client interaction a normal part of development, not a special privilege."

They revised: "How might we integrate client interaction into regular associate development so relationship skills are built systematically, not incidentally?"

They generated others:

- "How might we debrief after client interactions so associates learn from observation, not just observe?"

- "How might we help associates understand business context, not just legal analysis?"
- "How might we create safe spaces for associates to practice client-facing skills before doing them for real?"

Group 3: Career Paths and Partnership Clarity

Dwarkesh Jones worked with Elena Rodriguez, Priya Patel, and others on the career clarity challenge.

"I think there are two separate problems here," Elena said. "One is lack of clarity about partnership criteria. The other is the assumption that partnership is the only valuable path."

"Let's tackle them separately," Dwarkesh suggested. "First one: how do we create clarity?"

"The need is transparency," Priya said. "What are the actual criteria? Where am I relative to those criteria? What's the realistic timeline?"

They drafted: "How might we communicate partnership criteria and timelines so associates understand expectations and can track their own progress?"

"But that assumes partnership is the goal," Elena noted. "What about the second problem—multiple paths?"

The group was quiet for a moment, recognizing this was harder.

"What if the problem is that we only value one kind of success?" Dwarkesh said slowly. "What if we need to value different contributions differently?"

They drafted: "How might we create multiple valued career paths so lawyers can succeed through different strengths that include origination, service excellence, leadership, specialization?"

Elena looked at it and nodded. "That's the question. Can this firm create a model where my success as a service lawyer is genuinely valued equal to someone else's success as a rainmaker?"

"That's going to require compensation redesign, status markers, and partnership tiers. That's a total redesign of . . . everything," Priya observed, suddenly feeling overwhelmed.

"Which is why it's a good HMW," Dwarkesh said, trying to help her regain balance in the exercise. "It's focused on the core issue of valuing different paths without prescribing exactly how."

Other HMWs they generated:

- "How might we provide honest assessments earlier so associates can make informed career decisions?"
- "How might we help associates identify their strengths and align career paths with those strengths?"
- "How might we make transitioning between paths like practice, management, in-house, and back to firm normal rather than failure?"

Group 4: Billable Work vs. Development

Tom Brennan found himself with Jessica Park, Michael Solomon, and others tackling perhaps the hardest problem of all, the tension between billable pressure and development needs.

"This feels impossible," Jessica said bluntly. "Development takes time. Time is revenue. How do we square that circle?"

"Maybe that's the wrong framing," Tom said, thinking out loud. "What if development could be billable?"

"How?" Michael asked skeptically.

"I don't know yet—that's the solution we need to design. But the HMW should focus on the problem: we need associates to develop skills, and we need revenue, and those two things used to be perfectly aligned. Now, they're beginning to feel incompatible."

They started drafting different approaches:

"How might we fund associate development without depending on client billables?"

"That's one angle," Jessica said. "But it might limit our thinking. What if clients would pay for development if we framed it right?"

"How might we structure engagements so client work and associate development happen simultaneously?"

"Or," Michael suggested, "what if the issue is how we price, not what we do?"

"How might we move to pricing models that create space for associate development rather than penalizing non-billable time?"

Tom was writing all of these down. "I think these are all valid HMWs addressing different facets of the same problem."

They added others:

- "How might we create protected development time that's valued equally to billable time?"
- "How might we use efficiency gains from AI to invest in systematic training rather than just billing more?"

Sharing and Selection

Lucy called time and had each group share their strongest HMW statements. As they wrote them on flip charts, patterns emerged.

From Group 1:

"How might we create structured feedback systems so associates receive regular developmental guidance that helps them understand their progress and priorities?"

From Group 2:

"How might we integrate client interaction into regular associate development so relationship skills are built systematically, not incidentally?"

From Group 3:

"How might we create multiple valued career paths so lawyers can succeed through different strengths that include origination, service excellence, leadership, and specialization?"

From Group 4:

"How might we move to pricing models that create space for associate development rather than penalizing non-billable time?"

Lucy stepped back and looked at the four statements. "These are excellent. Do you see how they're connected?"

She drew arrows between them on the whiteboard. "You can't solve feedback without time for feedback. You can't create time without changing pricing. You can't change pricing without defining what value you're delivering, including how well-developed your lawyers are. And you can't have multiple career paths without clarity about what success looks like in each path."

"They're all part of the same system redesign," Julian said, standing, setting his coffee down and rolling up his sleeves. "Which is exactly what we need to understand. We're not fixing one thing. We're redesigning how we develop lawyers from the ground up."

He looked around the room at partners and associates who had, just an hour ago, been on opposite sides of empathy interviews. Now they were co-designers, working together on problems they both experienced.

"Tomorrow we'll ideate solutions," Lucy said. "But first, we need lunch and then this afternoon, we're tackling the other internal challenge of business development and go-to-market strategy. Because that's connected, too. If we're developing lawyers differently, we need to think about how they develop business differently."

As people filed out toward lunch, the conversations were intense but productive. Associates felt heard. Partners felt committed. And everyone recognized they'd just articulated problems that had been festering unspoken for years.

"That was gutsy," Tom Brennan said to Julian as they walked toward the dining room. "Giving associates that platform to be honest about where we're failing them."

"Had to be done," Julian replied. "Can't design better systems if we're not honest about why current systems aren't working."

"The question now is whether we can actually deliver on the redesign, or whether this becomes just another consultation that leads nowhere."

Julian stopped and looked at his CFO. "That's what Thursday and Friday are for. But Tom, we can't go back. Not after this. We've opened the conversation. If we close it without action, we'll lose every talented associate in this room within eighteen months."

Tom nodded slowly. "Then we'd better design something worth implementing."

Through the windows, clouds started accumulating over the mountains. Inside, something else was building, too: a shared understanding of problems that ran deeper than anyone had wanted to admit, and a fragile but growing belief that maybe, together, they could actually solve them.

Chapter 17

From Rainmakers to Building the Hive

The lunch conversations had been dominated by the morning's revelations about associate development. Partners who had conducted empathy interviews were still processing what they'd heard. Associates felt both vulnerable and hopeful that maybe, finally, someone was listening. Some continued to worry they'd said too much and would be penalized in the long term for not being team players. They started ruminating on how unfair this set up was, being encouraged to complain *to* the partners, the very people who paid their salaries and controlled their destinies, directly about a system *they* had created.

As people returned to the conference room, they found the seating rearranged again. The team workshop stations were gone. In their place, a huge U-shape table faced the front where Lucy stood with Tom Brennan and a new slide on screen: **From Solo Practice to Team Sport**.

"This morning we examined how we develop individual lawyers," Lucy began. "This afternoon, we're going to examine how we develop business, and why our current approach might be fundamentally at odds with everything else we're trying to build."

She clicked to show a stark image: a single tree standing alone in a field, and beside it, a beehive teeming with coordinated activity.

"Most law firms, and that includes ours, operate on what we've all come to know as the 'rainmaker model.' Individual partners are responsible for generating their own work. They own their client relationships. They get credited for originations. Their compensation reflects their personal book of business. That partner would then work with several associates to support their clients' work, scaling their ability to serve more clients.

"This made sense when law was simpler," she continued. "When clients needed help with relatively discrete legal problems, and one good lawyer could handle most of what the client needed. Maybe they brought in another partner for certain parts of a client's legal problems, but they remained the primary originating and relationship partner over time. But that world is gone."

Julian spoke from his seat. "Our average engagement now involves 3.2 practice areas. Our largest clients work with an average of seven different partners across five offices. And yet our business development model still assumes individual partners operating independently."

Lucy nodded. "Which brings us to what I call 'building the hive,' moving from autonomous rainmakers to a model where one partner might continue to bring in the work, but the work is coordinated across teams and a compensation model develops that more equitably rewards different types of work on client matters. But before we can design what that looks like, we need to understand why the current model persists and what problems it creates."

She turned to Tom. "Tom, can you walk us through the reality of how our compensation system works?"

The Compensation Reality

Tom Brennan stood, looking somewhat uncomfortable but committed to transparency. He pulled up a slide showing a simplified compensation formula:

Partner Compensation = Base + (Origination Credit × Rate) + (Quality/Service Factor) + (Leadership Factor)

"This is simplified," he said, "but it captures the basics. Every partner has a base compensation level. Then we add four factors, with origination credit being by far the largest multiplier."

He clicked to show the weightings: Origination 60%, Quality/Service 25%, Leadership 15%.

"What this means in practice," Tom continued, "is that a partner who originates $3 million in work will make significantly more than a partner who provides excellent service on $3 million of someone else's work. Even if both partners work the same hours and deliver the same quality."

Marcus Reed raised his hand. "But that makes sense, doesn't it? The person who brings in the work is taking the business development risk, investing in relationships, creating opportunities for everyone else. Without them, the whole firm would go under. And if we don't reward them for that, they go to another firm that does, taking their business with them."

"That's the traditional logic," Tom agreed. "And there's validity to it. But let me show you what else this creates."

He clicked to a new slide showing anonymized data, with three partners' compensation over five years with their origination versus service hours.

"Partner A originates heavily, works less on matters, makes $1.2 million. Partner B services more than originates, works more total hours, makes $750,000. Partner C does pure service work, extremely high quality, makes $600,000."

"Now, which partner is most valuable to the firm?"

Sarah Williams spoke up. "Depends on what we value. Partner A brings in revenue. But Partners B and C execute the work that keeps clients coming back."

"Exactly," Tom said. "But our compensation system sends a clear message that origination is what we value most. Everything else is secondary. But we need to generate excellent service that distinguishes the firm from our peers to keep clients coming back. We want all boats to rise, including the partners who bring in the business, by designing a compensation model that makes it easier for them to originate business in the first place when they know we have robust systems in place to serve the client once they engage us. This also all relates to our earlier discussion about associate development systems. These are not isolated conversations. If we're doing a better job at developing our associates and building their skills and we're creating better compensation models that ensure our service partners stand at the ready to do exceptional work once new clients are in the door, we work as a busy hive that coordinates rather than a group of rainmakers operating under a shared firm brand name."

People nodded slowly. It made sense on paper. William Klept was fuming inside. This was exactly what he feared as soon as he heard about this retreat. He'd made his career, and his money, being a peerless rainmaker, and there was *no way* he was sticking around if the firm was going to start chipping away at his compensation. Do these people know how hard it is to grind it out outside the walls of the firm, building relationships, taking the risks necessary to find new opportunities, mending fences when an associate screwed up an assignment or another partner made a strategic error? He took all the risks, found all the opportunity, and essentially fed everyone else at the firm. There was no way he was sharing his haul with others who sat and waited in their offices to do basic legal work. But he wasn't going to speak up now. These initiatives never took off because the business model and politics never supported it in the end, so he nodded along with everyone else as if this all made perfect sense.

The Ripple Effects

Lucy took over again. "Let's talk about what this creates. This morning, we heard from associates about their experience. Let me pull out a few themes that connect directly to our business development model."

She clicked through quotes from the morning interviews, displayed on screen without names:

"I have no idea how to generate work, how to build a client relationship from scratch, how to identify opportunities. Nobody's teaching me."

"I'm becoming a really good service lawyer, but I don't know if that's valued enough for partnership."

"The partnership track assumes I'll figure out origination somehow, but there's no structure for learning it."

"These are symptoms of a system that treats business development as an individual trait you either have or don't have, rather than a skill set we systematically develop," Lucy said.

She turned to the partners. "How many of you learned business development through formal training?"

No hands went up.

"How many learned through trial and error, watching senior partners, maybe getting mentored informally?"

Most hands went up.

"And how many of you," Lucy asked more quietly, "have struggled to teach business development to associates because you're not entirely sure how to articulate what you do that works?"

After a pause, several hands rose—including, notably, Robert Kim's.

"This is the problem," Lucy said. "We have an individual-based, tacit-knowledge approach to business development in an environment that increasingly requires team-based, sophisticated, systematized client service."

She clicked to show data from corporate clients:

- 73% of our clients prefer to work with integrated legal teams rather than individual lawyers
- 81% value firms that can provide cross-practice solutions without them having to coordinate
- 64% tell us they have stopped working with firms specifically because of poor internal coordination

"Our clients are asking for teams," Lucy said. "But we're still organized around solo practitioners."

The Current State: What We Do Now

Maggie McNamee spoke up from her seat. "Can we be specific about what this looks like in practice? I think we're dancing around some uncomfortable realities."

"Please," Julian said. "Let's name them."

Maggie stood. "Okay. I have clients who need corporate work, employment advice, and environmental compliance. That's three different partners. In theory, I should bring in my colleagues, we should serve the client as a team, everyone should share credit."

"In practice? I'm worried that if I bring in Dwarkesh for corporate work and he does a great job, he'll build a direct relationship with my client and start getting credit for work I originated. So I keep him at arm's length. I'm friendly and professional, but I'm protecting my origination."

The room was very quiet.

"And," Maggie continued, "when we do collaborate, we end up arguing about credit. Who gets the origination? Who gets the service credit? Who brought the client in originally versus who expanded the relationship? It's awkward, it creates tension, and it makes collaboration feel risky rather than valuable."

Dwarkesh nodded. "I've experienced the same thing from the other side. I know partners who have clients that could benefit from my M&A expertise. But they don't bring me in because they're worried about credit splitting or relationship dilution."

Alex Rivera, never one to shy away despite his junior status, raised his hand tentatively. "And from an associate perspective, we see this. We watch partners operate in silos. Nobody models collaborative business development. So we learn that successful lawyers protect their turf and build individual books of business."

"Which perpetuates the model for another generation," Lucy said, "even though the model doesn't serve clients well anymore and limits the firm's ability to grow revenue and sustain its health."

The Knowledge Hoarding Problem

Lisa Martinez spoke up from the operations side. "There's a related issue, which is knowledge hoarding. When business development is individual, knowledge about clients stays in individual partners' heads."

She stood and moved to the front. "I can't tell you how many times I've tried to create a firm-wide CRM system or client database, and partners resist. I used to think it was a tech adoption issue, but I came to realize it's because they don't want to document their client relationships, share their contact strategies, or make their knowledge accessible to others."

"Because," Robert Kim said, somewhat defensively, "those relationships are what we've built our careers on. They're our value to the firm."

"I understand that fear," Lisa said gently. "But it creates real problems. When a partner retires or leaves, client relationships leave with them. We lose institutional knowledge. And we can't serve clients proactively because nobody except one partner knows what's happening across the relationship."

Tom added, "From a financial perspective, it also means we can't value the firm accurately. If client relationships are personal rather than institutional, the firm itself has less value. That matters for succession planning, for potential acquisitions, for everything."

The Client Experience

Lucy pulled up a slide showing a client journey map, a timeline of a hypothetical corporate client's interactions with the firm over two years.

"Let's look at this from the client's perspective. They hire us for an acquisition in January. They work with Partner A in Corporate. Great experience. In March, they have an employment dispute. Partner A refers them to Partner B. But Partner B doesn't know anything about the client's business, their culture, their priorities, so they start from scratch."

She traced the timeline. "In June, they need environmental compliance advice. Partner C gets involved. Again, starting over. By September, they need litigation support. Partner D. Each time, the client has to re-explain their business, their challenges, their preferences."

"From their perspective, they're working with four individual lawyers who happen to have the same letterhead. They're not experiencing a firm, but a collection of solo practitioners."

She clicked to show a quote from yesterday's client panel: *"I wish more of my outside counsel would be proactive, calling me about new regulations, thinking about my business even when I'm not actively engaging you. That's partnership."*

"How can we be proactive," Lucy asked, "when four different partners all have partial information about this client, but nobody has a complete picture? When there's no system for sharing knowledge across the relationship? When everyone's protecting their origination credit?"

The Team-Based Alternative

Lucy's tone shifted from diagnostic to aspirational. "So what would team-based business development actually look like? Let me paint a picture."

She clicked to show a different client relationship model that showed circles connected by lines, representing integrated teams.

"Instead of Partner A 'owning' a client and bringing in others as needed, imagine a relationship team. Three to five partners from different practices, supported by senior associates and a relationship manager. They collectively understand the client's business, industry, and needs.

"They meet regularly and proactively instead of just when there's active work. They discuss the client's strategic challenges, anticipate needs, identify opportunities. They make joint pitches. They share credit based on contribution, not ownership.

"When the client calls with a problem, they don't need to explain context because the team already knows. When someone goes on vacation, others can step in seamlessly. When a partner eventually retires, the relationship is institutional and doesn't leave with them."

Robert Kim raised his hand. "That sounds good in theory. Obviously, we all get it. But practically, how do you determine credit? If five people are on a team but one person does most of the work, how do you split compensation fairly?"

"That's exactly the question we need to answer together," Lucy said. "And it's one of the HMW statements we'll develop this afternoon."

Connected to Associate Development

Lucy pulled up the morning's HMW statement: *"How might we integrate client interaction into regular associate development so relationship skills are built systematically, not incidentally?"*

"Notice how this connects to business development?" she said. "If partners operate solo, they can maybe mentor one or two associates closely. But if teams are working together, multiple associates can observe and participate in client relationships. They see how different partners contribute. They learn business development as part of regular work, not as a mysterious skill that some people just 'have.'"

Jessica Park nodded. "That would completely change the experience. Instead of hoping I somehow figure out how to originate work by year seven, I'd be learning it from year one by being part of client teams."

"And," Lucy continued, "it connects to the multiple career paths problem. If we only value origination, we only have one kind of successful partner. But in a team model, you can be valuable in different ways. Maybe you're brilliant at identifying new opportunities within existing clients. Maybe you're exceptional at cross-selling different services. Maybe you're amazing at client service that generates deep loyalty. All of those become valued contributions."

She clicked to show the afternoon's work ahead: **Building the Hive: Designing Team-Based Business Development**.

Cross-Role Workshop: Developing HMW Statements

"We're going to work differently this afternoon than this morning," Lucy said. "No interviews because you already understand the problem from your own experience. Instead, we're going straight to problem definition."

She reorganized the room into five cross-functional teams, deliberately mixing rainmakers with service partners, senior people with junior people, practice groups, and even including Lisa from operations and several other senior business leads on teams.

"Each team will develop HMW statements for one aspect of team-based business development. Twenty minutes to generate at least three HMWs per team. Then we'll share and synthesize."

She assigned the focus areas:

Team 1: Credit allocation and compensation in team-based models

Team 2: Knowledge sharing and relationship transparency

Team 3: Teaching business development skills systematically

Team 4: Client team structure and coordination

Team 5: Transitioning from individual to team mindsets

"Remember your training from yesterday and this morning," Lucy said. "Start from pain points and observations, not solutions. Keep it focused but open. Test for neutrality. Look for the Goldilocks zone between too broad and too narrow."

The teams formed and dove in.

Team 1: Credit Allocation and Compensation

Tom Brennan found himself working with Maggie McNamee, John Forte, Alex Rivera, and two other partners, a true cross-section.

"The elephant in the room," Maggie said, "is that team-based BD threatens how rainmakers currently make money. We need to acknowledge that."

"But the current system also limits growth," one of the partners said. "I could generate more work if I felt comfortable bringing others into my relationships. But I'm protecting my credit."

"So what's the underlying need?" Tom asked, facilitating. "What would make team-based BD feel safe instead of threatening?"

"Fairness," John suggested. "A system where everyone who contributes gets recognized appropriately, not equally but fairly based on actual contribution."

"And transparency," Alex added, not afraid to contribute in spite of his junior status and total lack of experience as a partner. "If partners know how credit will be allocated up front, they can decide whether to collaborate. It's the ambiguity that makes it risky."

They started drafting HMWs:

"How might we allocate origination and service credit in team-based relationships so contributions are recognized fairly and transparently?"

"That's good," Maggie said. "But it doesn't address the bigger comp question: how do we reward collaboration itself?"

They added: "How might we redesign partner compensation to reward collaborative business development, not just individual origination?"

"How might we create credit-sharing agreements that protect relationship originators while incentivizing team expansion of that relationship?"

"How might we make service excellence and client retention as valuable as new business origination in compensation decisions?"

Tom was writing quickly to try and capture the group's ideas as rapidly as they were emerging. He knew as he wrote how fraught these questions were and hoped Lucy and Julian knew what they were doing. They were asking the partners to reimagine the entire compensation philosophy and they were inviting the associates and of counsel into the conversation as they did. It was extremely risky.

Team 2: Knowledge Sharing and Relationship Transparency

Lisa Martinez was working with Dwarkesh Jones, Jessica Park, Robert Kim, and others on the knowledge and systems piece.

"The problem," Lisa said, "is that client information lives in people's heads and inboxes. We have CRM systems, but people don't use them. Why?"

"Because it takes time," Dwarkesh Jones said honestly. "Time I could be billing or doing other work."

"And because it feels like giving away my competitive advantage," Robert admitted. "If everyone knows everything about my clients, what makes me special?"

"But that's exactly the mindset we need to shift," Jessica said. "If the firm collectively knows more about a client, the firm serves them better. Which should make everyone more valuable, not less."

They drafted HMWs:

"How might we create knowledge-sharing systems that feel valuable to contributors, not just extractive?"

"How might we make client relationship information easily accessible across the firm so teams can serve clients proactively?"

"How might we help partners see knowledge-sharing as enhancing rather than threatening their value?"

"How might we reduce the time burden of documenting client information so it becomes natural workflow rather than extra work?"

Lisa added one more: "How might we visualize client relationships across practice groups so opportunities for collaboration become obvious?"

Team 3: Teaching Business Development Skills

Sarah Williams worked with Priya Patel, Michael Solomon, and several others on systematic BD skill development.

"The morning interviews were damning," Sarah said. "Associates have no idea how to develop business because we don't teach it."

"Because most of us don't know how to teach it," Michael admitted. "I learned by trial and error. I don't know how to systematize that."

"But other professions do this," Priya said. "Consultants teach business development from day one. Why can't we?"

They brainstormed the underlying needs: demystifying BD, building skills progressively, creating safe practice opportunities, learning from both successes and failures.

Their HMWs emerged:

"How might we teach business development skills progressively so associates build capabilities from year one rather than scrambling to figure it out on their own at year six?"

"How might we demystify client development so it feels like a learnable skill set rather than an innate personality trait?"

"How might we create safe opportunities for associates to practice BD skills like pitching, networking, identifying opportunities, without high stakes?"

"How might we help partners articulate what they do that works so BD knowledge becomes transferable rather than tacit?"

"How might we celebrate and learn from both successful and unsuccessful BD attempts so the firm collectively gets better?"

Team 4: Client Team Structure and Coordination

Lucy joined a team with Alex Rivera, Elena Rodriguez, and others on the structural question of how teams actually function.

"If we're going to have client teams," Lucy said, "we need to figure out how they're organized, who's on them, how they coordinate."

"The question is scale," one partner said. "Do we do this for all clients? Just major clients? How do we decide?"

"And composition," Alex added. "Who's on a client team? Just partners? Associates too? What about staff?"

They developed HMWs:

"How might we structure client service teams so roles and responsibilities are clear but flexible as client needs evolve?"

"How might we determine which client relationships benefit from team-based approaches versus individual partner management?"

"How might we integrate associates into client teams early so associates develop alongside client relationships rather than being added later?"

"How might we coordinate across client teams so people can contribute to multiple relationships without overwhelming their capacity?"

"How might we include client-facing staff (project managers, relationship coordinators) as valued team members rather than administrative support?"

Team 5: Mindset and Culture Change

Julian had joined this team himself, working with Robert Kim, Marcus Reed, and several younger attorneys on perhaps the hardest question of cultural transformation.

"This is ultimately about identity," Julian said. "For a lot of us, being a rainmaker is who we are. It's how we see ourselves as successful lawyers."

"But that identity is isolating," Marcus said. "And it makes succession planning nearly impossible. When you retire, your clients leave with you because they're your clients, not the firm's."

"So what would a different identity look like?" Robert asked. "What does it mean to be a successful partner in a team-based model?"

They worked through what success might mean: building strong client relationships that outlast any individual lawyer, developing others who extend your impact, contributing specialized expertise even when you don't originate work, orchestrating teams that solve complex problems.

Their HMWs focused on cultural and mindset shifts:

"How might we help rainmakers see team-based business development as amplifying rather than threatening their impact?"

"How might we celebrate team-based client wins as prominently as individual originations?"

"How might we redefine partnership success to include team-building and knowledge-sharing, not just personal book of business?"

"How might we create transition paths so established rainmakers can gradually shift from individual to team-based approaches without threatening their livelihood?"

"How might we make collaboration the default expectation rather than the exception that requires special effort?"

Synthesis and Selection

After twenty-five minutes of intense work, Lucy called the teams back together. Each team shared their strongest HMW statements, and she wrote them on flip charts at the front.

When all five teams had presented, she stepped back to look at the collection of statements covering the wall.

"Twenty-three distinct HMW statements about business development transformation," she said. "Do you see the themes?"

She started grouping them with different colored markers:

COMPENSATION/INCENTIVES (6 statements)

KNOWLEDGE/SYSTEMS (4 statements)

SKILL DEVELOPMENT (5 statements)

STRUCTURE/COORDINATION (5 statements)

CULTURE/MINDSET (3 statements)

"Like the other issues we've tackled, these challenges are all interrelated," Lucy said. "They're different facets of the same transformation. You can't change compensation without changing culture. You can't build systems without changing behavior. You can't teach BD skills without creating structure for practice."

Julian stood and moved to the front. "I want to point out something important. This room just spent twenty-five minutes collaboratively developing problem statements about issues that affect all of us differently. Rainmakers worked with service partners. Senior people worked with junior people. And you created questions we can tackle better together than any of you could have created alone."

He gestured to the walls covered in HMW statements. "That's what building the hive actually looks like. Not everyone doing the same thing, but everyone contributing their perspective and expertise to a shared challenge."

Lucy clicked to show three HMWs she'd selected as priorities for Thursday's ideation work, drawn from across the categories:

> **"How might we redesign partner compensation to reward collaborative business development, not just individual origination?"**
>
> **"How might we teach business development skills progressively so associates build capabilities from year one rather than scrambling at year six?"**
>
> **"How might we structure client service teams so roles and responsibilities are clear but flexible as client needs evolve?"**

"These three connect to everything else," she explained. "Compensation drives behavior. Skill development creates capability. Structure enables coordination. If we can design good solutions to these three, many of the other HMWs become easier to address."

She looked around the room. "Tomorrow, we're going to take all the HMW statements we've developed this week, ranging from client service from Tuesday to associate development from this morning to business development and compensation systems from this afternoon, and we're going to generate solutions. Lots of solutions. Wild solutions. Practical solutions. Solutions we've never tried before."

"But tonight," Julian said, "I want you to sit with what we've surfaced. We've spent two days naming problems that many of us have felt but never articulated together. That's progress. Tomorrow we move to designing solutions. And Friday, we'll decide which solutions to pilot and how to implement them."

He paused, looking at the HMW statements covering the walls. "We came here to design our future. What you're looking at is the very messy, maybe overwhelming guts of a blueprint for that future, expressed as questions we need to answer together."

Evening Reflection

As people filed out toward dinner, the conversations reflected the day's emotional journey. The morning's associate interviews had been uncomfortable for many and cathartic for others. The afternoon's business development workshop had been less personal but equally challenging because they asked people to reimagine systems that determined their livelihoods.

At a terrace table, Maggie McNamee sat with Marcus Reed and Dwarkesh Jones, watching the sun set behind the mountains.

"I spent fifteen years building my book of business," Marcus said quietly. "Learning to network, building relationships, figuring out how to generate work. And now we're talking about fundamentally changing how that's valued."

"Are you worried?" Maggie asked.

"A little," he admitted. "But I guess I'm also intrigued. The current model can be exhausting. And frankly, I'm not sure it's sustainable. I can only maintain so many relationships personally. If we could build teams that serve clients better and share the load, that might actually be better for everyone, including me. I just don't know how the math would work, especially if we're already under financial pressure like every other mid-sized firm is."

Dwarkesh nodded. "I've always been more of a service partner than a rainmaker. Under the current system, I'm perpetually less valued no matter how well I serve clients. The idea that we might create multiple paths to success is appealing to me, obviously. But I don't see how we change it when it negatively impacts the rainmakers so much, and I don't want them to leave the firm, obviously. We can't survive without work to do and there's no work together without the clients they bring in. Maybe they should make much more money than the rest of us. I mean, I'm not trying to argue against my own interests, but let's face it. They have a lot more value out in the market, so shouldn't they have a lot more value right here at the firm?"

"In a way, I think you're arguing in *favor* of your own interests by sticking to the current model," Maggie observed.

Inside, Robert Kim was having dinner with Sarah Williams and several younger attorneys, an unusual combination that the retreat had enabled.

"I keep thinking about what Julian said," Robert told them. "That we just demonstrated collaborative effort by actually defining our problems together. I've spent my whole career thinking of myself as an individual lawyer. The idea of being part of a team is foreign to me. But watching how we worked this afternoon, I can see the potential."

"Will the rainmakers actually go for this, though?" Priya Patel asked bluntly. "No offense, but the current system benefits the people with the most power to resist change."

Robert considered this honestly. "Some won't. Some will see this as threatening everything they've built. But some of us . . ." he paused, surprising himself, "some of us are tired. Tired of the isolation, tired of the competition, tired of seeing talented people leave because they can't figure out how to succeed here. If there's a better way, I'm open to considering it."

At the leadership table, Julian debriefed the day with Lucy, Tom, and Lisa.

"The compensation conversation is going to be the hardest," Tom said. "We're asking people who've succeeded wildly under the current system to accept a different system where they might make less money."

"Maybe," Lucy said. "Or maybe they make different money. If team-based approaches let us serve larger clients more effectively, if we can generate more work by being better coordinated, if we reduce the client losses that happen when partners retire or lateral, maybe there's more money for everyone, just allocated differently."

"That's pretty optimistic," Tom chuckled. He liked Lucy a lot, but this kind of illogical optimism was her Achilles' heel.

"The associate development conversation was easier," Lisa observed. "Because everyone has lived through it and agrees the current system is broken. The question is whether we're willing to invest in fixing it."

Julian looked tired but somehow also energized by the discussions. "Three days in, and we've gone from 'here's why we need to change' to 'here are the specific problems we need to solve.' Tomorrow we start generating actual solutions. That's when it gets real."

"That's when we find out if people are willing to think beyond incremental adjustments," Lucy agreed. "Tomorrow we need them to be bold, to imagine fundamentally different ways of working, to let go of 'that's how we've always done it' and embrace 'what if we tried something completely new?'"

"Do you think they're ready for that?" Julian asked.

Lucy looked out at the dining room, at partners and associates and staff having conversations they'd probably never had before. "I think we're about to find out."

Through the windows, the last light faded from the mountains. Tomorrow would bring ideation: the brainstorming, the wild ideas, the prototypes sketched on whiteboards and refined through feedback that comes with it. They'd taken three days to build awareness, differing levels of desire, and knowledge about the need for transformation. Now they'd test whether they could actually develop *ability*, the capacity to design and implement something genuinely new.

The HMW statements covered the walls of the conference room like a map of unexplored territory. Tomorrow they'd start charting courses through that territory, trying to find paths from the firm they were to the firm they needed to become.

It was ambitious. Maybe too ambitious. But sitting with the status quo was the riskier course of action. Not after three days of honest conversation about what wasn't working and why.

The only way forward was through. Together.

Reader Reflection

Incentives and Behavior

Tom Brennan showed how the compensation formula dictates firm culture.

1. **The Hoarding Instinct:** Does your compensation system reward partners for sharing work or hoarding it? If a partner introduces a colleague to a client, do they lose money or power?

2. **The "Solo" Experience:** Put yourself in your client's shoes. Do they experience your firm as a coordinated team, or as a collection of solo practitioners sharing a letterhead?

3. **Valuing the "Minders":** Every firm has partners like Maggie McNamee—excellent service lawyers who may not be top rainmakers. Does your firm have a way to value and retain them, or are they treated as marginalized partners?

Chapter 18

Ideation

Undoubtedly, by Thursday morning, the firm's participants were tired. The first three days had asked a lot from them, and today would require even more. It would ask them to move from listening and synthesizing into action and ideation. It would not be easy, but it was necessary if they were to have a shot at solving the problems they'd defined together.

People filed into breakfast with a sense of anticipation mixed with nervousness. The walls of the conference room were still covered with HMW statements from Tuesday and Wednesday, a visual reminder of the problems they'd defined together.

"I have no idea what to expect," Jessica Park said to Priya Patel over coffee. "Lucy keeps saying we're going to 'ideate,' but I don't know what that actually means."

"I think it means brainstorming," Priya replied. "But probably with some structure. Lucy doesn't seem to do anything without a framework."

At a nearby table, Robert Kim was having a similar conversation with Dwarkesh Jones. "I'm comfortable with analysis. I'm comfortable with evaluation. I'm less comfortable with . . . creativity on demand."

Dwarkesh smiled. "That might be exactly why we need someone to teach us how to do it."

At 9:00 a.m., people settled into the conference room to find it completely rearranged. Three distinct areas had been created, each with its own workspace, whiteboards, and mountains of supplies: Post-its, markers, large sheets of paper, timer displays.

Lucy stood at the front, practically vibrating with energy. Inside she was so tired, but today was what she'd waited all week for; what she'd waited her whole career for, really. She could sleep Saturday. Today, she was up at dawn, in spite of her fatigue. "Good morning! Today we move from understanding and defining problems to generating solutions. This is the Ideate stage of design thinking. For most lawyers, it's the hardest part of the process."

She clicked to a slide: **Why Lawyers Struggle with Ideation**.

"Let me be direct about what's about to happen and why it might feel uncomfortable. Lawyers are trained to spot issues and to look at any idea and immediately identify what could go wrong. You're rewarded throughout your careers for finding flaws, anticipating problems, and being skeptical."

Several people nodded, and some smiled knowingly, recognizing themselves.

"But ideation requires the opposite mindset," Lucy continued. "You need to generate possibilities without immediately evaluating them. You need to suspend judgment, embrace—or at least tolerate—wild ideas, and resist the urge to explain why something won't work."

She advanced to the next slide: **Three Traps We're Going to Avoid**.

Trap #1: Issue Spotting

"Your instinct will be to immediately critique every idea. 'That violates ethics rules.' 'Clients would never accept that.' 'That's too expensive.' Those statements might all be true, but evaluating ideas during generation kills creativity before it starts."

Trap #2: Social Convergence

"When brainstorming publicly, groups naturally converge around the most socially acceptable, obvious ideas. Nobody wants to be the person who suggests something that sounds stupid. So we all play it safe, and safe ideas rarely solve hard problems."

Trap #3: Self-Censoring

"Similarly, you'll have ideas you don't share because you pre-judge them as unlikely to work. But sometimes the 'bad' ideas contain kernels of insight that lead to breakthrough solutions. If you self-censor, the group never gets those kernels."

Alex Rivera was absorbing all of this. It explained so much about why brainstorming usually failed. He'd experienced all three traps before.

"So," Lucy said, "we're going to use three specific techniques designed to overcome these traps and generate ideas you wouldn't normally consider. Each technique forces you out of conventional thinking patterns."

She displayed the three methods:

1. **Worst Possible Idea**—Generate intentionally terrible solutions
2. **Crazy 8s**—Eight ideas in four minutes, sketched not written; the time compression eliminates the ability to self-censor
3. **Lateral Inspiration**—Steal shamelessly from other industries and consider how to adapt to a legal context

"We're going to split into three groups," Lucy explained. "Each group focuses on one problem area: Client Service, Associate Development, or Business Development. Each group will use all three techniques on two HMW statements from your area."

She clicked to show the assignments:

GROUP 1—CLIENT SERVICE (Tables 1, 2, and 3)

HMW #1: How might we communicate with our clients so they feel confident that the firm understands their need for clarity once a matter is ongoing and they have less visibility into its status?

HMW #2: How might we reimagine the client intake process so that in-house counsel feel collaboration begins before engagement?

GROUP 2—ASSOCIATE DEVELOPMENT (Tables 4 and 5)

HMW #1: How might we create multiple valued career paths so lawyers can succeed through different strengths that equally value origination, service excellence, leadership, and specialization?

HMW #2: How might we create structured feedback systems so associates receive regular developmental guidance that helps them understand their progress and priorities?

GROUP 3—BUSINESS DEVELOPMENT (Tables 6 and 7)

HMW #1: How might we redesign partner compensation to reward collaborative business development, not just individual origination?

HMW #2: How might we structure client service teams so roles and responsibilities are clear but flexible as client needs evolve?

"You'll spend about twenty minutes on each technique," Lucy said. "I'll explain each one before you start, and I'll be circulating to keep you on track. The goal is quantity, not quality. Generate as many ideas as possible. Wild ideas are encouraged. Judgment is forbidden."

She looked around the room with a slight smile. "This is going to feel weird and possibly uncomfortable. That's how you'll know it's working. Questions before we begin?"

Tom Brennan raised his hand. "What do we do with all the ideas we generate? How do we decide which ones are worth pursuing?"

"Great question, but that's this afternoon's work," Lucy replied. "This morning is pure generation. This afternoon we'll prototype and refine. Tomorrow we'll select which to pilot. But you can't evaluate ideas you haven't generated yet, so we need to maximize the raw material first."

Technique 1: Worst Possible Idea

Lucy moved to a whiteboard at the front. "First technique: Worst Possible Idea. This reverses the ideation process entirely. Instead of trying to solve the problem, you're going to deliberately generate the worst possible solutions you can imagine."

The room laughed nervously.

"I'm serious," Lucy said. "For the next ten minutes, your goal is to come up with ideas that would make the problem worse, that clients would hate, that would be unethical or illegal or completely impractical. The more terrible, the better."

Sarah Williams looked confused. "Why would we do that?"

"Two reasons," Lucy explained. "First, suggesting bad ideas helps us create conditions for psychological safety by lowering the stakes and lightening the mood, which means people share more freely. Second, bad ideas often contain inverse insights; if the worst solution is X, maybe the best solution is the opposite of X. Or bad ideas expose assumptions we didn't know we were making."

She turned to the Client Service Group. "You're going to start with your communication HMW: 'How might we communicate with our clients so they feel confident that the firm understands their need for clarity once a matter is ongoing and they have less visibility into its status?' Give me the worst possible ways to handle client communication. Go."

Group 1: Worst Possible Client Communication

At the front of the room, Group 1 gathered around their workspace. Jessica Park, Dwarkesh Jones, Sarah Williams, Tom Brennan, and about eight others stared at the HMW statement.

"Worst possible ideas," Dwarkesh said. "Okay. How about: only communicate with clients through certified mail sent to wrong addresses?"

People laughed, and someone wrote it on a Post-it.

"Never respond to client emails or calls," Jessica suggested. "Make them chase us."

"Bill them for time spent not communicating with them," Tom added with a grin.

The ideas started flowing, as did the laughs:

- "Use only legal jargon, especially Latin, in all communications. Make it as incomprehensible as possible"
- "Send updates at random times, like 3 a.m. emails, calls during their vacation"
- "Provide updates only when something goes catastrophically wrong, and don't offer any solutions"
- "Assign a different associate to every client call so no one knows the history"
- "Create elaborate phone trees that clients have to navigate to reach anyone"
- "Charge exorbitant consultation fees for answering basic status questions"

- "Only communicate in fifty-page memos, even for simple updates"
- "Ghost clients for months, then surprise them with completed work they hate and a huge invoice"

Sarah was writing them all down, laughing despite herself. "Okay, this is actually revealing. If you look at them closely, they're all exaggerations of things we sometimes actually do."

"The fifty-page memo for simple updates is not that far from reality," Jessica admitted.

"And ghosting clients then surprising them; isn't that basically what happened in Rebecca's story about the settlement discussions?" Dwarkesh observed.

Lucy had walked over and was listening. "See? The worst ideas are exposing patterns in current practice. Now flip them. What's the opposite of these terrible approaches?"

The group started converting:

- Opposite of "only communicate when catastrophe": **Proactive communication even when nothing's wrong**
- Opposite of "use only jargon": **Lead with plain language, follow with legal detail if needed**
- Opposite of "different associate every time": **Consistent point of contact who knows the relationship**
- Opposite of "fifty-page memos": **Brief executive summary with optional detail appendix**
- Opposite of "ghost then surprise": **Regular check-ins to ensure alignment throughout**

"These are actually good ideas," Tom said, surprised. "We just generated them backwards."

Technique 2: Crazy 8s

While Group 1 was finishing their worst possible ideas, Lucy moved to the Associate Development Group to introduce the next technique.

"Crazy 8s," she explained, handing each person a sheet of paper divided into eight boxes. "You have four minutes to sketch eight different ideas. One idea per box, thirty seconds per idea. The catch: you must sketch, not write. Don't worry about artistic quality; stick figures are fine. The point is to think visually and move fast."

She held up a timer. "Your HMW is: 'How might we create multiple valued career paths so lawyers can succeed through different strengths, origination, service excellence, leadership, specialization?' Eight ideas for career paths in four minutes. Go."

Group 2: Career Path Sketches

Robert Kim stared at his blank sheet, marker in hand, already uncomfortable. "I can't draw."

"Doesn't matter," Maggie McNamee said beside him, already sketching in her first box. "Just go."

The timer started.

Robert sketched a ladder in box 1, then crossed it out and drew multiple paths diverging from a single point. "Different routes to . . . something."

In box 2, he drew stick figures of different sizes with different labels: "Rainmaker," "Expert," "Leader," "Service."

Maggie was faster, already on box 3. She'd sketched:

- Box 1: A tree with different types of fruit (representing different valued contributions)
- Box 2: A video game skill tree with different branches to unlock
- Box 3: A restaurant with different specialized roles, like chef, sommelier, host

Priya Patel was sketching frantically:

- Box 1: Multiple tracks on a racing course, all leading to a finish line labeled "Success"
- Box 2: A university with different majors, all valuable
- Box 3: An orchestra with different instruments, all essential
- Box 4: A law firm organizational chart with multiple "partner" tiers, each valued differently

Alex Rivera was thinking about tech companies:

- Box 1: Individual contributor track and management track, parallel and equal
- Box 2: Rotating assignments where you try different paths before committing
- Box 3: Quarterly reviews where you assess your own path preference
- Box 4: "Choose your own adventure" career pathing

The timer went off. People looked up, most having filled five to seven boxes.

"Don't evaluate yet," Lucy said. "Just put your sheets in the middle and everyone take sixty seconds to look at what others created."

As they reviewed the sketches, patterns emerged. Several people had drawn paths that diverged but remained equal in value. Multiple people referenced other professions or industries that ranged from video games to restaurants to orchestras to tech companies. Someone had drawn a lattice structure where you could move between paths, not just pick one forever.

"What are you noticing?" Lucy asked.

"Lots of us thought about other industries," Maggie observed. "Restaurants, orchestras, tech companies. These are all places that already have multiple valued roles."

"And the movement between paths," Priya added. "You're not locked in forever, but instead you can shift as you develop."

"And status markers," Robert said, pointing to a sketch showing different partner titles. "We need ways to signal success in each path so that 'equity partner' isn't the only prestigious designation."

Lucy smiled. "You just generated lots of different conceptual models in four minutes. Some might be terrible when we evaluate them later. But you couldn't have generated them through traditional discussion. The time pressure and visual format forced different thinking and didn't give you time to decide first whether to share them with the group. You just had to get them out there."

Technique 3: Lateral Inspiration from Other Industries

Lucy called everyone together for the final technique. "Last method, and this one requires the most imagination. We're going to steal shamelessly from other industries."

She clicked to show images from different sectors: hospitals, consulting firms, sports teams, tech companies, fast food restaurants, hotels.

"Every industry has solved problems similar to yours, except they're in different contexts. Professional development? Medical residencies have been doing that for decades. Team-based service delivery? Consulting firms built their entire model around it. Complex compensation for diverse contributions? Look at how venture capital firms, creative agencies, or even professional sports teams handle it."

She distributed a handout:

LATERAL INSPIRATION GUIDE

Pick an industry that's different from law, then ask:

- How do they handle [our problem]?
- What's their equivalent of our challenge?
- What have they tried that worked or failed?
- What would their solution look like if we adapted it?

"Each group is going to pick two analogous industries and brainstorm adaptations," Lucy said. "Twenty minutes. Be specific. Don't just say 'be like tech companies.' Say 'tech companies do X for Y reason, we could adapt it as Z.'"

Group 1: Client Communication Inspiration

Group 1 clustered around their workspace, looking at their HMW about ongoing client communication.

"What industry is really good at keeping customers informed when they can't see what's happening?" Jessica asked.

"Package delivery," Dwarkesh suggested. "FedEx, UPS, Amazon. You get constant updates about where your package is."

"Airlines," Sarah added. "Flight tracking, gate changes, delay notifications."

"Medical care," Tom said. "My doctor's office sends me appointment reminders, test results, follow-up instructions."

They started adapting:

From Package Delivery:

- "Client portal showing where matters are in process, like package tracking"
- "Automatic notifications at key milestones"
- "Estimated completion dates that update as circumstances change"
- "Exception alerts when something unusual happens"

From Airlines:

- "Proactive notifications of delays or schedule changes before client asks"
- "Easy rebooking options when plans change"
- "Status updates that explain WHY there's a delay, not just that there is one"
- "Mobile app with real-time matter updates"

From Healthcare:

- "Post-interaction summaries sent automatically"
- "Clear next steps after every client contact"
- "Patient portal style access to all documents and communications"
- "Preventive outreach—'based on your industry, here's a regulatory change coming'"

Jessica was writing furiously. "These are concrete. 'Matter tracking portal' is something we could actually build."

"And some don't require technology," Sarah noted. "'Proactive notifications of delays before client asks, for example. We could do that tomorrow with better process discipline."

Group 2: Career Path Inspiration

Group 2 was wrestling with their multiple career paths HMW.

"Who else has this figured out?" Maggie asked. "Multiple ways to succeed without one being the 'real' path?"

"I've heard about Netflix doing this," Alex offered. "Individual contributor track that goes as high as management track. You can become a distinguished engineer without managing people."

"Consulting firms," Priya suggested. "They have different partner types, like client service partners, subject matter experts, and office managing partners."

"Professional sports," someone added. "Players, coaches, general managers, and scouts. They're all critical, all valued differently."

They started extracting principles:

From Tech:

- "Parallel tracks with equivalent compensation potential"
- "Title systems that signal seniority without implying one path is superior"
- "Distinguished [specialty] partner—like Distinguished Engineer"
- "Regular calibration to ensure paths remain truly equal"

From Consulting:

- "Partner types defined by strength: Client Partners (origination), Delivery Partners (service), Expert Partners (specialization), Leadership Partners (management)"
- "Shared governance across partner types"
- "Transparent about what each path requires"
- "All paths represented in firm leadership"

From Sports:

- "Recognition systems for different contributions (MVP, Best Defensive Player, Coach of Year)"
- "Career transitions built in (player to coach, player to management)"
- "Team success valued over individual statistics"

Robert was nodding slowly. "The Netflix example is compelling. They solved exactly our problem of how to retain brilliant people who don't want to manage but deserve senior status and compensation."

"And the consulting model of partner types," Maggie added. "We could create Client Partners, Service Partners, Expert Partners, Leadership Partners who have equity and are all valued, but who succeed through different strengths."

William Klept couldn't believe what he was hearing, and he especially couldn't believe Julian was allowing all of this to happen out in the open, in front of associates, staff, and counsel. This is the kind of discussion that needs to take place in a closed-door meeting among equity partners only, if at all. And he didn't think it should *ever* take place. Rainmakers are the lifeblood of the firm. If Julian thinks his spreadsheets are telling a terrifying story now, just wait until he sees what they look like when rainmakers are neutered and start to lateral to firms that properly value them. William heard his wife's voice in his head. "Deep breaths, Billy, deep breaths." He quietly practiced the breathing techniques from his new meditation app and heard the instructor's soothing British accent in his head. "In through the nose, out through the mouth. . . ."

Group 3: Client Team Structure Inspiration

Group 3 was exploring their HMW about structuring client service teams.

"Who builds effective teams with clear roles but flexibility?" Marcus asked.

"Hospitals," Tom suggested immediately. "Every patient has a care team that includes an attending physician, residents, nurses, specialists. Roles are clear, but the composition changes based on patient needs."

"Emergency response teams," Lisa added. "Fire, police, EMT who all coordinate across agencies with clear protocols."

"Film production," one of the younger partners suggested. "Director, producers, cinematographer, editor. It's a creative process where everyone has a role, but the team forms and reforms for each project."

"Software development," Alex said. "Agile teams, scrum masters, clear methodology for coordination."

They started extracting models:

From Hospitals:

- "Client 'attending partner' who coordinates the team"
- "Regular team rounds with brief check-ins to coordinate"
- "Handoff protocols when team members change"
- "Escalation pathways for complex issues"
- "Different specialties consulted as needed, not all present constantly"

From Emergency Response:

- "Incident command system with a clear leader for each client situation"
- "Pre-defined roles that activate based on situation type"
- "Communication protocols everyone follows"
- "After-action reviews to improve team performance"

From Film Production:

- "Project-based teams that form, work intensively, then dissolve"
- "Producer role (client relationship manager) separate from director role (matter leader)"
- "Clear creative brief (engagement parameters) that guides everyone"
- "Credits that acknowledge everyone's contribution"

From Software Development:

- "Sprint planning equivalent with regular team planning sessions"
- "Standup meetings equivalent that includes brief daily check-ins"
- "Retrospectives on what worked, what didn't, and how to improve"
- "Product owner role of someone who represents client needs to the team"
- "Visible backlog of work so everyone knows priorities"

Marcus was energized. "The hospital model is almost exactly what we need. 'Attending partner' for the relationship, specialists who rotate in and out as needed, regular coordination meetings, clear handoff protocols."

"And I love the film production separation of producer and director," Lisa said. "The person managing the client relationship doesn't have to be the person doing the technical legal work. Those are different skills."

Aggregating Ideas

After ninety minutes of intense ideation using all three techniques, Lucy called everyone back together. The conference room looked like a creativity explosion. The walls were covered with Post-its, whiteboards were filled with sketches and bullet points, sheets of paper were filled with rapid-fire ideas covering every table.

"Look around," Lucy said. "You've generated hundreds of ideas this morning. You! Lawyers, trained to spot issues and evaluate critically, just spent ninety minutes generating possibilities without judgment."

She walked among the workspaces. "Some of these ideas are probably terrible. Some might be brilliant. Most are somewhere in between. But that's exactly what ideation is supposed to produce. You generated the raw material that you can now refine, combine, and prototype."

Julian stood and moved to the front. "I've been watching you work, and I'm struck by something. The energy in this room is completely different from Monday morning. Monday, you were anxious and skeptical. Now you're engaged and creative. Why?"

Sarah Williams raised her hand. "Because we're designing solutions actively, not thinking and analyzing out of the gate."

"And because the problems are real," Jessica added. "We defined them ourselves. We know they need solving."

"And because the techniques gave us permission to be weird," Alex said, laughing. "Worst possible ideas, crazy sketches, stealing from other industries. I know this is serious in the end, but today was actually *fun*, like play. I can't remember the last time I felt that way."

Lucy clicked to show the afternoon's agenda. "This afternoon, we're moving to the Prototype stage. We're going to take some of these ideas and build rough versions we can test. Not perfect solutions, but quick prototypes that let us learn fast."

She looked around the room. "But first, lunch. Let these ideas percolate. Talk to each other about what you generated. Start thinking about which ideas have enough potential to be worth prototyping. And get ready for the afternoon, when we make some of this real."

Lunch Conversations: Processing Creativity

The dining room buzzed with unusual energy. People were still talking about the morning's exercises, sharing ideas across groups, building on each other's thinking.

At one table, Robert Kim was telling Maggie McNamee about the Netflix idea. "I never thought of creating a 'Distinguished Expert Partner' track with equivalent status to equity partner but focused on technical excellence rather than origination. But why couldn't we?"

"The medical residency model for associate development," Maggie replied. "Structured rotations through different practice areas, dedicated teaching faculty, clear competency milestones. It's not that different from what we need."

At another table, Jessica Park and Priya Patel were excitedly discussing the client portal idea inspired by package tracking. "What if clients could log in and see: matter opened, preliminary research complete, draft under review, ready for client feedback, just like tracking a package?" Jessica said.

"And get automatic notifications at each stage," Priya added. "Plus exception alerts if something unexpected happens. The technology exists. We just never thought to apply it this way."

Tom Brennan sat with Lisa Martinez and several others, working through compensation model ideas. "The team origination pool concept is interesting," he said, scribbling on a napkin. "Instead of individual credit, revenue goes into team pools. Partners get compensated based on team performance plus individual contribution."

"The consulting firm partner types model could work with that," Lisa suggested. "Different partner types, different compensation ranges, but all equity participants. Client Partners focus on origination, Service Partners on delivery, Expert Partners on specialization."

Near the windows, Lucy and Julian were observing the conversations with satisfaction.

"They're building on each other's ideas, combining concepts, and starting to evaluate feasibility," Julian noted.

"That's what happens when you generate enough raw material," Lucy said. "The best ideas emerge from combining and refining, not from trying to get it perfect on the first try."

"This afternoon is going to be trickier." Julian said. "Taking ideas from interesting to testable. That's where we find out if we can actually build something or if we're just generating fantasy solutions."

"I know," Lucy said, trying to sound confident, but feeling deeply anxious about this next step. She sighed deeply and stepped forward, "Let's see what happens."

As lunch concluded, people began filtering back toward the conference room.

The firm had spent three days building awareness and knowledge. Now they were building ability and the capacity to actually design new approaches. They were in the messy, exhilarating middle of creation.

For lawyers trained to analyze and critique, the experience of creating without immediate judgment was weird, but for many in the room, surprisingly liberating. Now, could they maintain that creative mindset through the next phase of building prototypes that would test whether their ideas actually worked?

Chapter 19

Prototyping

After lunch, people returned to find the conference room reorganized yet again. The three problem-area workspaces remained, but now each had been expanded with additional tables, fresh whiteboards, and new materials. Now, the participants found foam core boards, colored paper, scissors, tape, and stacks of blank templates labeled "Service Blueprint," "User Journey Map," and "Prototype Canvas."

Lucy stood at the front with visible excitement. "This morning you generated hundreds of ideas. This afternoon, we're going to make some of them real, or at least real enough to test. Welcome to the Prototype stage of design thinking."

She clicked to a slide showing the five design thinking stages with "Prototype" highlighted:

Empathize → Define → Ideate → PROTOTYPE → Test

"Prototyping is where creativity meets reality," Lucy began. "You take promising ideas and build rough versions that are just developed enough to test whether the concept has merit, but not so polished that you're afraid to change or abandon them."

Julian spoke from his seat. "I want to be clear about what we're doing this afternoon and why. By the end of today, we need eight to ten concrete prototypes that we can evaluate tomorrow morning. Not perfect solutions, but testable concepts. We're using an abbreviated version of something called an Innovation Tournament to select which prototypes to pilot and build detailed implementation plans for."

Lucy nodded. "So we have three phases this afternoon. First, we're going to do a first round of filtering from this morning's work and select the most promising ideas. As Julian noted, we need about eight to ten total. Second, we'll form prototype teams around those ideas. Third, you'll build rough prototypes that make your concepts tangible. Let's get started."

Phase 1: First Round of Filtering

"Each problem area is going to do this separately," Lucy explained. "Client Service groups, you're going to gather in the front workspace. Associate Development, you're in the middle. Business Development, you're in the back. You have forty minutes."

She distributed a one-page guide:

IDEA SELECTION FRAMEWORK

Step 1: Share All Ideas (15 minutes)

- Each group shares the ideas generated this morning across all three techniques
- Post everything on the walls without filtering yet
- Look for patterns, overlaps, and complementary concepts

Step 2: Affinity Clustering (10 minutes)

- Group similar ideas together
- Combine ideas that work better together
- Identify themes emerging across your morning work

Step 3: Selection Criteria (5 minutes)

Evaluate ideas against:

- **Impact**: Would this significantly improve the problem we're solving?
- **Feasibility**: Could we actually implement this in the next 6–12 months?

- **Innovation**: Does this represent real change vs. incremental adjustment?
- **Strategic Fit**: Does this align with where we want to go as a firm?

Step 4: Dot Voting (10 minutes)

- Each person gets 5 votes (dots)
- Vote for ideas you want to prototype
- Can put multiple dots on one idea if you feel strongly
- Select top 3–4 ideas from your problem area

"This is convergent thinking," Lucy explained. "This morning was divergent because our goal was to generate as many ideas as possible. Now we converge so we can focus on the most promising ones. Both are necessary. You can't evaluate what you haven't generated, and you can't implement everything you generate."

The three groups dispersed to their workspaces.

Client Service Group: Convergence

The three Client Service groups merged at the front workspace. The group included about fifteen people total. Jessica Park, Dwarkesh Jones, Sarah Williams, Tom Brennan, and others gathered around tables now covered with Post-its and sketches from the morning.

"Let's start by getting everything visible," Sarah said, taking the facilitation lead. "Each group, put your best ideas from all three techniques on the wall."

They began posting and organizing. The wall quickly filled:

Communication Ideas:

- Real-time matter portal (package tracking analogy)
- Proactive exception alerts before client asks
- Weekly executive summaries (brief + optional detail)
- Consistent point of contact for each client

- Post-interaction summaries sent automatically
- Mobile app for status updates
- Scheduled check-ins even when nothing is happening

Intake Ideas:

- Co-design workshops at intake (design sprint format)
- "Day in the life" shadowing before proposal
- Collaborative scoping sessions
- Client brings their team to intake meeting, we bring ours
- Intake as ongoing conversation, not one-time event
- Prototype solution during intake, test before engagement
- Joint success criteria development

"I'm seeing patterns," Dwarkesh observed. "A lot of ideas about making information more accessible and transparent. And a lot about involving clients earlier and more deeply in the process."

They started clustering:

TRANSPARENCY CLUSTER:

- Matter portal
- Automated updates
- Executive summaries
- Status notifications

PROACTIVE ENGAGEMENT CLUSTER:

- Scheduled check-ins
- Exception alerts
- Preventive outreach about industry changes

COLLABORATIVE INTAKE CLUSTER:

- Co-design workshops
- Joint scoping
- Success criteria development
- Client team + our team from start

CONSISTENT EXPERIENCE CLUSTER:

- Dedicated point of contact
- Handoff protocols
- Post-interaction summaries

"Now let's combine some of these," Jessica suggested. "What if the matter portal idea included automated updates AND proactive alerts AND executive summaries? That's one integrated solution, not three separate ones."

They began merging:

IDEA 1: "Client Command Center"

- Real-time portal showing matter status
- Automated milestone notifications
- Weekly executive summaries
- Exception alerts for delays or issues
- Mobile access
- Document repository
- Direct messaging to matter team

IDEA 2: "Intake as Co-Design"

- Multi-session intake process
- Client brings their full team, we bring ours
- Day 1: Understand client business and challenges
- Day 2: Collaborative scope approach

- Day 3: Define success metrics together
- Result: Shared engagement design, not our proposal to them

IDEA 3: "Proactive Partnership Model"

- Dedicated relationship coordinator (not biller, coordinator)
- Quarterly business reviews even without active matters
- Industry alerts and regulatory monitoring
- Scheduled check-ins at matter milestones
- Clear escalation paths
- Handoff protocols for consistency

IDEA 4: "Plain Language First"

- All client communications lead with executive summary
- Legal detail available but optional
- Recommendations stated clearly
- "What this means for your business" translation
- No unexplained jargon

Tom Brennan was writing evaluation notes.

"**Command Center** is high innovation, medium feasibility and requires technology investment.

Co-Design Intake is medium innovation, high feasibility and is mostly process change.

Proactive Partnership is medium innovation, medium feasibility and requires role creation.

Plain Language is low innovation but high impact and we could start tomorrow."

They did dot voting. Each person put sticky dots on the ideas they wanted to prototype.

Results:

- Client Command Center: 18 dots
- Intake as Co-Design: 22 dots

- Proactive Partnership Model: 15 dots
- Plain Language First: 11 dots

"Top three to prototype," Sarah declared. "Command Center, Co-Design Intake, and Proactive Partnership."

Associate Development Group: Convergence

In the middle workspace, the two Associate Development groups merged, bringing together about twelve people, including Robert Kim, Maggie McNamee, Priya Patel, Alex Rivera, and several others.

They went through the same process, posting ideas and clustering:

Career Paths Ideas:

- Multiple partner tracks (Client Partners, Service Partners, Expert Partners, Leadership Partners)
- Distinguished Expert Partner title (Netflix model)
- Transparent criteria for each path
- Ability to shift between paths
- Equal compensation potential across paths
- Different evaluation standards for different strengths
- Portfolio career model where you can combine different roles

Feedback/Development Ideas:

- Quarterly development check-ins (separate from performance reviews)
- Competency-based milestones at each year
- 360-degree feedback from peers, not just partners
- Real-time feedback on matters, not just annual reviews
- Development plans co-created by associate and mentor
- Protected development time (non-billable but valued)
- Learning cohorts that progress together

They clustered and combined:

IDEA 1: "Four Partner Paths"

- Client Partners (origination focus)
- Service Partners (execution excellence focus)
- Expert Partners (specialized technical depth)
- Leadership Partners (firm management/mentorship focus)
- All equity partners with equivalent status
- Clear criteria for advancement in each path
- Transparent about what each path requires and rewards
- Ability to move between paths

IDEA 2: "Competency Roadmap"

- Define specific competencies for each career stage
- Year 1-2: Foundation skills (research, drafting, analysis)
- Year 3-4: Independence skills (client interaction, matter management)
- Year 5-6: Strategic skills (business development, specialization)
- Year 7+: Leadership skills (mentorship, innovation)
- Associates can see exactly what they're working toward
- Development plans tied to competency building
- Assignments made intentionally to build specific competencies

IDEA 3: "Continuous Feedback System"

- Matter-based feedback (after each significant assignment)
- Quarterly development conversations (not performance reviews)
- 360-degree input from multiple partners and peers

- Real-time recognition system (visible acknowledgment of good work)
- Annual comprehensive review that synthesizes year's feedback
- Associates always know where they stand

They voted:

- Four Partner Paths: 20 dots
- Competency Roadmap: 16 dots
- Continuous Feedback System: 14 dots

"We're prototyping all three," Maggie said. "They're connected because you need paths to aim for, roadmaps to follow, and feedback to know if you're on track."

Business Development Group: Convergence

In the back workspace, the two Business Development groups merged, with about ten people, including Marcus Reed, Lisa Martinez, and others.

Their wall filled with compensation and team structure ideas:

Compensation Ideas:

- Team origination pools
- Collaboration multipliers
- Credit for different contributions (origination, service, mentorship, innovation)
- Base + team bonus structure
- Transition protections for current rainmakers
- Metrics beyond origination (client satisfaction, knowledge sharing, associate development)
- Shared risk and reward for client teams

Team Structure Ideas:

- Client attending partner + supporting cast (hospital model)
- Relationship manager separate from technical experts (film production model)
- Sprint-style team coordination meetings (software development)
- Clear handoff protocols
- Rotating specialties as needed
- After-action reviews for continuous improvement

They clustered and merged:

IDEA 1: "Team Compensation Pools"

- Major clients assigned to relationship teams (3–5 partners)
- Revenue from that client goes into team pool
- Individual compensation based on: base + share of team pool + individual contribution factor
- Contribution factor includes: client origination, service hours, client satisfaction scores, mentorship, knowledge sharing
- Protections for partners transitioning existing solo relationships to teams
- Phased implementation over 2–3 years

IDEA 2: "Client Care Teams" (hospital model adaptation)

- Every major client has an Attending Partner (relationship owner)
- Supporting team of specialist partners who contribute as needed
- Client Relationship Manager (non-lawyer) coordinates logistics
- Weekly team "rounds": brief check-ins to coordinate

- Clear protocols for bringing specialists in and out
- Shared client knowledge base everyone accesses
- Team responsible for proactive account management

IDEA 3: "Agile Account Planning"

- Quarterly planning sessions for each major client relationship
- Review: what's working, what's not, what opportunities exist
- Sprint-style short-term goals (90-day plans)
- Regular retrospectives on team performance
- Client included in some planning sessions (co-creation)
- Visible backlog of potential services/opportunities
- Celebrate team wins, learn from team losses together

IDEA 4: "Collaboration Credit System"

- Create formal recognition for collaborative behaviors
- Credit for introducing colleagues to your clients
- Credit for knowledge sharing and documentation
- Credit for mentoring associates in BD skills
- Credit for participating effectively on others' client teams
- Credit tracked and factored into compensation
- Make collaboration visible and valued

They voted:

- Team Compensation Pools: 17 dots
- Client Care Teams: 19 dots
- Agile Account Planning: 11 dots
- Collaboration Credit System: 13 dots

"Top three," Marcus declared. "Compensation Pools, Care Teams, and Collaboration Credits."

Phase 2: Prototype Team Formation

Lucy called everyone back together after forty-five minutes. Each group reported their three selected ideas:

Client Service:

1. Client Command Center
2. Intake as Co-Design
3. Proactive Partnership Model

Associate Development:

1. Four Partner Paths
2. Competency Roadmap
3. Continuous Feedback System

Business Development:

1. Team Compensation Pools
2. Client Care Teams
3. Collaboration Credit System

"Nine prototypes to build this afternoon," Lucy said. "Now we're going to reorganize one more time. You're going to self-select which prototype team you want to join. You can work on an idea from your original problem area, or switch to something else that excites you."

She displayed guidelines:

PROTOTYPE TEAM FORMATION

- Each team needs a minimum of 4–6 people
- Mix of perspectives valuable (partners + associates, different practices)
- Include at least one skeptic (or one person to adopt the role of the skeptic) because they'll help you strengthen the prototype
- Include someone with relevant expertise (tech for Command Center, finance for Compensation Pools)
- Aim for diversity of thought, not just enthusiasm

"You have five minutes to form teams," Lucy said. "Find the sign for the prototype you want to work on and gather there."

People moved around the room, gravitating toward different ideas. Some stayed with their morning groups, others switched. The resulting teams were notably mixed:

Client Command Center Team: Dwarkesh Jones, Jessica Park, two associates from different offices

Intake as Co-Design Team: Sarah Williams, several service partners, two mid-level associates

Proactive Partnership Model Team: Maggie McNamee, Marcus Reed, several junior partners, three associates

Four Partner Paths Team: Robert Kim, Julian (he joined this one), several other partners

Competency Roadmap Team: Lisa Martinez, John Forte, Maya Davis, three other associates, four partners

Continuous Feedback System Team: Elena Rodriguez, several associates from different years, two partners

Team Compensation Pools Team: Tom Brennan, Marcus Reed, two senior partners, one skeptical partner who had voted against it

Client Care Teams Team: Priya Patel, Michael Solomon, one operations person, two partners, two associates

Collaboration Credit System Team: Alex Rivera, several mid-level partners, two associates interested in BD

Lucy looked pleased with the mixing. "Good. Now, each team has a workspace with materials. You have two hours to build a prototype. Let me explain what that means."

Phase 3: Rapid Prototyping

Lucy pulled up a slide showing different prototype formats:

PROTOTYPE FORMATS

Service Blueprint—Map out the entire service experience, moment by moment

User Journey Map—Show what the user experiences at each stage

Role Play/Skit—Act out how the solution would work in practice

Mock-up—Sketch screens, forms, or physical materials

One-Pager—Describe the concept with key features and benefits

Process Flow—Diagram how the system works

Before/After Comparison—Show current state vs. proposed state

"Pick the format that best communicates your concept," Lucy said. "You're not building the finished product. You're building something rough that makes your idea tangible enough to test and get feedback."

She clicked through prototype examples from other organizations:

- The small cardboard box that eventually became the first ipod
- An early soda bottle/plunger contraption that later became the successful supersoaker toy water gun
- A cardboard mock-up of a mobile app
- A hand-drawn service blueprint for a hospital check-in process
- A role-play script for a new customer service interaction
- A before/after comparison showing process improvements

"The goal is 'low resolution, high concept,'" Lucy explained. "Don't get caught up in perfecting details. Focus on communicating the core idea clearly enough that someone can understand it, react to it, and help you improve it."

She distributed materials and set a timer. "Two hours. Make something real. Go."

Selected Prototype Vignettes

Client Command Center Team

Dwarkesh Jones spread out the materials on their table. "Okay, we're building a client portal. We should probably mock up what it would look like."

"Let's start with user needs," Jessica Park suggested. "What does the client actually need to see?"

She consulted the morning's notes. "Real-time status, upcoming milestones, who's working on what, how to reach the team, recent updates, documents."

They started sketching on a large foam board, creating a mock-up of a web interface:

Dashboard view:

- Matter status indicator (In Progress/Milestone Approaching/ Action Needed)
- Timeline showing completed steps and upcoming milestones
- Team roster with photos, roles, contact info
- Recent activity feed
- Document library
- Message center
- Budget tracker

One associate suggested, "What if we add an 'explain this to me' button next to legal terms? Click it and you get plain-language explanation."

"Yes," Dwarkesh said, sketching it. "And what about proactive alerts? Let's design what those notifications would look like."

They created sample notification templates:

"Milestone Update: Discovery responses filed yesterday. Next step: Review responses with you. Sarah will reach out this week to schedule."

"Budget Alert: Matter is at 75% of estimated hours. Current projection suggests we'll finish within budget, but we wanted you to know we're monitoring closely."

"Exception Notice: Opposing counsel requested extension on filing deadline. This delays timeline by two weeks. Do you want to discuss strategy implications? If so, let's schedule a call."

Jessica had shifted her focus to the business case. "Implementation cost: CRM integration, portal development, probably $150K–200K. Ongoing cost: relationship manager time to keep updated. Benefit: reduced client anxiety, fewer surprise billing issues, competitive differentiator."

After two hours, they had a foam board mock-up showing the interface, sample notifications printed on cards, and a one-page business case. It looked *very* rough, full of sketches and sticky notes, but the concept was clear.

Four Partner Paths Team

Robert Kim, Julian, and several others were tackling the multiple career paths challenge.

"We need to define each path specifically," Julian said. "What does a Client Partner do that's different from a Service Partner?"

They started with a grid:

	Client Partners	Service Partners	Expert Partners	Leadership Partners
Primary Focus	Origination & relationships	Execution & delivery	Technical specialization	Firm building & mentorship
Success Metrics	New client development, relationship expansion	Client satisfaction, matter quality, efficiency	Thought leadership, technical innovation	Associate development, culture building, strategic initiatives
Compensation	Base + origination credit + team participation	Base + quality metrics + client retention	Base + specialization premium + IP/publication credits	Base + leadership metrics + firm growth
Time Allocation	60% BD, 40% delivery	20% BD, 80% delivery	30% IP/thought leadership, 70% delivery	40% leadership, 60% delivery

Another partner was pushing on the details. "But what about transitions? Can I start as a Service Partner and become a Client Partner later?"

"Absolutely," Robert said, suddenly invested in this new model. "In fact, that should be encouraged. Most of us started as service lawyers and gradually developed into rainmakers. Why not make that official?"

They added a "Career Evolution" section showing possible paths:

- Associate → Service Partner → Client Partner
- Associate → Expert Partner (deep technical specialization)

- Associate → Service Partner → Leadership Partner
- Associate → blend of paths (50/50 Service + Expert)

Julian asked, "How do we ensure Service Partners are actually valued equally? Compensation is one thing, but what about status signals?"

They brainstormed:

- Equal voting rights in partnership decisions
- Service Partners represented in all leadership roles
- Recognition events celebrate all types of contribution
- Marketing materials showcase all partner types
- Clients see different partner types as equally senior
- Office assignments and perks not tied to origination

After two hours, they had a poster board showing the four paths, a compensation framework table, a career evolution diagram, and a list of "equality indicators" that would signal genuine parity.

Client Care Teams Team

Priya Patel's team was role-playing to prototype their idea.

"Let's act out what a client care team actually does," Michael Solomon suggested. "I'll be the client. Priya, you're the Attending Partner. He assigned another colleague the role of specialist partner and a final team member the role of relationship manager."

They set up a mock "weekly team rounds" meeting:

Priya (as Attending Partner): "Let's review our clients. Starting with Apex Manufacturing. What's happening?"

The Relationship Manager: "Three active matters: the acquisition due diligence, the employment dispute, and routine contract reviews. Acquisition is on schedule for closing next month. Employment litigation matter had a development when opposing counsel filed a motion yesterday."

Priya: "Our specialist, you're handling the employment matter. Do we need to brief the client before they see it in the news?"

Specialist Partner: "Yes, I'll call them this afternoon. Also, I think this motion reveals their strategy, so we should consider a counter-motion."

Priya: "Good. Let's schedule a call with the client tomorrow to discuss strategy together, not just report what we're doing. Our relationship manager should coordinate that and make sure we're all prepared."

They role-played several more scenarios:

- Bringing a new specialist onto a matter
- Proactive account review identifying new opportunities
- Handling a client complaint about responsiveness
- Transitioning relationships when a partner retires

After each role-play, they captured what worked:

- Regular coordination kept everyone aligned
- Relationship manager freed partners from logistics
- Clients got team consistency even when individual lawyers changed
- Proactive communication happened because team made it a priority
- Knowledge sharing was built into the structure

They created a service blueprint showing:

- Team composition decisions (when formed, who's included)
- Weekly coordination process (rounds)
- Client interaction protocols (who contacts client when)
- Knowledge management (shared files, briefing protocols)
- Handoff procedures (when specialists rotate in/out)
- Performance metrics (client satisfaction, team efficiency)

Phase 4: Gallery Walk

At 4:30, Lucy called time. "Prototypes on the walls. Everyone's going to do a gallery walk. This is where we circulate and look at what each team created. Ask questions, give feedback, note what resonates."

The nine prototype teams set up their work around the room like an art gallery. People circulated with sticky pads, leaving feedback on each prototype:

At the **Client Command Center** display:

- "Love the 'explain this' button. It makes legal lingo accessible and actionable"
- "Budget alerts before overages = trust building"
- "How often would portal need updating? Who does that?"
- "This could be competitive differentiator"

At the **Four Partner Paths** board:

- "Service Partners need to be on compensation committee or it won't feel equal"
- "Transition between paths is key; it can't be one-way doors"
- "What about associates who want to blend paths? 60/40 split?"
- "This changes recruiting because we can attract different personalities"

At the **Client Care Teams** space:

- "Relationship manager role is crucial because it frees partners for legal work"
- "Weekly rounds seem frequent—maybe bi-weekly for smaller clients?"
- "Love that knowledge stays with team, not just one person"
- "How do you prevent turf battles over who leads?"

At the **Competency Roadmap** area:

- "Finally—a clear answer to 'what should I be learning'"
- "Year 7+ still needs definition—leadership how?"
- "Could this help with lateral hiring? Know exactly what gaps to fill?"
- "Needs to connect to Four Partner Paths—competencies for each path"

At the **Team Compensation Pools** wall:

- "Transition protections for current rainmakers are essential"
- "How do you handle partners who contribute differently to same team?"
- "This requires sophisticated tracking—feasible?"
- "What if a team member isn't pulling weight—how do you address?"

After thirty minutes of circulation, people gathered back together. It seemed like everyone should be ready to collapse by this point in the day and week, but instead the room felt electric, with walls covered with ideas, feedback accumulating, and conversations happening in every corner.

Lucy stood at the front. "Look at what you built in two hours. Nine rough prototypes that make abstract ideas concrete. Tomorrow morning, you're going to present these in the next filtering stage of our Innovation Tournament. Judges will evaluate them on impact, feasibility, innovation, and strategic fit. The top ideas will move to pilot implementation."

Julian didn't want to push his colleagues too hard, given how much effort they'd expended this week already, but knowing what was on tap for Friday, he added, "Tonight, I want you to think about the hard questions people asked and get ready to make a compelling case tomorrow for why your idea should be piloted."

Lucy displayed the next slide in her deck, showing the full framework one more time:

Empathize ✓ (Tuesday: client panel, Wednesday: associate interviews)

Define ✓ (Tuesday/Wednesday: HMW statements)

Ideate ✓ (Thursday morning: three techniques)

Prototype ✓ (Thursday afternoon: nine concepts)

Test → (Friday and beyond: Innovation Tournament + pilot selection)

"Tomorrow we begin the final stage of design thinking, testing," Lucy said. "We find out which ideas are strong enough to become reality. Do just a bit more thinking and then get some rest. Tomorrow's the day we decide what we're actually going to do."

Evening: Refining and Reflecting

The dining room that evening was unlike any previous night. Prototype teams clustered together, still working, refining their presentations, addressing the feedback they'd received.

At one table, the Client Command Center team was debating implementation. "We need to address the 'who updates the portal' question," Dwarkesh said. "That's the feasibility concern everyone had."

"What if the relationship manager does it?" Jessica suggested. "Part of the Proactive Partnership Model. One person responsible for keeping client information current."

"That connects two prototypes," Dwarkesh noted. "Command Center + Proactive Partnership. Maybe they're really one integrated solution."

At another table, the Four Partner Paths team was strengthening their equality indicators. "We need to be specific about how Service Partners get represented in leadership," Robert insisted. "Not just 'they have a voice,' but 'two of five compensation committee seats reserved for Service Partners.'"

Julian was nodding. "And we need examples. Show what a Service Partner career actually looks like, from compensation progression to status markers . . . the whole path."

Nearby, the Team Compensation Pools team was working through their transition protections. Tom had spreadsheet printouts covering the table. "If we transition existing books for five years with declining weights, so 100% year one, 80% year two, etc., we can make the evolution financially safe while still moving toward team-based models."

"And we add bonuses for early adopters," another partner suggested. "Partners who voluntarily convert their solo relationships to teams get a premium for the first two years."

After a while, Julian moved to the table where Lucy sat so they could review the day's work.

"Nine viable prototypes," Julian said. "These are actually testable concepts with enough detail to pilot."

"And notice who's working together," Lucy pointed to the tables. "Associates and partners designing career paths. Robert Kim invested in designing a model that doesn't elevate rainmakers. Alex Rivera bringing enthusiasm and innovative cockiness to the partners' discussions. Jessica Park and Dwarkesh Jones building client systems. Old guard and new, skeptics and enthusiasts. Pretty cool."

"That's the beginning of a culture shift," Julian observed. "I just hope we can keep it going."

"Tomorrow's going to be interesting," Lucy said, inhaling deeply, fatigue setting in deeply now. "We're asking judges to pick winners. That could create competition and disappointment."

"Or," Julian countered, "it could create accountability. Not everything can be piloted. We need to choose. And the tournament format gives us a structured way to make those choices based on criteria, not politics. People will be disappointed, but at least they know it was fair because they saw it play out."

"We shall see," Lucy said, drumming her fingers on the table and standing, "humans are not very rational creatures."

Julian was surprised by Lucy's uncharacteristic cynicism.

"See you in the morning, friend," Lucy said to Julian, as she turned toward the hotel lobby. She needed rest for the final day. Rather than feeling relief at how well things were going, she felt a growing weight of responsibility for moving promising ideas forward. They couldn't lose steam after all this work and trust building. She also knew the groups whose ideas wouldn't move forward would be disappointed. Would they continue to support the ideas that did or check out and sour on change altogether?

Reader Reflection

Making It Real

The teams moved from abstract ideas to concrete prototypes in just two hours.

1. **The "Rough Draft" Fear:** Lawyers are trained to be perfectionists. What holds you back from sharing "rough" ideas or imperfect drafts with colleagues to get early feedback?

2. **Low-Tech Solutions:** The "Client Command Center" started as sketches on foam board. What expensive technology problem in your firm could be prototyped first with paper and pen to see if the *process* is right?

Chapter 20

The Pitches

Friday morning arrived with a different kind of nervous energy. People filed into breakfast knowing that today was decision day. The week of exploration and ideation would culminate in choices about what would actually happen next.

The conference room had been transformed overnight into a presentation venue. Chairs arranged theater-style facing a panel table at the front, not unlike *American Idol.* Nine prototype displays positioned along the side walls. A large screen showing the evaluation criteria:

INNOVATION TOURNAMENT JUDGING CRITERIA

Impact (30%): Will this significantly improve client service, associate development, or business development?

Feasibility (25%): Can we realistically implement this in the next 6–12 months?

Innovation (25%): Does this represent meaningful change vs. incremental adjustment?

Strategic Fit (20%): Does this align with the firm we want to become?

At the front of the room, a panel table had been set up with seven chairs and name placards:

Julian Justice, Managing Partner

Lucy Lex, Chief Innovation Officer

Rebecca Tisdale, General Counsel, Apex Manufacturing

Dr. James Wilson, Chief Legal Officer, Meridian Health Systems

Maria Santos, General Counsel, Pinnacle Retail Group

Dr. Sarah Conforti, Penn State Professor & LegalTech Futures

Professor Katherine Morrison, Duke Law School

As people settled into their seats, murmurs of surprise rippled through the room. The three general counsel had returned. The experts from earlier in the week were back. This was serious.

Lucy stood to open the proceedings. "Good morning, and welcome to our Innovation Tournament. This format, popularized by Professors Karl Ulrich and Christian Terwiesch at Wharton and used by companies ranging from Deloitte to Procter & Gamble has been used to select which innovations to pursue from large pools of ideas. This morning, we're going to do the same for our firm."

She gestured to the panel. "Our judges represent different perspectives we need to consider. Julian and I know the firm's strategic direction and constraints. Rebecca, James, and Maria represent our clients, and they'll evaluate whether these ideas actually serve client needs. Dr. Conforti and Professor Morrison bring expertise in the forces reshaping our profession."

Julian spoke from the panel table. "Each prototype team will have seven minutes to present, followed by five minutes of questions from the judges. We'll then deliberate and select the top three to four prototypes for immediate pilot implementation. Then we'll spend this afternoon building detailed implementation plans for those selected before we send you home for well-deserved rest. Or, more likely, catching up on your long neglected inboxes!" Everyone groaned.

He paused, looking around the room. "Before we begin, I want to be clear: not being selected doesn't mean your idea is bad. It means we can't pilot everything simultaneously. Some excellent ideas may need to wait, or may need more development, or may be too ambitious for our first wave of pilots."

"But," Lucy added, "the ideas that are selected will be resourced, supported, and tracked. This isn't theater; this is how we're actually making decisions about our firm's future."

She pulled up the presentation order, randomly selected that morning:

1. Continuous Feedback System
2. Client Command Center
3. Team Compensation Pools
4. Four Partner Paths
5. Intake as Co-Design
6. Competency Roadmap
7. Client Care Teams
8. Proactive Partnership Model
9. Collaboration Credit System

"First up," Lucy said, "Continuous Feedback System. Team, you're on."

Presentation 1: Continuous Feedback System

Elena Rodriguez and three associates moved to the front. Elena took the lead, visibly nervous but prepared.

"Right now, associates get feedback sporadically if at all," she began. "Annual reviews that feel like surprises. Track changes on documents with no explanation. Maybe a comment here or there. We never really know if we're developing well or struggling until it's too late."

She clicked to their prototype, a diagram showing multiple feedback loops:

MATTER-BASED FEEDBACK

- After each significant assignment (>20 hours)
- Standardized form: What went well, what to improve, skill areas demonstrated
- Takes partner 5 minutes, gives associate specific actionable guidance

QUARTERLY DEVELOPMENT CONVERSATIONS

- Not performance reviews, but development focused
- 30-minute conversations between associate and assigned mentor
- Review: skills building progress, areas to focus next quarter, career path alignment
- Co-create development goals

360-DEGREE INPUT

- Twice yearly
- Input from multiple partners and peers who've worked with the associate
- Aggregated anonymously, patterns identified
- Addresses blind spots that single reviewers miss

REAL-TIME RECOGNITION

- Visible system for acknowledging good work
- Partner sees excellent work → enters recognition in system → associate gets notification → appears in development file
- Makes positive feedback more frequent and visible

ANNUAL COMPREHENSIVE REVIEW

- Synthesizes year's feedback
- Tracks progress against development goals
- Informs compensation and advancement decisions
- No surprises because associate has been getting feedback all year

Another associate on the team took over. "Implementation requires three things: a simple technology platform, which could be built in our existing HR system for about $25K. Training partners on giving developmental feedback through a two-hour workshop. And cultural commitment means that feedback becomes expected, not optional."

Another associate team member added, "From our perspective, this changes everything. Instead of guessing whether we're doing well, we would actually know. We'd understand what to work on. We'd feel supported rather than evaluated."

Questions came quickly.

Dr. James Wilson: "I like this. In healthcare, continuous feedback is essential for resident development. But I'm concerned about the partner time burden. You're asking already busy partners to provide regular feedback. What's the incentive?"

Elena responded, "Two answers. First, matter-based feedback takes five minutes per assignment and immediately improves the associate's future work, which means time saved on the next matter. Second, we'd make feedback provision part of partner performance metrics. You get evaluated on how well you develop associates, and this gives you the structure to do it."

Professor Morrison: "The developmental conversation separate from performance review is crucial. When feedback is tied to compensation decisions, people get defensive. When it's purely developmental, they can actually hear it and learn from it. Have you thought about who conducts those quarterly conversations?"

One of the associates, a third year, nodded. "We envision a formal mentorship program where each associate has an assigned developmental mentor. That person is not necessarily someone they work with constantly, but someone committed to their growth. They conduct the quarterly conversations."

Maria Santos: "From a client perspective, anything that makes your associates better faster serves us. But I'm wondering about the 360-degree feedback. How do you prevent that from becoming a popularity contest?"

"We'd focus questions on observable behaviors and specific skills," Elena explained. "Not 'do you like working with this person' but 'rate their written communication clarity, their responsiveness, their collaboration effectiveness.' And it's patterns across multiple reviewers that matter, not individual opinions."

Lucy: "One implementation question. You're proposing this launch firm-wide immediately. Should you pilot with one practice group first?"

The team exchanged glances. "We discussed that," Elena said. "Our concern is that piloting creates inequality where some associates get better feedback than others based on which group they're in. We think it needs to be universal to be fair."

Time was called. The team returned to their seats, adrenaline clearly pumping. Elena smiled at her teammates. The idea of a formative development system was both invigorating and tantalizingly doable in their minds.

Presentation 2: Client Command Center

The Client Command Center team approached the front. Dwarkesh Jones, Jessica Park, and two associates.

"Three days ago, we heard from Rebecca, James, and Maria about communication failures," Jessica began, looking directly at the client panel. "Rebecca's surprise about ongoing settlement discussions without her input. James wanting concise answers instead of ten-page memos. Maria being shocked by bills because she didn't know work was happening."

She clicked to their foam board mock-up, now photographed and displayed digitally. "The Client Command Center solves this by giving clients real-time visibility into their matters. Think of it like package tracking, but for legal work."

Dwarkesh walked through the interface:

Dashboard showing:

- Matter status with visual indicators
- Timeline of completed and upcoming milestones
- Team roster with photos and contact info
- Recent activity feed
- Document library organized by matter
- Direct messaging to matter team
- Budget tracker showing spend vs. estimate

Automated notifications:

- Milestone completions
- Upcoming deadlines

- Budget alerts before overages
- Exception notices for delays or issues
- Weekly executive summaries

"The key innovation," Dwarkesh explained, "is that this shifts client communication from reactive to proactive. Instead of clients wondering what's happening and having to ask, they have visibility. Instead of us remembering to update them, the system prompts updates at logical points."

An associate showed sample notifications they'd drafted:

"Discovery responses filed yesterday. Next: review with you to discuss findings. Your attorney Sarah will reach out this week."

"Matter Budget Alert: We're at 65% of estimated hours with approximately 70% of work complete. Current projection: finish within budget. Questions? Contact Tom directly."

"Timeline Update: Opposing counsel requested extension. This shifts your deadline from July 15 to July 29. Want to discuss implications? Schedule a call here."

Questions:

Rebecca Tisdale leaned forward with visible interest. "This is exactly what I've been asking for. But my question is: who maintains this? If I have twenty active matters with your firm, someone has to update twenty portals. That's a lot of work."

Jessica answered, "That's why this connects to the Proactive Partnership Model. We envision a new FTE, a client relationship manager role. This would be someone dedicated to keeping client information current, coordinating communications, ensuring nothing falls through cracks. The portal is the technology, but the relationship manager is the human making sure it stays current."

Dr. Sarah Conforti: "I'm curious about the AI potential here. Could you use AI to automatically generate status updates based on document filing activity, calendar entries, and email communications? That would reduce the human update burden significantly."

"Absolutely," Dwarkesh said, energized. "We hadn't prototyped that far, but you're right! AI could draft status updates that humans then approve and refine. That could make this much more sustainable."

Maria Santos: "I love this. But I'm going to push on one thing. Most firms I work with would build this and then not use it properly. The portal would get out of date, the updates would stop or be wrong or inconsistent, and it would become one more abandoned technology project. How do you prevent that?"

Dwarkesh responded carefully, "That's our biggest implementation risk. We think it requires three things: dedicated relationship manager roles to maintain it, making portal accuracy part of partner performance metrics, and starting with a pilot of maybe five clients, to prove it works before scaling."

Julian: "Jessica, what's the investment and what's the return?"

"We estimated a development cost, including CRM integration of $175,000," Jessica said. "Ongoing cost, relationship manager salaries of maybe $150K per year for three people handling 100 major clients. Return is harder to quantify, but we think it would include reduced client attrition, faster client issue resolution, fewer billing disputes, and competitive differentiation. If we retain even two major clients who might have left, it pays for itself."

Presentation 3: Team Compensation Pools

The Team Compensation Pools team took the front. Tom Brennan, two senior partners, and one partner who'd been vocally skeptical about the concept.

Tom opened. "This is the most controversial prototype we're presenting today because it fundamentally changes how partners make money. Right now, individual origination drives compensation. We're proposing that major client revenue goes into team pools, and partners share based on contribution."

The skeptical partner, William Klept, spoke next, a deliberate choice by the team. "I opposed this idea initially. I've spent fifteen years building my book of business, and this felt like asking me to give it away. But here's what changed my mind."

He clicked to a slide showing client data. "Our average major client now works with 4.7 partners across 2.3 offices. When we try to serve them well, we're constantly having awkward conversations about credit allocation. Who gets the origination? Who gets the service credit? It's uncomfortable, it slows us down, and it makes us worse at serving clients."

"And," William continued, "I'm fifty-eight years old. When I retire, my client relationships will probably leave with me because they're my relationships, not the firm's. In the short term, this is great for me! But it's really bad for everyone else. It's bad for the firm, bad for the clients who lose continuity, and bad for younger partners who can't build on what I created."

William had decided that the only way through this miserable week was through, so he started mirroring all of the nonsense Lucy and her consultants were preaching. He had become so concerned about the future of the firm over the course of the week that he had already decided to look for a new place to practice as soon as he returned to the office. He'd already texted his wife to let her know and to ask her to cancel their social activities for the next few weeks so he could concentrate on finding a new role. For now, he would grin and bear it so that they could get out of this hotel conference room as soon as possible.

Tom took back over, showing the proposed model:

TEAM COMPENSATION STRUCTURE

Major clients (>$500K annual revenue):

- Assigned to relationship teams of 3–5 partners
- All revenue from that client goes into team pool
- Partners compensated: Base + (Team Pool Share × Contribution Factor)

Contribution factors:

- Client origination (bringing the client to firm)
- Service hours (billable work on client matters)
- Client satisfaction (survey scores)
- Team collaboration (peer ratings)
- Mentorship (developing associates on the team)
- Knowledge sharing (documenting approaches, updating systems)

Transition protections:

- Existing solo relationships grandfathered for 5 years
- Declining weights: 100% individual credit year 1, 80% year 2, etc.
- Early adopter bonuses for voluntarily converting solo to team relationships
- Protected minimum compensation for current top performers

Tom walked through financial modeling. "We ran this on our current top twenty clients. The result is that most partners make about the same total compensation, but it's distributed more fairly based on actual contribution. Top rainmakers who also service well make slightly more. Pure service partners make significantly more. Partners who rainmake but don't service much make slightly less, unless they lean into the mentorship and collaboration factors."

Questions:

Julian: "How do you prevent free-riding? The partner who doesn't pull their weight but benefits from the team pool?"

Tom responded, "The contribution factor addresses this. If you're on a team but not contributing meaningful hours, not attending team meetings, or getting poor peer ratings, then your contribution factor goes down. In extreme cases, the team can request your removal."

Rebecca Tisdale: "I like this from a client perspective because it incentivizes you to put your best people on my work, not just the people who need to bill hours. But I'm curious whether this means I'd have a single team that handles all my work. Because sometimes I need specialists from different areas."

"Great question," Tom said. "For major clients, yes, you'd have a core relationship team. But that team can bring in specialists as needed for specific matters. Those specialists might be on multiple teams. The core team owns the relationship and coordinates, but they're not a silo."

Professor Morrison: "This addresses a fundamental problem in professional services of how to reward collaborative behavior. But it requires significant trust. Partners have to believe the contribution factors will be assessed fairly. How do you build that trust?"

William Klept, having made peace with his decision and beginning to enjoy his new acting role of eager innovator, answered, "Transparency. The contribution factors and how they're weighted need to be completely clear upfront. And there needs to be a review process where partners can appeal or discuss if they feel their contribution was undervalued. It can't be a black box."

Dr. Sarah Conforti: "One observation: this model assumes relationship teams are relatively stable. But in an active lateral environment and an AI-augmented world where work gets done faster, might teams need to form and reform more dynamically? Have you thought about more fluid team structures?"

The team exchanged glances as they hadn't considered this. "That's a really good point," William admitted, feeling internally gratified to have his feeling that none of this would work confirmed. "We designed this assuming relatively stable client relationships. But you're right that faster cycle times might require more flexible teaming. We'd need to think through how contribution tracking works if teams are constantly changing."

Presentation 4: Four Partner Paths

Robert Kim and two other partners approached the front. Robert took the lead, surprising many in the room.

"I've been a partner at this firm for eighteen years," Robert began. "And for all eighteen years, there's been one definition of successful partner: someone who originates significant work, maintains client relationships, and brings in revenue. If you're brilliant at execution but not at business development, you're valued less. We obviously never *say* that, but we all feel it; it's cultural, not just here, but at most firms. If you want to focus on mentoring and firm building, you're seen as not contributing your share."

He paused. "This model is killing us. We're losing talented people who don't fit the rainmaker mold. We're forcing people into roles they're not suited for. And we're perpetuating a culture where only one type of contribution matters."

Another junior partner took over. "The Four Partner Paths model recognizes that partners create value in different ways. Not everyone should have to be a rainmaker."

She revealed their prototype poster showing four distinct paths:

CLIENT PARTNERS

- Focus: Origination and relationship development
- Success metrics: New client acquisition, relationship expansion, cross-selling
- Compensation: Base + origination credit + team participation
- Time allocation: 60% BD, 40% delivery

SERVICE PARTNERS

- Focus: Excellence in execution and delivery
- Success metrics: Client satisfaction, matter quality, efficiency, innovation in service delivery
- Compensation: Base + quality metrics + client retention bonuses
- Time allocation: 20% BD, 80% delivery

EXPERT PARTNERS

- Focus: Deep technical specialization and thought leadership
- Success metrics: Service execution, publications, speaking, technical innovation, peer recognition
- Compensation: Base + specialization premium + IP/knowledge credits
- Time allocation: 30% development, 70% delivery/thought leadership

LEADERSHIP PARTNERS

- Focus: Firm building, mentorship, strategic initiatives
- Success metrics: Associate development, culture building, successful strategic projects

- Compensation: Base + leadership metrics + firm growth
- Time allocation: 40% leadership, 60% delivery

Robert walked through the career evolution possibilities. "You're not locked into one path forever. Most of us probably start as Service Partners while we're learning to deliver excellent work. Some evolve into Client Partners as we develop business development skills. Others might become Expert Partners, specializing deeply. Others might move into Leadership Partners. And you can blend, so maybe you're 60% Service, 40% Expert."

Robert showed their "equality indicators." These were specific mechanisms to ensure paths are genuinely valued equally, and the group had spent significant time getting specific about what these might be:

- All partner types represented in firm leadership (2 of 5 compensation committee seats for non-Client Partners)
- Equal voting rights in partnership decisions
- Title structure that doesn't signal hierarchy (no "junior" or "service" labels)
- Marketing materials showcase all partner types
- Office space and perks not tied to origination
- Recognition events celebrate all forms of contribution

Questions:

Maria Santos: "I love this. But I'm going to be blunt. As a client, I want to know I'm getting excellent service. If someone's a Service Partner focused on delivery, that's probably who I want doing my work, not the rainmaker who's focused on bringing in the next client. So this might actually serve me better."

Robert nodded. "That's exactly right. Right now, we sometimes staff matters based on who needs billable hours, not who's best suited for the work. This system lets us match people to work based on their strengths."

Dr. James Wilson: "In medicine, we have something similar, with clinicians focused on patient care, researchers focused on advancing medical knowledge, administrators focused on running institutions. All are valued physicians. But it took decades to get there. What's your timeline for implementation?"

The junior partner answered, "We're proposing a two-year transition. Year one: define paths clearly, let current partners self-identify which path fits them, adjust compensation committee composition. Year two: fully implement differentiated evaluation and compensation. New partners admitted into specific paths from the start."

Professor Morrison: "The Expert Partner path is particularly interesting for legal education. Those partners could also teach at law schools, publish scholarship that's actually relevant to practice, bridge the theory-practice divide. Have you thought about how this connects to law school partnerships?"

"We haven't detailed that yet," Robert admitted. "But you're right. Since Expert Partners are incentivized to focus on thought leadership, they would be natural bridge figures. They could co-teach, supervise clinical programs, place top students as fellows. That could contribute to the law school–firm collaboration problem we discussed earlier in the week."

Julian: "The critical thing is that all four paths have equivalent status and equivalent compensation potential. A Service Partner at year ten should be able to make as much as a Client Partner at year ten if they're excelling in their domain." The team nodded, thrilled to hear Julian tacitly endorse their idea.

"That's exactly right," Robert said, "The goal is greater fairness across all roles."

Lucy: "Walk me through a scenario. I'm a mid-level associate trying to decide which path to aim for. How do I know? And what if I choose wrong?"

Robert responded, "We'd introduce path discussions in years four to five. You'd assess your own strengths with your mentor. You'd try different work to test your preferences. And critically, you can change paths. If you start as a Service Partner and discover you're actually good at business development, you can transition. These aren't permanent sentences."

William Klept, chimed in, "But how do you prevent Service Partners from being marginalized? Because we can create these titles, but if the culture still treats rainmakers as the 'real' partners, nothing changes."

Julian answered this one directly. "That's the leadership imperative. If we continue to primarily recognize and reward origination in how we talk about success, in who we promote to leadership roles, in subtle status signals, then this fails. It requires other leaders and me to actively celebrate Service Partner achievements, Expert Partner contributions, and Leadership Partner successes. It's a culture change as much as a structural change."

Brief Summaries of Remaining Presentations

Intake as Co-Design (Sarah Williams and team): The team role-played their proposed intake process, with three sessions featuring clients spanning a week, moving from understanding client's business challenges, to collaborative solution design, to joint success criteria. They emphasized that this transforms the client-firm relationship from the first interaction, making engagement feel like partnership rather than just a transaction. Judges were intrigued but concerned about the time investment. Rebecca Tisdale countered that she'd happily invest time in better intake if it meant better outcomes and fewer misalignments later.

Competency Roadmap (Lisa Martinez, Maya Davis and team): The team presented a detailed year-by-year competency framework showing exactly what skills associates should develop at each stage. Year 1-2: Foundation skills. Year 3-4: Independence. Year 5-6: Strategic capabilities. Year 7+: Leadership. They'd mapped specific activities, assignments, and training to build each competency intentionally rather than hoping associates picked things up through osmosis. Dr. Conforti noted this could integrate beautifully with AI training tools because the firm could use AI to help associates practice skills in safe environments before applying them with real clients.

Client Care Teams (Priya Patel, Michael Solomon and team): The team showed their service blueprint for relationship teams inspired by hospital care teams. Each major client gets an Attending Partner who coordinates, specialist partners who contribute as needed, and a relationship manager who handles logistics. They role-played a weekly "team rounds" meeting showing how coordination actually works. The judges appreciated the hospital analogy but wanted more specifics about when teams form, how specialists get allocated across multiple teams, and how this integrates with the compensation model.

Proactive Partnership Model (Maggie McNamee, Marcus Reed, team): This team focused on the relationship manager role as the key to proactive client service. Not a biller but a coordinator who maintains the Client Command Center, schedules quarterly business reviews, monitors for regulatory changes affecting clients, and ensures nothing falls through cracks. They showed how this role frees partners to do legal work while ensuring consistent client communication. Cost analysis showed one relationship manager could support fifteen to twenty major clients. Maria Santos said this would be a significant competitive differentiator and that most firms don't provide this level of proactive coordination.

Collaboration Credit System (Alex Rivera, several mid-level partners, two associates): The final presentation proposed formal tracking and crediting of collaborative behaviors, including introducing colleagues to your clients, knowledge sharing, cross-practice coordination, and mentoring. These contributions would be visible, tracked, and factored into compensation and partnership advancement. The team showed mock-ups of a simple tracking system and how credits would be weighted. Some judges worried about making collaboration transactional ("I'll introduce you to my client so I get a credit"). The team acknowledged this risk but argued that what gets measured gets valued, and collaboration is currently invisible and unrewarded.

Deliberation

After a full morning of presentations, Lucy called a thirty-minute break for the judges to deliberate privately. The room buzzed with nervous energy. Teams clustered together, debriefing their presentations, wondering how they'd done.

"Did you see Rebecca's face during Client Command Center?" Jessica whispered to her team. "She was nodding the whole time."

"Julian basically presented Four Partner Paths himself," someone else observed. "That's got to mean something."

"The compensation question is going to be hardest," Tom Brennan said to his team. "That requires the most trust and the biggest change."

After thirty minutes, the judges returned. Julian stood to deliver their decision.

"First, I want to say that every prototype presented this morning was viable. You could implement any of these and improve the firm. That made our decision difficult."

He paused. "We used the scoring criteria—impact, feasibility, innovation, strategic fit—but we also considered how prototypes connect to each other. Some ideas work better in combination. Some need to be implemented in sequence."

Lucy pulled up a slide showing the selected prototypes:

SELECTED FOR IMMEDIATE PILOT IMPLEMENTATION:

1. Client Command Center + Proactive Partnership Model

Combined into single pilot

- Merged because the technology needs the human role to succeed
- Pilot with 10 major clients
- 6-month implementation timeline

2. Four Partner Paths

- Phased 18-month rollout
- Begin with current partners self-identifying paths
- New partners admitted to specific paths
- Critical for recruiting and retention strategy

3. Competency Roadmap + Continuous Feedback System

Combined into integrated associate development program

- Roadmap provides structure, feedback system provides assessment
- Firm-wide implementation starting with current first and second-year associates
- 12-month rollout

UNDER CONSIDERATION FOR FUTURE IMPLEMENTATION:

4. Client Care Teams

- Excellent concept but requires compensation model clarity first
- Revisit in 6 months after Team Compensation Pools piloted

5. Intake as Co-Design

- Strong interest but significant time investment
- Pilot with 3 clients in Q4 after process designed

NOT SELECTED AT THIS TIME:

6. Team Compensation Pools

- Highest innovation score but highest implementation risk
- Requires extensive partner discussion and buy-in
- Form working group to develop detailed proposal over 6 months

7. Collaboration Credit System

- Valuable but needs integration with compensation redesign
- Incorporate concepts into Four Partner Paths evaluation metrics

Rebecca Tisdale stood from the panel to explain the client perspective. "We were unanimous that Client Command Center plus Proactive Partnership had to be selected. As clients, this directly addresses our biggest frustrations of communication gaps and lack of proactive coordination. We'd volunteer to be pilot clients."

Dr. Wilson added, "Four Partner Paths solves a professional development problem similar to what we faced in medicine. Creating multiple valued trajectories means you can recruit and retain different types of talent. It's strategically essential."

Professor Morrison spoke to the associate development selection. "The Competency Roadmap and Continuous Feedback System solve the problem we discussed Wednesday that neither law schools nor firms are systematically developing lawyers. This gives you structure to do it well. It's the foundation for everything else."

Julian took over. "I know some teams are disappointed. The Team Compensation Pools team did excellent work on a critical issue. But that change is so fundamental because it affects how every partner makes money, so it needs more time to build consensus and work through details. It's not rejected, it's deferred for proper development."

He looked around the room. "Similarly, Client Care Teams and Collaboration Credits are good ideas that need other pieces in place first. We're not saying no, we're saying not yet."

Lucy addressed the room. "This afternoon, we will all come back together to work on the three selected ideas to build detailed implementation plans. Everyone else, thank you so, *so* much! Your work this week matters even if your specific prototype wasn't selected. You've changed how we think, how we work together, and what we believe is possible."

Reactions

As people broke for lunch, the reactions were mixed.

Jessica Park's team was elated. "We're doing this," she said, almost disbelieving. "The Command Center is actually going to be built."

Elena Rodriguez looked both satisfied and thoughtful. "Four Partner Paths means I might actually have a future here. A path that fits what I'm good at."

The Competency Roadmap team was energized. "Finally, a real answer to 'how do we develop lawyers in an AI world,'" Maya Davis said.

But the Team Compensation Pools team sat together, processing disappointment. One of the new partners looked deflated. "We did all that work and it's 'under consideration'?"

Tom Brennan, always the realist, put his hand on their shoulder. "They didn't reject it. They said it needs more time because it's the most foundational change. That's actually respect for how important it is."

The Collaboration Credit System team was integrating their concepts into the Four Partner Paths implementation. "Our work is getting incorporated," Alex Rivera pointed out. "Just not as a standalone system."

Near the windows, Robert Kim stood with Maggie McNamee and Dwarkesh Jones, looking out at the mountains.

"Four Partner Paths was my team," Robert said quietly. "Three weeks ago, I would have opposed this idea. Now I helped design it and it's being implemented."

"That's what this week did," Maggie replied. "Changed what we think is possible. Changed what we're willing to try."

"And now we have to actually do it," Dwarkesh added. "Presentation is one thing. Implementation is another."

Through the windows, the Blue Ridge Mountains stood unchanged. But inside the Grove Park Inn, a law firm had just committed to changing major elements of how it developed lawyers, served clients, and structured success.

The question was whether the enthusiasm in this room could survive the reality of implementation when everyone returned to their offices, their demanding clients, and their normal routines.

Friday afternoon would begin to answer that question. That's when they'd have to translate these selected prototypes from inspiring concepts into specific action plans with timelines, resources, responsibilities, and accountability mechanisms.

The easy part of imagining change, as exhausting as it might have felt for these legal professionals, was over. The hard part of making change real was only about to begin.

Chapter 21

Building What Lasts

After lunch, people returned to find the conference room reconfigured one final time. Three distinct workspaces had been created, each labeled with one of the selected prototypes. At the front of the room, Lucy had written on the whiteboard:

REINFORCEMENT: Making Change Stick

The word "REINFORCEMENT" was circled and connected to the full ADKAR framework displayed beside it:

Awareness ✓

Desire ✓

Knowledge ✓

Ability ✓

REINFORCEMENT ← We are here

As people settled, the exhaustion was palpable. Five intensive days of learning, challenging assumptions, designing solutions. Several people looked at the afternoon agenda and another three hours of work, with visible fatigue. Everyone was eagerly awaiting the end of this transformative but tiring week.

Lucy stood at the front, acknowledging what everyone felt. "You're tired. I see it. This has been an intense week, and what I'm about to ask of you, an afternoon of detailed implementation planning, probably feels like the last thing you want to do.

"But here's why we're doing it anyway. Ideas don't implement themselves. Enthusiasm fades. Next week, you'll be back in your offices with urgent client emails, pressing deadlines, and a hundred reasons why 'we'll get to that innovation stuff later.' We called you here for a week because we are facing existential questions as a firm. We've learned why this week and we've developed ideas and selected several we want to pilot. But we need to spend these last precious hours together before we scatter to the wind developing plans for implementation."

"Reinforcement," she continued, clicking to a slide, "is the phase where most change initiatives fail. Not because the ideas are bad. Not because people don't care. But because we don't build the structures, accountability, and habits that make new behaviors stick when old pressures return."

Julian stood and moved to the front beside Lucy. He also looked drained, but his expression was more serious than it had been all week.

"I need to be honest with you about what's ahead," he began. "This week doesn't solve the challenges facing our profession or our firm. AI will keep advancing. Clients will keep demanding more for less. Talent will keep questioning whether law firm practice is worth pursuing. The forces we've been learning about are all accelerating and our structures are going to continue to make it difficult to respond without our working against them to adapt."

He looked around the room, making eye contact. "And the changes we've committed to today—Four Partner Paths, Client Command Center, Competency Roadmap—these make your lives harder in some ways, not easier. They ask you to work differently than you've been trained. They ask you to unlearn behaviors that have made you successful. They ask you to trust systems that don't exist yet."

The room was completely quiet.

"So why do it?" Julian asked. "Why stay at a firm that's asking you to change everything about how you work, when you could lateral to a competitor that would pay you the same or more, give you a similar title, and let you keep doing what you've always done?"

He paused, choosing his words carefully. "The answer is culture. That's it. That's the only sustainable differentiator we have."

He gestured around the room. "Look at what happened this week. Partners who disagreed about fundamental issues collaborated on solutions. Associates spoke honestly about where we're failing them, and we listened instead of defending. Skeptics became believers. Silos broke down. We designed things together that none of us could have designed alone."

"That culture, the one where we actually give a damn about each other, where we're willing to be vulnerable and honest? Where we believe we can build something better together? That's what you can't get at most firms. That's what I'm asking you to stay for and fight for."

He clicked to a slide showing three columns:

WHAT WE'RE NOT:

- Highest paying
- Biggest platform
- Most prestigious brand
- Easiest place to succeed

WHAT WE ARE:

- Most human-centered
- Most willing to evolve
- Most collaborative
- Most honest about challenges
- Most committed to developing people

WHAT WE'RE BECOMING:

- The firm that figured out how to thrive in transformation
- The place talented people choose because of how we work, not despite it
- A model for what law firms can be

"Culture is fragile," Julian said quietly. "It can be damaged quickly, by a few bad hires, by cynical leadership, by choosing short-term profit over long-term sustainability, by allowing old behaviors to creep back in when we get busy."

"So this afternoon isn't just about implementation planning. It's about building the reinforcement structures that protect what we're creating. It's about making explicit commitments to each other about how we'll work going forward. It's about choosing, every single day, to be the kind of firm we designed this week."

He looked at the three selected prototype workspaces. "The teams who designed the chosen prototypes are going to spend the next two hours beginning to build detailed implementation plans. We need timelines, resources, success metrics, accountability mechanisms. That's the tactical work.

"But everyone else is going to do something equally important. You're going to design the reinforcement structures that help all of us, including and especially me, stay committed when it gets hard. Because it will get hard. And we need systems that keep us on track when motivation fades."

Implementation Planning: Selected Prototypes

Lucy gestured to the three workspaces. "Teams for the selected prototypes, please go to your stations. Julian, Tom, Lisa, and I will rotate through to help you build realistic plans. Everyone else, stay here. We're going to tackle the reinforcement question together."

The three teams dispersed:

Client Command Center + Proactive Partnership Model Team

Jessica Park, Dwarkesh Jones, Maggie McNamee, Marcus Reed, and several others moved to workspace one, where templates were laid out:

- 6-month implementation timeline
- Resource requirements (budget, technology, people)
- Pilot client selection criteria
- Success metrics
- Risk mitigation plan
- Communication strategy

Four Partner Paths Team

Robert Kim and team members gathered at workspace two with similar templates, plus:

- Partner self-identification process
- Compensation committee restructuring plan
- New partner admission criteria for each path
- Equity and status signal checklist
- 18-month phased rollout schedule

Competency Roadmap + Continuous Feedback System Team

Lisa Martinez, Elena Rodriguez, and others at workspace three faced templates including:

- Competency definitions by year and practice area
- Feedback platform selection and customization
- Partner training curriculum on developmental feedback
- Mentor assignment process
- Integration with existing HR systems
- Firm-wide rollout schedule

The teams dove in, the earlier exhaustion temporarily forgotten as they grappled with real implementation challenges.

At the Client Command Center workspace, tension emerged almost immediately.

"Who actually maintains this portal?" one associate asked. "If it's partners, it won't happen. If it's associates, it's more non-billable work we're evaluated negatively for doing."

"That's why we merged it with Proactive Partnership," Jessica said. "The relationship manager role is the key. But that means creating new positions. Tom, what's realistic?"

Marcus Reed was already working numbers on his laptop. "If each relationship manager handles fifteen major clients, and we pilot with ten clients, we need one person. Starting salary probably $80–90K. Can we hire someone in three months?"

"Probably," Maggie said, "but they need training in our systems, our client relationships, our work. At least thirty days. So we may be looking at six months before the portal is actually maintained properly."

Dwarkesh was sketching the technology timeline. "Portal customization: six weeks. CRM integration: four weeks. Those can overlap. Testing: two weeks. We're looking at eight to ten weeks, after the four-month hiring and onboarding process, before it's live, assuming we start immediately."

Jessica raised a concern. "But we haven't selected the pilot clients yet. Who should they be? We need clients who'll be patient with a new system but also demanding enough to test whether it really works."

"Rebecca, James, and Maria," Marcus said immediately. "They're already invested in our success after participating this week. And they're sophisticated enough to give us honest feedback."

The team mapped out their timeline:

Months 1–3: Hire relationship manager, select technology platform, brief pilot clients

Month 4: Customize portal, train relationship manager, integrate systems

Month 5: Test with pilot clients, refine based on feedback

Months 6–7: Full pilot operation, gather data, adjust

Month 8: Evaluate results, decide on expansion

"Success metrics?" Maggie prompted.

They brainstormed:

- Client satisfaction scores (survey after 3 and 6 months)
- Client-initiated contact frequency (should decrease if we're proactively communicating)
- Billing dispute rate (should decrease with better transparency)
- Matter status accuracy (portal reflects reality >95% of time)
- Partner and associate time spent on client updates (should decrease)

"Risk mitigation?" Dwarkesh asked.

"Biggest risk is portal becomes out of date," Jessica said. "Mitigation: make portal accuracy part of matter leader performance review. If your matters' portals aren't current, that's a problem."

"Second risk: clients don't use it," Maggie added. "Mitigation: relationship manager proactively engages clients, walks them through features, incorporates their feedback."

At the Four Partner Paths workspace, Robert Kim was facilitating a difficult conversation.

"We need current partners to self-identify which path fits them," he said. "But how do we ensure people are honest about their strengths rather than just claiming to be Client Partners because that's historically been most valued?"

"Maybe we don't let people just claim a path," Julian suggested. "Maybe it's based on data like actual origination patterns, client satisfaction scores, service hours, and then you discuss with leadership where you fit."

Another partner pushed back. "That feels top-down. The whole point is creating paths that value different contributions. If leadership is assigning people to paths based on historical metrics that favor rainmakers, we're just recreating the old hierarchy with new labels."

"What if it's a combination?" Robert proposed. "You self-assess based on where you want to focus going forward. Leadership provides feedback based on where you've demonstrated strength historically. There's a conversation. You reach an agreement. And critically, you can shift paths later if your initial choice doesn't fit."

They worked through the process:

Month 1–2:

- Communicate Four Paths framework to all partners and ask for volunteers to participate in pilot program
- Provide self-assessment tool to pilot participants
- Partners reflect and discuss with practice group leaders

Month 3–4:

- Individual conversations between each partner in pilot and management committee
- Reach agreement on initial path designation
- Document commitments and expectations for each path

Month 5–6:

- Restructure compensation committee (add Service Partner representation)
- Define specific evaluation criteria for each path
- Communicate to associates about how to make partner so they understand what they're working toward

Month 7–18:

- Operate under new framework as associates join partnership, gather feedback quarterly
- Address issues and refine
- Begin admitting new partners, both laterals and in-house promotions, into specific paths

Julian had joined the group to listen. After a few minutes, he interrupted. "Compensation committee restructuring is crucial," he emphasized. "If Client Partners still control all compensation decisions, Service Partners will never be truly equal."

They drafted specific changes:

- Expand compensation committee from 5 to 7 members
- Mandate at least 2 Service Partners, 1 Expert Partner, 1 Leadership Partner
- No single partner type can comprise majority
- Decisions require supermajority (5 of 7) to ensure cross-path buy-in

"Equality indicators need to be specific and measurable," Robert said, working from their prototype. "Not aspirational, but enforceable."

They created a checklist:

Status Equality Checklist (Assessed Annually):

- ☐ Compensation committee composition meets diversity requirement
- ☐ All partner types represented in firm management roles
- ☐ Marketing materials feature partners from each path
- ☐ Partnership announcements celebrate diverse paths to partnership
- ☐ Office space allocation not correlated with origination
- ☐ Recognition events acknowledge all types of contributions
- ☐ Internal communications about "successful partner" include diverse examples
- ☐ Associate mentorship includes exposure to all partner types
- ☐ Lateral partner recruiting seeks diverse paths, not just rainmakers

"If we don't hit all these indicators, we're failing," one partner said. "This can't be window dressing."

At the Competency Roadmap workspace, the team was wrestling with scope.

"We need to define specific competencies for each year, for each practice area," Lisa Martinez said, looking at a blank template. "That's a massive undertaking."

"We can't do it all today," another team member acknowledged. "But we can build the framework and identify who's responsible for filling in details."

They created a project structure:

Phase 1 (Month 1–3): Framework Development

- Define competency categories (technical skills, client skills, business skills, leadership)
- Create year-by-year progression for each category
- Pilot with one practice area (Litigation) to test framework

Phase 2 (Month 4–6): Practice Area Customization

- Each practice group defines specific competencies within framework
- Associates and junior partners participate in defining what actually matters
- Create library of assignments/experiences that build each competency

Phase 3 (Month 7–9): Integration with Feedback System

- Launch technology platform for matter-based feedback and quarterly conversations
- Train all partners on providing developmental feedback (required 2-hour workshop)
- Assign mentors to each associate for quarterly development conversations

Phase 4 (Month 10–12): Full Implementation and Refinement

- All associates have competency-based development plans
- Regular feedback loops operating
- Gather data on what's working and adjust

A mid-level associate on the team raised the hardest question. "Who owns this? If it's just HR or professional development, it won't have teeth. If it's practice group leaders, will they make time for it?"

"We need a dedicated role," Lisa said. "Someone whose job is making this work, coordinating across practice groups, training partners, ensuring the system operates consistently."

"That's a significant investment," Maya Davis noted. "A senior person at maybe $200K plus benefits. Is the firm willing to make that commitment?"

They noted it as a critical resource requirement. Without dedicated ownership, this would become "everyone's responsibility" which meant no one's responsibility.

They defined success metrics:

Associate Satisfaction Metrics:

- % of associates who feel clear about development expectations (target: 80%+)
- % who feel they receive regular developmental feedback (target: 75%+)
- % who believe they're building skills intentionally vs. haphazardly (target: 70%+)

Retention Metrics:

- Associate retention at 3-year mark (current: 65%, target: 75%+)
- Exit interview reasons (shift from "unclear development" to other factors)

Quality Metrics:

- Partner satisfaction with associate work product
- Client feedback on associate performance
- Time to independence on common tasks

"We need to be honest that some of this is long-term," Elena Rodriguez said. "We won't see retention improvements in year one. This is a two-to-three-year investment before results are really visible."

Reinforcement Structures: The Larger Group

While the implementation teams worked, Lucy was leading the remaining fifty or so participants through a different exercise.

"I want to remind you about a concept from Amy Edmondson called psychological safety," Lucy began. "She defines it as a belief that you won't be punished or humiliated for speaking up with ideas, questions, concerns, or mistakes."

She showed them a slide with research findings. "Edmondson studied teams across many industries. What she found is that the highest performing teams aren't the ones where everyone is brilliant and never makes mistakes. They're the teams where people feel safe enough to admit mistakes, ask questions, challenge ideas, and learn from failures.

"This week," Lucy continued, "you've experienced psychological safety. Associates told partners uncomfortable truths about where we're failing them. Skeptics voiced concerns openly. People proposed wild ideas without fear of being mocked. Junior people challenged senior people's assumptions. That's psychological safety in action.

"But psychological safety is fragile. One sarcastic comment about a 'stupid idea,' one punishment for admitting a mistake, one instance of shooting the messenger, and it starts to erode. That's when people start sweeping issues under the rug. We lose collective sight of the problems we should be tackling together. Our culture weakens and the business suffers. People learn it's safer to stay quiet, play it safe, pretend everything's fine."

She looked around the room. "If we're going to sustain what we've built this week, we need to protect and reinforce psychological safety. So let's design the structures that do that."

She distributed a framework and worksheets:

REINFORCEMENT STRUCTURE DESIGN

1. **What behaviors do we want to become habits?**

   List specific behaviors that support our transformation

2. **What prevents those behaviors in normal work life?**

   Identify barriers, like time pressure, competing priorities, old habits, fear

3. **What structures make the desired behaviors easier and more likely?**

   Design systems, processes, rewards, defaults that enable good behavior

4. **What accountability mechanisms ensure we actually follow through?**

   Create ways to track, review, and course-correct

The group broke into four teams to tackle different aspects:

Team 1: Communication and Transparency

This group focused on sustaining the open, honest communication experienced this week.

Desired behaviors:

- Associates speaking up about problems without fear
- Partners admitting when they don't know something
- People raising concerns early rather than waiting until crisis
- Honest feedback flowing in all directions
- Acknowledging mistakes quickly

Barriers:

- Fear of looking incompetent
- Hierarchy and power dynamics
- Billable hour pressure leaves no time for communication
- History of shooting the messenger
- "Everything's fine" culture

Reinforcement structures they designed:

Monthly All-Hands Meetings

- Julian shares firm challenges openly, including things not going well
- Celebrates people who raised problems early
- Q&A where anyone can ask anything, answers given honestly
- "Failure of the month": what we tried that didn't work and what we learned

Anonymous Feedback Channel

- Digital suggestion box monitored by Lucy
- Quarterly report on themes and firm responses
- Guarantees psychological safety for raising hard issues

"Speak Up" Recognition

- Quarterly recognition for people who raised valuable concerns or asked hard questions
- Message: we value honesty over pretending everything's perfect

Pre-Mortems Required for Major Projects

- Before launching significant initiatives, team asks "what could go wrong?"
- Explicitly surface concerns before problems emerge
- Creates permission to be skeptical without being dismissed

Team 2: Learning and Development

This group tackled sustaining the learning orientation demonstrated this week.

Desired behaviors:

- Partners investing time in associate development
- People trying new approaches and learning from results
- Sharing knowledge openly rather than hoarding
- Attending training even when busy
- Giving and seeking feedback regularly

Barriers:

- Billable hour pressure makes development feel like luxury
- Partners not rewarded for time spent teaching
- Fear that trying new things might fail
- Knowledge hoarding as competitive advantage
- Training seen as "nice to have," not essential

Reinforcement structures they designed:

Protected Development Time

- 10% of associate time explicitly protected for development activities
- Not billable but tracked and valued in performance reviews
- Includes: training, shadowing, practice skills, reflection

Partner Development Scorecard

- Each partner tracked on: associates mentored, training provided, knowledge shared
- Factored into compensation as 10% weight
- Makes development an explicit responsibility, not optional

Learning Labs (Monthly)

- Two-hour sessions where people share new approaches, tools, or learnings
- Safe space to present work-in-progress, get feedback
- Attendance tracked, celebrated
- Partners and associates present together to create status-neutral sharing

Innovation Fridays (Quarterly)

- Four times a year, no client work scheduled (unless emergencies require)
- Firm-wide day for: learning new tools, experimenting with processes, strategic thinking
- Message: staying current isn't optional, we build time for it

Knowledge-Sharing Credits

- Points awarded for: writing practice guides, documenting processes, training others, updating systems
- Credits tracked and recognized in compensation discussions
- Makes knowledge sharing visible and valued

Team 3: Accountability and Measurement

This group designed systems to ensure commitments made this week actually happen.

Desired behaviors:

- Following through on implementation plans
- Tracking progress honestly
- Adjusting course when things aren't working
- Holding each other accountable with respect
- Celebrating progress and learning from setbacks

Barriers:

- Busy-ness overtakes strategic priorities
- No one specifically responsible for follow-through
- Measuring transformation is harder than measuring billable hours
- Fear of admitting we're not succeeding
- Letting things slide when uncomfortable

Reinforcement structures they designed:

Transformation Dashboard (Public)

- Posted in common areas and firm intranet
- Shows progress on each pilot: timeline, milestones, metrics
- Updated monthly with transparency about what's working and what's not
- Everyone can see if we're following through

Monthly Leadership Check-ins

- Management committee reviews transformation progress
- Each prototype has a sponsor who reports status
- Red/Yellow/Green status with specific blockers identified
- Publicly commits to next month's actions

Quarterly Transformation Town Halls

- Julian presents progress on all transformation initiatives
- Honest about successes and struggles
- Takes questions, adjusts course based on feedback
- Associates and partners can hold leadership accountable

Peer Accountability Pods

- Groups of 5–6 people across levels/practices
- Meet monthly to discuss: what am I doing differently? what's hard? where am I stuck?
- Support and gentle accountability
- Makes transformation personal, not just institutional

Annual Transformation Assessment

- Every partner and associate surveyed: are we living our commitments?
- Results published transparently
- Leadership must respond to gaps between commitments and reality
- Repeated annually to track cultural evolution

Team 4: Celebrating Change and Managing Resistance

This group tackled the emotional and cultural dimensions of sustaining transformation.

Desired behaviors:

- Trying new approaches even when uncertain
- Supporting colleagues who are struggling with changes
- Celebrating experimentation whether it succeeds or fails
- Calling out behaviors that undermine transformation
- Choosing to stay and build rather than leave when it's hard

Barriers:

- Change is uncomfortable and scary
- Old behaviors feel safer and are easier
- Early attempts at new approaches often stumble

- Some people genuinely preferred old ways
- Cynicism is easier than hope

Reinforcement structures they designed:

Transformation Stories (Monthly Newsletter)

- Feature people doing the work differently
- Both successes and instructive failures
- Makes the abstract concrete: "here's what client-centric actually looks like"
- Associates and partners featured equally

Early Adopter Recognition

- People who pilot new approaches get public recognition
- Even if the approach doesn't work, we recognize the courage to try
- Message: experimentation is valued, not just success

Resistance Protocols

- Explicit permission to voice concerns and skepticism
- But distinction between: "I'm concerned about X" (productive) vs. "this will never work" (undermining)
- If someone consistently undermines transformation, have direct conversation
- In extreme cases, may not be right fit for firm going forward

Exit Interviews with Learning Focus

- When people leave, understand why
- If leaving because of transformation changes, we can learn from that

- If leaving because we didn't transform enough, we learn from that too
- Use departures as data about what's working and what's not

Celebration Rituals

- Quarterly event celebrating transformation progress
- Not just "we succeeded" but "we tried, we learned, we're evolving"
- Stories of courage, vulnerability, growth
- Partners and associates honored equally

Integration and Commitment

After two hours, both the implementation planning teams and the reinforcement structure teams reported out. The room had generated:

- Four detailed implementation plans with timelines, budgets, metrics, and accountability
- Four categories of reinforcement structures with specific mechanisms to sustain change
- Approximately thirty concrete commitments about how work would be different

Lucy captured it all on a master timeline showing what would happen and when over the next eighteen months.

Julian stood at the front, looking at the accumulated work of the week, with walls covered in HMW statements, prototypes, implementation plans, reinforcement structures.

"This is remarkable," he said quietly. "Five days ago, we arrived here with anxiety and skepticism. Today we have a roadmap for transforming nearly every major system in our firm."

He paused. "But we can't end today without acknowledging something. Some of you will leave. Not immediately, maybe not this year. But transformation is hard, and not everyone will want to do this hard work. Some people will decide they preferred the old way, or that another firm offers an easier path, or that the changes we're making don't align with what they want their career to be."

The room was very quiet.

"And that's okay," Julian continued, surprising people. "I mean it. If you look at what we're building and decide it's not for you, that's a totally valid choice. I absolutely get it. This is not what most people sign up for when they join a law firm. Better to know that now and transition thoughtfully than to stay and be miserable or undermine what we're creating.

"But," and his voice strengthened, "for those of you who are choosing to stay, who are choosing to be part of building this, I'm asking for a real commitment. Not just 'I'll try' or 'I'll see how it goes.' I'm asking you to commit to doing the hard work of changing how you work, even when it's uncomfortable. To commit to supporting your colleagues through their struggles with change. To commit to speaking up when you see us slipping back into old patterns."

He looked around the room. "Because here's what I've learned this week. The culture we've experienced here, including the honesty, the collaboration, the creativity, and the mutual respect; that's not magic. It's a choice. A choice we make every day in how we treat each other, how we communicate, how we handle conflict, how we respond to mistakes and failures."

Julian pulled up the final slide for the week:

THE CHOICE WE'RE MAKING

We choose to:

- Value all contributions, not just origination
- Develop people intentionally, not hope they figure it out
- Communicate proactively, not just respond when asked
- Serve clients as teams, not solo practitioners
- Learn from failures, not hide them
- Speak honestly, even when uncomfortable
- Support each other's growth, not just compete
- Build something that outlasts any individual
- Be the firm that figured out how to thrive in transformation

"This is what we're choosing to be," Julian said. "Not what we've always been. Not what's easiest. But what we believe we can become together."

He turned to Lucy. "Lucy has one final exercise." A collective audible groan, followed by the good-humored laugh of a group who had gone through a lot together.

"I know! I know!," said Lucy, "but this is a short one, and I promise you'll thank me later."

Personal Commitments

Lucy distributed index cards to everyone. "I want you to write two things. First, one specific behavior you personally commit to changing based on this week. Not 'I'll be better', but a specific, observable behavior."

"Second, how you'll know you're succeeding in that commitment. A way to measure your own progress."

The room fell silent as people wrote. After several minutes:

"Now share it with one person near you," Lucy said. "Tell them your commitment. They'll be your accountability partner. They'll check in with you in 30 days and 90 days to see how you're doing."

Pairs formed. Quiet conversations:

Robert Kim to Dwarkesh Jones: "I commit to asking associates 'what would make you better at this?' before giving them assignments, not just telling them what to do. I'll know I'm succeeding if associates tell me they understand why their work matters."

Jessica Park to Priya Patel: "I commit to speaking up in meetings when I see decisions being made without considering associate perspective. I'll know I'm succeeding if partners start asking 'how does this affect associate development?' before I have to raise it."

Tom Brennan to Marcus Reed: "I commit to presenting financial information as opportunities, not just constraints. Saying 'here's what we could invest in if we made this change' rather than 'we can't afford that.' I'll know I'm succeeding if people come to me with ideas instead of avoiding financial discussions."

Maggie McNamee to Alex Rivera: "I commit to introducing junior lawyers to my clients within the first months of working together, not waiting until they've 'proven themselves.' I'll know I'm succeeding when clients start copying the associates on emails instead of sending messages only to other senior lawyers and me."

Sarah Williams to Elena Rodriguez: "I commit to protecting development time, for myself and for people I supervise. Setting aside billable work that would encroach on protected learning time. I'll know I'm succeeding if I actually attend the monthly Learning Labs."

Lucy collected the cards. She promised people would get them back in thirty days as reminders. "These personal commitments are as important as the institutional structures. Remember ADKAR because culture is made of individual choices, repeated daily, until they become who we are."

Closing

Julian returned to the front for the final time. "Before we leave, I want to acknowledge several realities about what happens Monday morning.

"You'll return to full inboxes. Demanding clients. Urgent deadlines. All the pressures that make strategic work feel like a luxury. Within a week, the intensity of this experience will start to fade. Within a month, if we're not careful, we'll slip back into old patterns because old patterns are comfortable and familiar.

"The five forces driving transformation—AI advancement, client pressure, intergenerational dynamics, hybrid work, and regulatory shifts—those aren't solved by this week's work. They're ongoing, accelerating pressures that will keep pushing us to evolve.

"And the changes we've committed to: Four Partner Paths, Client Command Center, and Competency Roadmap, these will be hard. You'll have days where you wonder why we're doing this. Days where the old way seems easier. Days where you question whether it's worth it."

He paused, looking around the room at faces that were exhausted but engaged, challenged but hopeful.

"So why do it? Because the alternative is worse. The alternative is slowly becoming irrelevant. Slowly losing the people we most want to keep. Slowly transforming into just another law firm where money is the only thing holding people together or being absorbed into a culture completely unlike our own and losing everything we've built and continue building together.

"Because our culture is our competitive advantage."

He clicked to a final image: a photo taken Tuesday morning during the breakfast conversations. People leaning in, engaged, animated. Partners and associates talking as equals. Laughter and intensity mixed together.

"Look at this. Look at what we've built this week. This is what we're fighting to preserve and expand. Not the specific prototypes, which might succeed or fail. But this: the way we worked together. The honesty. The collaboration. The belief that we can build something better.

"So here's my commitment to you," Julian said. "I will keep us accountable to what we designed this week. I will champion the changes we selected, resource them properly, and track progress transparently. I will call out behavior that undermines our culture. I will celebrate people who do the hard work of changing. And I will have honest conversations with people, including myself, when we're not living up to our commitments.

"But I can't do this alone. Culture is built by all of us, through every interaction, every decision, every day."

He looked at Lucy. "Lucy, anything to add?"

Lucy stood beside him. "Just this. You came here Monday not knowing what to expect. Some of you were skeptical. Some were anxious. All of you were uncertain."

"You're leaving with something concrete in the form of implementation plans, reinforcement structures, and personal commitments. But more importantly, you're leaving with proof that transformation is possible. You experienced it. You did it together. And that memory of what it feels like to work this way is what will sustain you when it gets hard."

"Because you'll remember: we did hard things together this week. We can do hard things together going forward."

Departure

As the session ended, people didn't rush out. They lingered, talking in small groups. Exchanging contact information with their accountability partners. Taking photos of the walls covered with their week's work. Promising to stay connected.

At the front of the room, Rebecca Tisdale, Dr. Wilson, and Maria Santos gathered with Julian and Lucy.

"This was remarkable," Rebecca said. "I've been to a lot of law firm retreats and usually it's just presentations about finances. This felt different. Genuine."

"Because it was," Maria added. "You did real work. Made real commitments. Built promising solutions. If you follow through on even half of what you designed this week, you'll be five years ahead of your competitors."

Dr. Wilson nodded. "The key is sustaining the energy and commitment when the daily pressures return. That's where most transformation efforts fail, not in ideation, but in implementation."

"That's what the reinforcement structures are for," Lucy said. "Making it easier to do the new behavior than the old. But you're right; it will be hard."

"Then keep us involved," Rebecca suggested. "Bring us back in six months to evaluate the Client Command Center pilot. Let us hold you accountable to what you promised. Use us as external pressure when internal resistance builds."

Julian smiled. "We will. You're part of this now. Partners in our transformation, not just clients receiving services."

Near the windows, Robert Kim stood with several younger attorneys, looking out at the mountains one last time.

"What did you think?" Priya Patel asked him.

Robert was quiet for a moment. "A month ago, if someone had told me I'd help design a system that devalues the rainmaker model I've built my career on, I would have said they were crazy."

"And now?" Alex Rivera prompted.

"Now I think maybe it's crazy to keep doing what we've always done when the world has changed. Maybe the courage is in being willing to evolve, even when it means rethinking everything you thought made you valuable."

He turned from the window. "I still have doubts. I still worry we're making promises we can't keep. But I also know this: if we don't try this, in five years we'll be just another struggling mid-size firm being acquired by someone who figured out transformation before we did."

"So we try," Elena Rodriguez said simply. "We stumble, we adjust, we keep trying. And maybe we actually build something special."

Throughout the room, similar conversations. Lawyers who'd arrived Monday as skeptics or cynics leaving Friday as tentative believers. Not because they'd been sold a fantasy, but because they'd experienced a different way of thinking and could imagine it continuing.

The afternoon sun slanted through the windows, illuminating the walls covered with their week's work, of problems defined, solutions designed, commitments made. Tomorrow, people would travel home. Monday, they'd return to their offices, their clients, their real lives.

The question was whether what they'd built this week could survive that return to reality.

Julian and Lucy knew the answer wouldn't come quickly. It would come in small choices, repeated daily, by many people in fifteen offices who'd spent a week imagining a different future and now faced the harder work of building it and leading others in living it.

As the last participants filed out, the conference room stood empty. Walls still covered with Post-its. Whiteboards still filled with frameworks. Prototypes still displayed along the sides. Evidence of five days of intense, uncomfortable, generative work.

Inside the Grove Park Inn, something had changed over the last week. Not the complete transformation they'd imagined because that would take years, if it happened at all. But the belief that transformation was possible. The experience of working differently. The commitment to try.

And sometimes, that is enough to start.

Reader Reflection

The Monday Morning Test

Julian and Lucy acknowledged that the real work would begin when everyone returned to their desks.

1. **The "Busy" Trap:** When you return to your desk and the urgent client emails pile up, what is the *one* strategic commitment you will protect time for?

2. **Psychological Safety:** The firm built a culture where associates could speak honestly to partners. Does your team have a mechanism (like the "Anonymous Feedback Channel" or "Learning Labs") to keep that channel open?

3. **Your Personal Commitment:** If you were to fill out the index card Lucy handed out, what represents the specific behavior *you* need to change to help your firm evolve? (e.g., "I will stop hoarding client contacts," or "I will give developmental feedback after every major assignment").

Epilogue

Part 1: Six Months Later

Charlotte, NC, September 15, 2027, 7:47 p.m.

Julian Justice poured two glasses of bourbon in his office, the Charlotte skyline glittering through the floor-to-ceiling windows. Lucy Lex sat in the chair across from his desk, looking as exhausted as he felt.

"I got another resignation letter today," Julian said, handing her a glass. "Marcus Reed."

Lucy's face fell. "Marcus? He was so enthusiastic at the retreat. He co-designed the Proactive Partnership model."

"I know." Julian sank into his chair. "He said the pace of change was slower than he'd hoped. He's going in-house at one of his clients. Better work-life balance, fewer politics, more direct impact."

Lucy sipped her bourbon. "That's six partners in six months."

"Seven if you count Elena Rodriguez, who would have made partner, going to that boutique firm in September." Julian rubbed his eyes. "Every exit interview says something similar: 'loved the vision, couldn't wait for implementation,' or 'too much uncertainty,' or 'other opportunities came along.'"

"Some of them are probably excuses," Lucy said. "William Klept admitted he hated the Four Partner Paths concept and only went along because he thought it would die quietly. When we actually started implementing it, he was out."

"But not all of them are excuses," Julian countered. "Marcus was genuine. And he's right; we're moving slower than we promised. The Client Command Center took four months to launch instead of two. The Competency Roadmap is still half-built. The Four Partner Paths implementation has been a chaotic mess of arguments about compensation committee composition."

He stood and walked to the window, staring out at the city. "There are days I wonder if we should have just taken the Wagner merger. Clean, simple, certain. Instead, we're bleeding talent, exhausting everyone who stayed, and I'm not even sure it's working."

Lucy was quiet for a long moment. "Do you want the optimistic version or the realistic version?"

"Realistic. I'm too tired for platitudes."

"Okay. Realistic: Year one of major transformation always sucks. Always. We're asking people to change behaviors they've practiced for decades while also doing their regular jobs. Of course, some people are leaving because they didn't actually want to change, or they wanted change to be easier than this, or they got recruited away by firms offering more money for less disruption. That's human nature. It's rational."

She set down her glass. "And yes, implementation is slower than we hoped. Technology always takes longer than promised. The relationship manager hiring was delayed because we couldn't find the right person. The competency definitions required way more detail work than we anticipated. Partner self-identification for Four Paths turned into an emotional nightmare for people whose identities are wrapped up in being rainmakers."

"So it's a disaster," Julian said flatly.

"I didn't say that." Lucy stood and joined him at the window. "You asked for realistic. Here's the rest: the Client Command Center is live with twelve clients now, and client satisfaction scores are up 23% for those clients—23%, Julian. That's huge."

She counted on her fingers. "The three general counsel who participated in the retreat? They're evangelizing about us to their peer networks. Rebecca Tisdale introduced us to two new potential clients specifically because of how we work now. Maria Santos included us in an RFP we normally wouldn't have been considered for because, in her words, 'you're doing something different.'"

"Associate retention is up," Lucy continued. "Not dramatically, but we've lost fewer third and fourth years this fall than we did last year. And the ones who are staying are saying it's because of the feedback system and the clarity about development. Maya Davis told me last week she'd turned down a recruiter call because 'I can actually see my career path here now.'"

Julian turned to look at her. "But seven partners left."

"Seven-ish partners left," Lucy agreed. "Three of whom were going to leave anyway because they were already checked out before the retreat. Two left for legitimate personal reasons that had nothing to do with transformation. William Klept and Marcus Reed? Those hurt. But

Julian, we have 150 partners. Losing two who didn't actually want what we're building might not be a bad thing."

"It feels bad."

"Of course it does. You put your reputation on the line for this. You asked people to trust you, and some of them didn't. That's personal." She paused. "But do you know what else happened?"

Julian waited.

"Robert Kim is now actively mentoring three associates on business development skills. Robert Kim, who six months ago thought the whole transformation was consultant nonsense. He's teaching people how to develop client relationships because he's a Leadership Partner now and that's what Leadership Partners do."

"Maggie McNamee redesigned her entire practice around the Client Care Team model," Lucy went on. "She has a relationship manager, she coordinates with three other partners on her major clients, and she told me it's the first time in five years she hasn't felt like she's drowning. She's actually enjoying practice again."

"Jessica Park presented at a legal tech conference about our Client Command Center. Got approached by three firms asking for advice. Jessica, who was about to leave a year ago because she couldn't see a future here."

Lucy's voice softened. "And Priya Patel told me last week that for the first time in her career, she feels like she has permission to be good at what she's actually good at instead of pretending to be someone she's not. That's Four Partner Paths working, even if the implementation has been messy."

Julian returned to his desk and refilled his glass. "So what you're saying is it's not a disaster, but it's also not the triumphant transformation we envisioned."

"Exactly. It's the messy middle. Where most transformations die because leaders give up when they don't see immediate results, or because the people who leave make more noise than the people who stay, or because six months feels like forever when you're exhausted."

She sat back down, looking directly at him. "The question is: do you still believe we're building something worth building? Not whether it's easy. Not whether everyone's happy. But whether the culture we're creating where Robert Kim mentors associates and Maggie McNamee actually enjoys her work and Priya Patel feels like she can be herself is worth fighting for."

Julian was quiet for a long time, swirling bourbon in his glass.

"You know what struck me last week?" he finally said. "I was walking past the associates' area and heard laughter. Not nervous laughter or sarcastic laughter. Genuine laughter. Three senior associates working on something together, clearly enjoying themselves."

"I stopped and listened for a minute. They were workshopping a pitch for a new client using the co-design intake method. Taking turns role-playing the client, giving each other feedback, refining their approach. And they were having fun."

He looked at Lucy. "When I was an associate, work was terrifying. You hoped you didn't screw up, hoped the partner wouldn't yell at you, hoped you'd somehow figure out what you were supposed to be learning. Fun was never part of it."

"If we're building a place where associates can actually enjoy developing their skills, where partners like Maggie can enjoy practicing law again, where someone like Priya doesn't have to pretend to be something she's not, then yeah, that's worth fighting for."

Lucy smiled. "So you don't regret not taking the merger?"

"Wagner called again two weeks ago. Wanted to revisit conversations. Bigger offer this time." Julian smiled slightly. "I told her to bug off."

"Professionally phrased, I hope."

"Extremely professionally. Something about 'pursuing our current strategic direction.'" He raised his glass. "We're doing this. Messy, slow, imperfect, and oh my God, exhausting, but we're doing this."

Lucy raised hers to meet his. "Then let's do it better in year two. Because we've learned a lot about what doesn't work."

"Like what?"

"Like we tried to implement everything at once. Four major pilots simultaneously was too much. People got overwhelmed. Next year, we will sequence better and finish one thing before starting the next.

"Like we underestimated how much training partners need. We gave them one workshop on developmental feedback and expected them to be good at it. They need ongoing coaching, not one-and-done training."

"Like we didn't celebrate wins enough. We were so focused on what wasn't working that we forgot to recognize what was. Robert Kim's transformation is remarkable, and we should be telling that story more."

Julian had put his glass down to jot notes. "What else?"

"We need to bring the retreat group back together. They need to see progress, give feedback, help solve problems. We made them co-designers then disappeared for six months. That breaks trust."

"So we do another retreat?"

"Absolutely. One year anniversary. Show them what we've learned, what we're changing, what's next. Make it a reinforcement structure, an annual ritual where we assess honestly and recommit."

Julian nodded slowly. "March again?"

"March again. Same place. Some different players. But the same core: we take time to step back, reflect, and decide together where we go next."

Julian looked at his calendar. "Six months until the next retreat. Let's make sure we have something worth reporting."

"Then let's get to work."

They clinked glasses one more time before returning to their laptops, their to-do lists, their relentless pursuit of a vision that was taking shape slowly, imperfectly, but unmistakably.

Outside, Charlotte glittered in the September night. Inside, two leaders chose, yet again, to keep building something that would outlast them both.

Part 2: One Year After the Retreat

Grove Park Inn, Asheville, NC, March 13, 2028, 9:00 a.m.

Julian Justice stood at the front of the same conference room, looking out at faces both familiar and new. Seventy-five people this time, more than last year. Some faces were missing: Marcus Reed, Elena Rodriguez, William Klept, and a few others who'd found different paths. But new faces had joined, including three lateral hires attracted by the firm's reputation for innovation, two associates from the most recent recruiting class who'd specifically sought out the firm because of what they'd heard, Rebecca Tisdale, and Sarah Conforti from Penn State who'd asked to attend to hear updates about the first retreat's outcomes.

The energy was different than last year. Less anxious, more comfortable and curious. The returning participants knew what to expect. The newcomers had heard stories but didn't quite know what to expect yet.

Julian waited for the room to settle, then began.

"Good morning, and welcome to our second annual transformation retreat. For those who were here last year, welcome back. For those who are new, welcome to something that might be the strangest experience of your legal career."

A few nervous laughs.

"Last year, we spent a week examining why transformation was necessary and designing solutions to problems we'd been ignoring for years. We left here energized, committed, ready to change everything. And then we returned to reality."

He clicked to a slide showing a timeline of the past twelve months with major milestones marked.

"I'm going to be completely honest about what happened in year one. Not the sanitized version we might put in a recruiting brochure, but the actual, messy, complicated truth. Because if we're building a culture of honesty, it starts with leadership acknowledging what really happened."

He advanced to the next slide: **Year One: What We Promised.**

The slide showed the four selected prototypes from the Innovation Tournament:

- Client Command Center + Proactive Partnership Model
- Four Partner Paths
- Competency Roadmap + Continuous Feedback System
- Plus reinforcement structures to sustain change

"Here's what we actually delivered," Julian said, clicking to a new slide: **Year One: What We Built.**

CLIENT COMMAND CENTER + PROACTIVE PARTNERSHIP

✓ Launched (4 months late)

✓ Currently serving 15 major clients

✓ Client satisfaction scores up 14% for participating clients

✓ Three relationship managers hired and trained

✓ Portal usage rate: 73% of clients logging in at least weekly

✓ Billing dispute rate down 45% for portal clients

- ✗ Struggled with portal updates—still not fully automated
- ✗ Cost more than projected ($240K vs. $175K budgeted)
- ✗ Some partners resist updating portal information

Status: Working but needs refinement

"Translation," Julian said, "this was our biggest success. Clients love it. Rebecca Tisdale is in this room again because she specifically asked to come back and see what else we're building. But we learned that technology alone doesn't solve cultural problems because we still have partners who don't prioritize keeping client information current."

He advanced to the next result.

FOUR PARTNER PATHS

- ✓ 37 partners self-identified into paths
- ✓ Compensation committee restructured (now includes 2 Service Partners, 1 Expert Partner)
- ✓ First partner admitted directly to Service Partner track (hired laterally)
- ✓ Evaluation criteria differentiated by path
- ✓ Marketing materials updated to feature all partner types
- ✗ Significant pushback from some Client Partners about compensation changes
- ✗ Lost 2 partners who disagreed with path valuations
- ✗ Associate confusion about which path to aim for
- ✗ Status equality still questioned with subtle signals that Client Partners more valued

Status: Implemented but culturally incomplete

"Four Partner Paths has been our most controversial change," Julian said bluntly. "Some partners embraced it immediately. Robert Kim became a Leadership Partner and is thriving. Maggie McNamee is a Service Partner and loving the clarity. But we lost William Klept and one other partner who genuinely believed this devalued what they'd built their careers on."

"And honestly? We're still working on the culture piece. We say all paths are equal, but our behavior doesn't always match our words. Service Partners still don't feel truly equal. That's on leadership, and especially me, to fix. I would value your help in building better ways to do that."

Robert Kim spoke from the audience, startling people. "Can I say something?"

Julian nodded.

Robert stood. "A year ago, I was skeptical about this whole thing. I thought that Four Partner Paths especially was going to destroy what made successful lawyers successful. I was wrong."

He looked around the room. "I'm a Leadership Partner now. I focus on mentoring, on building systems, on developing the firm's future. And I'm happier than I've been in ten years. I make slightly less money than I did, but I enjoy my work more. I go home earlier. Not 'early,' mind you, but earlier. I have better relationships with the people I work with."

"That said," Robert continued, "Julian's right that the culture shift is incomplete. Some partners still treat Leadership Partners and Service Partners as 'less than.' That needs to change. But the structure is working; we just need to keep leaning into it."

He sat down. Julian nodded his thanks.

"Next," Julian said, clicking forward.

COMPETENCY ROADMAP + CONTINUOUS FEEDBACK SYSTEM

- ✓ Roadmap created for all major practice areas
- ✓ Feedback platform implemented
- ✓ 68% of matters now receive structured feedback
- ✓ Quarterly development conversations happening for 85% of associates
- ✓ Associate satisfaction with development support up 41%
- ✓ Junior and mid-level associate retention up 18%
- ✗ Partner training inadequate, with many still giving poor feedback
- ✗ Some practice groups adopted fully, others barely using it

- ✗ Associates in non-participating groups feeling left behind
- ✗ Competency definitions still being refined
- ✗ No one "owns" the system firm-wide yet

Status: Promising but inconsistent

"The associate development work is probably our most meaningful long-term investment," Julian said. "We're finally answering the question 'how do you develop lawyers in an AI-augmented world?' with actual structure instead of hope."

"But implementation has been wildly uneven. Some practice groups have embraced this completely. Litigation and Corporate have integrated it fully. Tax and Employment are lagging. That creates inequality, with some associates getting great development, and others feeling like nothing has changed."

He looked at Jessica Park and Priya Patel in the audience. "The associates who've experienced the full system, like Jessica, Priya, and others, are evangelizing to their peers. That's how culture spreads. But we need to make it universal, not optional."

He clicked to the final assessment.

REINFORCEMENT STRUCTURES

- ✓ Monthly all-hands meetings launched (attendance averaging 72%)
- ✓ Quarterly transformation town halls happening
- ✓ Learning Labs occurring monthly (attendance lower than hoped)
- ✓ Transformation dashboard posted publicly
- ✓ This retreat—we're here, we're doing it again
- ✗ Peer accountability pods mostly dissolved after 3 months
- ✗ Protected development time still encroached upon by client work
- ✗ Knowledge-sharing credits never fully implemented
- ✗ Innovation Fridays happened twice then got abandoned

Status: Some structures stuck, others failed

"Here's what we learned about reinforcement," Julian said. "The structures that work are the ones that happen publicly and regularly. Monthly all-hands, quarterly town halls, this annual retreat became habits because they were scheduled, public, and I personally championed them."

"The structures that failed were the ones that depended on distributed responsibility without clear ownership. Peer accountability pods sounded great but fizzled because no one was specifically responsible for making them happen. Innovation Fridays died because client emergencies took precedence or people were working remotely, so we didn't protect the time fiercely enough."

He paused, looking around the room. "So that's the honest accounting. Some successes, some failures, lots of messy middle."

Julian clicked to a new slide: **What This Actually Cost Us**.

The room tensed.

DEPARTURES (12 months):

- 7 partners left (4 for transformation-related reasons, 3 for other reasons)
- 12 associates left (lower than previous year's 18)
- 3 staff members left

FINANCIAL:

- Revenue flat (neither growth nor decline)
- Profit per partner down 3.2% (industry average: down 1.8%)
- Transformation investment: $847,000 (technology, training, consulting)

TIME:

- Estimated 3,200 billable hours redirected to transformation work
- Leadership time: significant (not fully quantified)

EMOTIONAL:

- Exhaustion, frustration, anxiety, doubt
- Also: excitement, hope, engagement, meaning

"I'm not going to sugarcoat this," Julian said. "Transformation cost us money, time, and people. We're slightly less profitable than we were. We lost partners we wanted to keep. We exhausted everyone who stayed. By traditional law firm metrics, year one was not a success."

He let that sit for a moment.

"But here's what else happened," Julian said, his voice shifting.

He clicked to a new slide: **What We Actually Built**.

CLIENT RELATIONSHIPS:

- 5 new clients specifically attracted by our approach
- 3 existing clients expanded relationships
- Client satisfaction scores: up 19% overall
- Retention rate: 94% (up from 89%)
- RFP win rate: 38% (up from 31%)

TALENT:

- Associate retention: up 18%
- First-year recruiting: accepted offers up 15%
- Lateral associate interest: up significantly
- New hires cite "culture" and "development" as top reasons

CULTURE METRICS:

- Engagement survey: 76% engaged in transformation programming (up from 61%)
- Trust in leadership: 71% (up from 54%)
- Belief firm is "heading in right direction": 79% (up from 47%)
- Willingness to recommend firm to colleagues: 82% (up from 58%)

EXTERNAL RECOGNITION:

- Featured in 3 legal publications as an innovator
- Speaking invitations to present our approach
- Law schools asking to study our model
- Clients referring other potential clients

Julian walked away from the screen to the center of the room.

"Here's what I've come to understand. The traditional metrics of revenue, PPEP, and hours billed measure efficiency. They measure how well we're operating the old model. And by those metrics, transformation looks expensive."

"But other metrics also matter, including client loyalty, talent retention, cultural health, and strategic positioning. Those measure whether we're building something sustainable. Something that will outlast any individual lawyer or client. Something that attracts the people and clients who want to work differently."

"And by those metrics, we're winning."

He clicked to a photo from last year's retreat of the conference room walls covered in Post-its, people clustered around prototype displays, animated conversations everywhere.

"Last year, we imagined a different future. This year, we're living it. Imperfectly, incompletely, but unmistakably."

Julian's voice softened. "I know year one was hard. I know some of you wondered if this was worth it. I know you've had moments of doubt. I certainly have."

"But look around this room. Seventy-seven people from fifteen offices, taking time away from billable work, to keep building what we started. That's not obligation. That's commitment."

"We have new people here who chose to join a firm specifically because of what we're doing. We have clients like Rebecca who are so invested in our success that they keep coming back to help. We have associates who've turned down recruiters because they can see a future here now. We have partners like Robert who've rediscovered why they loved practicing law in the first place."

"This year, we're going deeper rather than wider. Instead of launching new initiatives, we're finishing what we started.

He clicked to his final slide: **Year Two: What We're Building Next**.

Year Two Priorities:

1. **Complete the culture shift around Four Partner Paths**—Make status equality real, not aspirational
2. **Scale Client Command Center** to all major clients—Make it excellent, not just functional
3. **Fix Competency Roadmap implementation**—Make it universal and consistent
4. **Develop next generation of firm leadership**—Create clear paths to leadership roles
5. **Reimagine pricing and compensation**—Finally tackle the compensation pool model from last year

"That last one," Julian said, pointing to item five, "yes, we're finally ready. Tom Brennan and a working group have been developing a team-based compensation model. We're going to workshop it this week, refine it, and pilot it in year two. Because we've learned that you can't fully shift to team-based client service without shifting compensation incentives."

He paused. "We're also going to do something new this year. We're going to fail faster and learn quicker. Last year, we held onto structures that weren't working like Innovation Fridays and accountability pods for too long because we didn't want to admit they failed. This year, we'll run ninety-day experiments, assess honestly, and either scale or kill them quickly."

Julian looked at Lucy, who stood and joined him at the front.

"The framework for this week is similar to last year," Lucy said. "But informed by twelve months of learning. We're going to:

- Examine what worked and why
- Understand what failed and why
- Refine our existing initiatives based on real data
- Design solutions to new problems that emerged

- Build better reinforcement structures
- Recommit to the culture we're creating"

"For those who are new," Lucy continued, looking at the lateral hires and recent recruits, "this week will feel intense and strange. You're going to see partners admit mistakes. Associates challenge assumptions. People collaborate across hierarchy in ways that don't happen at most firms. That's the culture we've built and it's one where honesty and collaboration matter more than hierarchy and pretense."

Julian took over for the close. "Before we begin today's sessions, I want to say one more thing."

He looked around the room, making eye contact with as many people as he could.

"Last year, I asked you to commit to doing hard work even when it's uncomfortable. To support each other through change. To speak up when you see us slipping into old patterns. Many of you made that commitment and honored it. Some didn't, and that's why they're not here."

"This year, I'm asking for the same commitment again. But I'm also making a commitment to you."

He clicked to a slide showing simple text:

LEADERSHIP COMMITMENT

We will:

- Keep you informed honestly about progress and challenges
- Resource the changes we ask you to make
- Celebrate successes and learn from failures publicly
- Hold ourselves accountable to the same standards we hold you
- Choose culture over short-term profit when they conflict
- Keep listening even when the feedback is uncomfortable
- Build something worth the sacrifice we're asking you to make

"That's my promise," Julian said. "Not that it will be easy. Not that we'll be perfect. But that we'll keep trying, keep learning, keep building something that matters."

"So let's get to work."

As people broke for the first session, the conversations reflected the shift from year one's anxiety to year two's informed commitment. The returning participants were orienting the newcomers, sharing stories from implementation, explaining what to expect.

Near the coffee station, Maggie McNamee was talking with one of the new lateral partners.

"What's it actually like?" the new partner asked. "The Client Command Center. Does it work in practice?"

Maggie smiled. "It's imperfect. Sometimes portal updates are late. But compared to where we were a year ago, with no idea if our clients were getting what they needed, it's very different. They now know where their matters stand, when to expect outreach from us, the next material action in the matter, and an estimate of budget to work performed. They love it and we keep improving it all the time."

At another table, Robert Kim was explaining Four Partner Paths to a newly hired Service Partner.

"Will I actually be valued equally?" the new partner asked skeptically. "Or is this just marketing?"

Robert was honest. "It's a work in progress. Some people fully believe it, some are still adjusting. But I can tell you this: I make less money than I did as a rainmaker, and I'm happier. The work is more meaningful. The relationships are better. The pressure is different. It's not absent, but different."

Near the windows, Rebecca Tisdale was talking with Julian and Lucy about what she'd observed.

"You asked us to hold you accountable," Rebecca said. "Here's my accountability report: Client Command Center is excellent. You've delivered on that promise. I tell other GCs about it constantly. But I want to see more progress on proactive partnership. The relationship manager role is great, but I still sometimes feel like I'm chasing you for information rather than you anticipating my needs."

"Fair," Julian said. "That's cultural, not structural. We have the tools, but some partners still default to reactive communication. We need to make proactive outreach an explicit evaluation criterion."

"Exactly," Rebecca said. "And that's why I keep coming back. You actually listen to feedback and adjust. Most firms thank you politely and change nothing."

Throughout the room, these conversations unfolded. They were honest, direct, and forward-looking. Not one pretended the past year was perfect, but they also didn't dwell on failures. The group was acknowledging the work ahead while recognizing the progress made.

Dr. Sarah Conforti pulled Lucy aside. "You should be really proud. I've studied change management in dozens of organizations. Most transformation initiatives are dead by month six. You're still at it at month twelve and building on what you've learned. The firm is lucky to have you."

"It doesn't always feel like growing," Lucy admitted. "Some days it feels like we're barely holding on."

"That's what successful transformation feels like from the inside," Dr. Conforti said. "From the outside, you've built something genuinely different. The culture in this room—the honesty, the collaboration, the commitment—that's rare. Especially in law firms."

"Let's see if we can sustain it for another year," Lucy said.

"Or twenty," Dr. Conforti replied. "If you can make this an annual ritual, with this level of reflection and recommitment, you'll have built something that outlasts any individual leader."

As the morning sessions began, Julian stood at the back of the room, watching his colleagues engage with the day's agenda. A year ago, he'd stood in almost the same spot, anxious about whether anyone would buy into the need for transformation. Now he was watching people who'd lived through innovation's messy reality choosing to keep going.

The work would never be finished. The culture would always need tending. The commitment would need to be renewed constantly.

But for seventy-seven people gathered in a conference room in Asheville, North Carolina, that was no longer a burden.

It was a choice they kept making together.

And that choice was about building something that might actually last.

THE END

Or perhaps more accurately:

THE MESSY MIDDLE

A Note on the Use of Artificial Intelligence

This book argues that the future of the legal profession lies not in resisting technology, but in leveraging it to elevate human expertise. In the spirit of that message, I want to be transparent that I used generative AI during the creation of this manuscript. I used these tools as a "co-intelligence" and specifically, I used them to pressure-test ideas, organize research, and refine the structure of the narrative arc.

But the story, the characters, and the strategic insights within these pages are entirely human. They are born from my own writing and the frameworks I teach to law firms and lawyers, and all of it reflects the lessons, observations, failures, and triumphs of over two decades in the legal profession. As with law firms in the future, the technology provided the leverage, but the architecture, craftsmanship, judgment, and the vision for a better future is entirely my own.

Appendix A

Main Takeaways: A Chapter-by-Chapter Guide to Law Firm Transformation

Chapter 1: The Reckoning

- Recognize that external market pressures require proactive firm transformation, not reactive crisis management.
- Confront uncomfortable financial realities (flat or declining revenue, partner departures, client losses) as catalysts for change.
- Accept that what made the firm successful in the past may not sustain it in the future.
- Commit leadership time and resources to examining fundamental business model questions.
- Consider bringing in outside expertise to facilitate transformation.

Chapter 2: The Call to Action

- Create dedicated time and space away from daily operations to focus on strategic transformation.
- Frame transformation as proactive leadership rather than reactive crisis management to inspire confidence and momentum.
- Include diverse voices (partners, associates, staff) in transformation conversations from the beginning.

Chapter 3: Welcome to the Retreat

- Recognize that people approach change from different postures—skeptic, realist, optimist, futurist—and each perspective has value.
- Anticipate that informal conversations before formal sessions reveal the real concerns, anxieties, and hopes people bring to transformation work.
- Mix seating and groupings across practice groups and seniority levels to break down silos and encourage fresh perspectives.

Chapter 4: The Keynote

- Build Awareness first: people must understand why change is necessary before they can commit to it.
- Use data, financial projections, and concrete client examples to make the case for change compelling and undeniable.
- Frame the choice as being architects of the firm's future versus being shaped by forces beyond your control.

Chapter 5: Leading Change—ADKAR in Our Firm

- Use Jeffrey Hiatt's ADKAR framework (Awareness, Desire, Knowledge, Ability, Reinforcement) to structure change management.
- Ground organizational change in personal experience: people understand transformation better when they first reflect on changes they've navigated in their own lives.
- Cultivate Desire by connecting firm transformation to individual benefits and professional meaning.
- Recognize that Knowledge of what to do and Ability to do it are separate skills requiring different development.
- Plan for Reinforcement from the start, as change initiatives fail most often in sustaining new behaviors.

Chapter 6: What Comes Next

- When designing a retreat, create frequent informal spaces for honest conversation, as breakthrough insights often emerge during breaks.
- Acknowledge skepticism openly rather than dismissing it, as resisters often raise legitimate concerns.
- Recognize that some partners will never embrace change and plan accordingly.
- Use peer-to-peer dialogue to process new ideas, not just top-down presentations.
- Allow time for emotional processing when challenging long-held assumptions about the profession.

Chapter 7: How We Got Here—The Evolution of Legal Practice

- Understand that the legal profession's history holds keys to the structures that prevent innovation in the modern firm.
- Recognize that resistance to change is not new; the profession has always had tension between tradition and innovation.
- Learn from historical patterns: those who adapt thrive, those who resist become obsolete.
- Use historical perspective to reduce fear and increase confidence that transformation is possible.
- Connect current challenges to broader patterns of professional evolution.

Chapter 8: The Five Forces of Convergence

- Recognize the 2008 financial crisis as a permanent reset of client expectations around cost and efficiency.
- Understand generational workforce shifts: new lawyers hold different views about how they want to navigate their careers than the generations that built the firm.

- Leverage COVID's demonstration that remote work is viable and that clients accept new service delivery models.
- Monitor regulatory changes that are opening legal services to non-lawyer ownership and alternative providers.
- Prepare for AI's impact as the most transformative force since the personal computer.
- Understand that these five forces are converging simultaneously, creating unprecedented pressure for change.
- Develop strategic responses to each force rather than hoping they will subside.

Chapter 9: Generative AI—The Catalyst Force

- Accept that AI will automate significant portions of traditional legal work (research, document review, drafting).
- Shift focus of service and development of new lawyers from tasks AI can do to capabilities only humans provide (judgment, creativity, strategy, relationships).
- Invest in AI literacy for all lawyers, not just technology specialists.
- Begin developing and piloting new pricing models as AI reduces time required for traditional billable work.
- Create AI usage policies that address ethics, confidentiality, and quality control.
- Reimagine associate development when foundational tasks are automated.
- Position AI as augmentation (co-intelligence), not replacement of human lawyers.

Chapter 10: Moving to Client-Centricity Through Design Thinking

- Shift from lawyer-centric to client-centric service design.
- Apply the Stanford d.school five-stage design thinking process: Empathize, Define, Ideate, Prototype, Test.
- Recognize that lawyers are trained to solve problems quickly, but design thinking requires slowing down to understand the context in which the end user exists first.
- Challenge the assumption that legal expertise means understanding client needs. Sometimes lawyers focused on answering the legal question miss latent client needs that can strengthen service and lead to future ways to support the client.
- Create systems for regularly gathering and acting on client feedback.
- Design services around client experience, not just legal outcomes.

Chapter 11: Empathy Workshop

- Practice empathy interviewing: ask questions without judgment, exhibit only curiosity, and ask "why" until you exhaust an area.
- Use empathy maps to organize insights systematically.
- Consider introducing empathy exercises with non-legal topics (like airport travel) before applying to client service. This allows lawyers to learn the framework in a personal and low-risk way before exploring ways design thinking can enhance their legal work.
- Recognize that everyone's experience of the same environment differs dramatically based on their circumstances.

- Suspend judgment and resist the urge to explain or solve during empathy work.
- Understand that empathy reveals layers people don't volunteer unless asked with genuine curiosity.

Chapter 12: Empathy Interviews with General Counsel

- Invite actual clients to provide honest feedback about their experience with outside counsel.
- Accept that some clients perceive billable hour incentives as misaligned with their success.
- Recognize that small acts of human empathy (acknowledgment, encouragement) can shift client relationships from transactional to a partnership.
- Acknowledge that clients want partnership, not just vendor relationships.

Chapter 13: Defining Client Problems

- Use "How Might We" (HMW) statements to frame problems as opportunities rather than constraints.
- Start HMW statements with action verbs (help, enable, redesign) to invite momentum.
- Keep the user/stakeholder at the center of problem statements.
- Check scope: too broad creates chaos, too narrow limits creativity, find the Goldilocks zone.
- Avoid embedding solutions in problem statements ("automate" prescribes; "help clients feel confident" invites options).
- Generate many HMW statements before selecting the strongest ones.
- Test for neutrality: if someone can immediately guess your solution, the statement is too prescriptive.

Chapter 14: Turning the Lens Inward: Design Thinking for Internal Transformation

- Apply design thinking to internal stakeholders (associates, partners, staff), not just external clients.
- Recognize that associates are "users" of development systems; their experience determines retention.
- Understand that partners trying to develop business are "users" of go-to-market systems.
- Acknowledge that you have more control over internal systems, making redesign both easier and harder.
- Map internal stakeholder experiences with the same rigor applied to client empathy work.
- Accept uncomfortable truths about how internal systems actually function versus how you claim they work.
- Connect internal transformation to external client service, as unsupported professionals cannot serve clients to the best of the firm's ability.

Chapter 15: Reimagining Associate Development

- Question whether the traditional apprenticeship model works when AI handles foundational tasks.
- Address the existential financial question: if clients stop paying for junior associate time, how does training get funded?
- Create structured development pathways rather than hoping associates learn through osmosis.
- Develop competency frameworks that define what associates should learn at each stage.
- Build mentorship into partner responsibilities with accountability, not just encouragement.

- Consider multiple career paths so not everyone must become a rainmaker to succeed.
- Design development systems for the future, not replications of how current partners were trained.

Chapter 16: Empathy Interviews: Understanding Associate Experience

- Have partners interview associates they don't regularly work with for fresh perspective.
- Listen to hear when associates feel overwhelmed, isolated, anxious, and uncertain about their progress.
- Understand that associates often don't know if they're doing well because feedback may be sporadic.
- Recognize that hybrid work has increased isolation and made informal learning harder.
- Consider that associates are anxious about developing skills that may be obsolete in an AI world. Listening to these concerns without defensiveness or urgency to solve these challenges contributes to trust in the firm.
- Create safe space for honest feedback without fear of career consequences.

Chapter 17: From Rainmakers to Building the Hive

- Recognize that the solo rainmaker model doesn't scale and creates fragile client relationships.
- Understand that current compensation systems may reward individual origination, undermining collaboration.
- Design team-based client service models where relationships survive individual departures.

- Consider team origination pools where revenue is shared more evenly based on collective contribution from business originators, service providers, and leaders.
- Accept that changing compensation is the hardest cultural shift because it affects partner income.
- Build systems for proactive client development, not just reactive service delivery.

Chapter 18: Ideation

- Avoid three traps: issue spotting (immediately critiquing), social convergence (playing it safe), and self-censoring (not sharing unusual ideas).
- Use Worst Possible Idea technique: generate intentionally terrible solutions, then flip them to find insights.
- Use Crazy 8s: sketch eight ideas in four minutes to bypass overthinking and self-censorship.
- Use Lateral Inspiration: steal shamelessly from other industries and adapt for a law firm context.
- Generate quantity first, quality later; evaluation kills creativity during generation.
- Embrace wild ideas because bad ideas often contain kernels that lead to breakthroughs.
- Suspend judgment throughout ideation, even when ideas seem impractical.

Chapter 19: Prototyping

- Build rough prototypes quickly to test concepts before investing heavily.
- Filter ideas using criteria: feasibility (can we do it?), desirability (do users want it?), viability (does it work financially?).

- Create prototypes that are just good enough to test, not polished enough to feel precious.
- Use service blueprints, journey maps, and role-plays to make abstract ideas tangible.
- Identify assumptions embedded in your prototype that need testing.
- Design feedback mechanisms to learn from early users.
- Accept that prototypes will be imperfect; that's the point of testing.

Chapter 20: The Pitches

- Use an Innovation Tournament format to evaluate and select crowdsourced ideas for prototyping and piloting.
- Evaluate prototypes on Impact, Feasibility, Innovation, and Strategic Fit.
- Include diverse perspectives on the judging panel (clients, academics, leadership).
- Prepare clear, concise pitches that explain the problem, solution, and implementation plan.
- Anticipate tough questions and prepare honest answers about risks and challenges.
- Select a manageable number of initiatives to pilot rather than trying everything at once.
- Commit resources (people, money, time) to selected pilots.

Chapter 21: Building What Lasts

- Reinforcement is where most change initiatives fail; plan for it from the start.
- Create detailed implementation plans with owners, milestones, metrics, and accountability.

- Build visible progress tracking so everyone can see momentum.
- Establish regular rituals (monthly meetings, quarterly reviews, annual retreats) to sustain commitment.
- Celebrate wins publicly to build positive momentum.
- Address resistance directly rather than hoping it will fade.
- Assign dedicated project leadership; transformation doesn't happen on top of regular jobs.
- Plan for the "messy middle" when enthusiasm fades and reality sets in.

Epilogue

- Accept that year one of transformation will be hard: some people will leave, implementation will be slower than hoped.
- Measure both traditional metrics (revenue, PPEP) and transformation metrics (client satisfaction, retention, engagement).
- Distinguish between people who leave because they don't want change versus legitimate personal reasons.
- Celebrate the culture shifts (partners mentoring, associates enjoying development, people finding meaning).
- Learn from what didn't work to make improvements in year two and beyond
- To avoid pilot overload, sequence initiatives rather than launching everything simultaneously.
- Create annual retreats as reinforcement rituals to assess progress and recommit.
- Lead with honesty about challenges alongside recognition of progress.
- Keep choosing transformation even when it's exhausting, because a law firm's survival depends on proactive change.

Appendix B

McNamee, Weiss & Oh Transformation Retreat Agenda

Designing Our Future: A Five-Day Intensive

The Omni Grove Park Inn, Asheville, NC

MONDAY: The Case for Change

8:00–9:00 AM | Continental Breakfast & Registration

Sunset Terrace

9:00–9:30 AM | Opening Keynote: "The Inflection Point"

Speaker: Julian Justice, Managing Partner

- The timeline of disruption: 2008 to Present
- The "Spreadsheet at Midnight": Why incremental change is failing
- The call to be architects of our own future

9:30 AM–12:00 PM | Leading Change: ADKAR in Our Firm

Facilitator: Lucy Lex, Chief Innovation Officer

- Understanding the psychology of change
- **Exercise:** Personal Change Reflection & Sharing
- **Assessment:** Rating our firm's Awareness, Desire, Knowledge, Ability, and Reinforcement

12:00–1:30 PM | Lunch

Seated tables mixed by practice group and seniority

1:30–2:45 PM | "How We Got Here: The Evolution of Legal Practice"

Guest Speaker: Professor Ethan Rover, Stanford Law School

- The Cravath System and its unintended consequences
- The rise and fall of the billable hour monopoly
- Regulatory moats vs. modern innovation

2:45–3:00 PM | Break

3:00–3:45 PM | "The Five Forces of Convergence"

Facilitator: Lucy Lex

- Analysis of the five drivers reshaping the industry
- **Small Group Activity:** Cross-Force impact analysis

3:45–5:00 PM | "Generative AI: The Catalyst Force"

Guest Speaker: Dr. Sarah Conforti, Penn State University & LegalTech Futures

- The "Secret Cyborg" problem
- Impact on the leverage model and business of law
- Opportunities: Scaling expertise and new value propositions

6:00–8:00 PM | Welcome Dinner

Conversations on the Terrace: Processing the "Five Forces"

TUESDAY: Moving to Client-Centricity

8:00–9:00 AM | Breakfast & Reflection

Table Topic: "What surprised you most yesterday?"

9:00–10:30 AM | "Introduction to Design Thinking"

Facilitator: Lucy Lex

- Shifting from lawyer-centric to client-centric mindsets
- The 5 Stages: Empathize, Define, Ideate, Prototype, Test
- **Exercise:** The Airport Experience (Empathy Interviewing Practice)

10:30–10:45 AM | Break

10:45 AM–12:00 PM | Analyzing the Airport Exercise

- Debrief: How empathy reveals hidden needs
- Mapping emotional journeys vs. logistical steps

12:00–1:30 PM | Working Lunch: The Client Panel

Guest Panelists: Rebecca Tisdale (Apex Mfg), Dr. James Wilson (Meridian Health), Maria Santos (Pinnacle Retail)

- **Activity:** Live empathy interviewing with General Counsel
- Understanding the "Black Box" of client frustrations

1:30–3:00 PM | Synthesis & Definition

- Mapping client insights: Communication gaps, pricing misalignment, lack of partnership
- **Workshop:** Crafting "How Might We" (HMW) Statements for Client Service

5:00 PM | Evening Free

Informal small group dinners & discussion

WEDNESDAY: Reimagining Internal Systems

8:00–9:00 AM | Breakfast

9:00–10:30 AM | "The Broken Apprenticeship Model"

Guest Speaker: Professor Katherine Morrison, Duke Law School

- The theory-practice divide
- Why "osmosis" fails in a hybrid, AI-augmented world
- The Leadership Imperative: Competency-based development

10:30–10:45 AM | Break

10:45 AM–12:30 PM | Empathy Work: The Associate Experience

- **Exercise:** Partners interview Associates
- Uncovering the reality of feedback, career paths, and skill development
- **Synthesis:** Identifying systemic barriers to growth

12:30–1:30 PM | Lunch

1:30–3:00 PM | "Building the Hive: Business Development & Compensation"

Facilitators: Lucy Lex & Tom Brennan, CFO

- Moving from the "Rainmaker" model to Team-Based Service
- The Compensation Reality: Incentives vs. Behavior
- **Exercise:** Developing HMW Statements for Internal Systems (Career Paths, Comp, BD)

3:00–5:00 PM | Problem Definition & Team Selection

- Refining the final list of "How Might We" challenges
- Selecting focus areas for Thursday

6:00–8:00 PM | Group Dinner

THURSDAY: Ideation & Prototyping

8:00–9:00 AM | Breakfast

9:00–10:45 AM | Radical Ideation

Facilitator: Lucy Lex

- **Technique 1:** Worst Possible Idea (Overcoming fear of failure)
- **Technique 2:** Crazy 8s (Visualizing rapid solutions)
- **Technique 3:** Lateral Inspiration (Stealing from other industries)

10:45 AM–12:00 PM | Convergence

- Filtering and selecting the top concepts
- Formation of 9 Prototype Teams

12:00–1:00 PM | Working Lunch

- Teams begin conceptualizing their solutions

1:00–4:30 PM | Rapid Prototyping Laboratory

- Teams build low-fidelity prototypes (Mock-ups, Service Blueprints, Role-plays)
- **Focus Areas:**
  - Client Service
  - Associate Development
  - Business Development

4:30–5:30 PM | The Gallery Walk

- Teams display prototypes
- Peer feedback and iteration

Evening | Team Working Dinners

Refining pitches for the Innovation Tournament

FRIDAY: Commitment to Action

8:00–9:00 AM | Breakfast

9:00–11:30 AM | The Innovation Tournament

- **The Pitches:** 7-minute presentations from the Prototype Teams
- **The Panel:** Julian, Lucy, Guest Experts, and Client Guests
- **Judges' Deliberation & Selection:** Choosing the pilot initiatives

11:30 AM–12:30 PM | Lunch

12:30–3:00 PM | Implementation & Reinforcement

- **Track A (Selected Teams):** Detailed Implementation Planning (Resources, Timeline, Metrics)
- **Track B (General Group):** Designing Reinforcement Structures (Culture, Accountability, Rituals)

3:00–4:00 PM | Closing Session

- Presentation of the Year 1 Roadmap
- **Activity:** Personal Commitment Cards
- **Closing Remarks:** Julian Justice—"The Choice We're Making"

Appendix C

Cast of Characters

Firm Leadership

Julian Justice: Managing Partner. A veteran of the firm who realizes the traditional metrics of success are masking a coming crisis. He initiates the retreat to save the firm from a merger or decline.

Lucy Lex: Chief Innovation Officer. A former litigator turned innovation leader who designs the retreat curriculum and serves as the primary facilitator and change agent, pushing the firm to embrace design thinking.

Tom Brennan: Chief Financial Officer. The firm's realist who provides the sobering financial data that underscores the urgency of change, specifically regarding the threat AI poses to the billable hour model.

Lisa Martinez: Director of Legal Operations. An implementation expert who has long fought against knowledge hoarding and inefficient processes.

Partners

Robert Kim: Partner, Real Estate. A traditionalist who is initially skeptical of "innovation" but undergoes a significant transformation over the course of the book.

Maggie McNamee: Partner. Granddaughter of a firm founder who represents the firm's cultural legacy and warmth.

Sarah Williams: Partner, Employment Law. A pragmatic leader and working parent who is eager for efficiency but concerned about the practical implementation of new ideas.

Dwarkesh Jones: Partner. Represents the "practical middle" of the partnership, experienced enough to know the traditional model but new enough to leadership to know it must change.

Marcus Reed: Partner, Regulatory. A partner whose client's blunt warning about becoming a competitor serves as a wake-up call.

William Klept: Partner. A vocal skeptic regarding compensation changes who pushes back on the innovation ideas the firm participants propose.

Associates/Counsel

Michael Solomon: Counsel. Stuck in "up or out" limbo, he represents valuable lawyers who don't necessarily fit the traditional rainmaker track.

Jessica Park: Associate. A high performer and working parent who is considering leaving the firm due to burnout.

Elena Rodriguez: Associate. A top performer who candidly admits she plans to leave because the path to partnership is opaque.

John Forte: Associate. A strong service lawyer who feels lost regarding business development expectations.

Alex Rivera: Associate. A tech enthusiast and "secret cyborg" who is eager for the firm to adopt AI and modernize.

Priya Patel: Associate. A thoughtful member of the firm's AI pilot group who worries about how automation will affect her skill development and judgment.

Maya Davis: Associate. Represents the new generation of talent; she feels isolated and unsure of how to learn in an unstructured environment.

Clients

Rebecca Tisdale: General Counsel, Apex Manufacturing. A direct and candid leader who is frustrated by lack of communication and being excluded from strategy.

Dr. James Wilson: Chief Legal Officer, Meridian Health Systems. Emphasizes the need for lawyers to provide concise business answers rather than legal treatises.

Maria Santos: General Counsel, Pinnacle Retail Group. Focused on budget predictability and value, she challenges the firm on the misaligned incentives the billable hour creates.

Guest Experts

Professor Ethan Rover: Stanford Law School. A legal historian who sets the stage by explaining the origins of the Cravath System and the billable hour.

Dr. Sarah Conforti: Professor of Computer Science (Penn State) & Founder of LegalTech Futures. An expert on Generative AI who moves the firm from fear of technology to strategic adoption.

Professor Katherine Morrison: Duke Law School. An expert on the "theory-practice divide" in legal education who challenges the firm to take ownership of associate development.

Bibliography and Selected Readings

Books

Barton, Benjamin H. *Fixing Law Schools: From Collapse to the Trump Bump and Beyond.* New York: NYU Press, 2019.

Edmondson, Amy C. *The Fearless Organization: Creating Psychological Safety in the Workplace for Learning, Innovation, and Growth.* Hoboken, NJ: Wiley, 2018.

Hiatt, Jeffrey M. *ADKAR: A Model for Change in Business, Government and our Community.* Loveland, CO: Prosci Learning Center Publications, 2006.

Kelley, Tom, and David Kelley. *Creative Confidence: Unleashing the Creative Potential Within Us All.* New York: Crown Business, 2013.

Mollick, Ethan. *Co-Intelligence: Living and Working with AI.* New York: Portfolio, 2024.

Terwiesch, Christian, and Karl T. Ulrich. *Innovation Tournaments: Creating and Selecting Exceptional Opportunities.* Boston, MA: Harvard Business Press, 2009.

Articles, Reports & Studies

American Bar Association. *Legal Education and Professional Development: An Educational Continuum* (Report of the Task Force on Law Schools and the Profession: Narrowing the Gap). Chicago, IL: American Bar Association, 1992 (The "MacCrate Report").

CBRE. *2024 U.S. Law Firm Office Benchmarking Survey.* Dallas, TX: CBRE Research, 2024.

Furlong, Jordan. "Private Equity at the Gate." *Law21*, September 6, 2023.

Harvard Law School Center on the Legal Profession. "The Impact of Artificial Intelligence on Law Firms' Business Models." Cambridge, MA: February 24, 2025.

Institute for the Advancement of the American Legal System (IAALS). *Foundations for Practice: The Whole Lawyer and the Character of the Legal Profession.* Denver, CO: University of Denver, 2016.

Legal Services Corporation. *The Justice Gap: Measuring the Unmet Civil Legal Needs of Low-income Americans.* Washington, DC: Legal Services Corporation, 2022.

Major, Lindsey & Africa. *2023 Millennial Survey.* Hanover, MD: Major, Lindsey & Africa, 2023.

Richard, Larry. "Herding Cats: The Lawyer Personality Revealed." *Report to Legal Management* 29, no. 11 (August 2002).

Thomson Reuters Institute. "Motivating Lawyers to Participate in Law Firm's Return-to-Office Policies." *Legal Blog*, April 27, 2022.

Thomson Reuters Institute. *Stellar Performance: Skills and Progression for the Modern Lawyer.* Eagan, MN: Thomson Reuters, 2021.

Thomson Reuters Institute and Georgetown Law Center on Ethics and the Legal Profession. *2024 Report on the State of the US Legal Market.* Eagan, MN: Thomson Reuters, 2024.

Utah Office of Legal Services Innovation. *Sandbox Activity Report.* Salt Lake City, UT: December 2023 (March 2024).

Westfahl, Scott, and David B. Wilkins. "The Leadership Imperative: A Collaborative Approach to Professional Development in the Global Age of More for Less." *Stanford Law Review* 69, no. 6 (June 2017): 1667–1740.

www.ingramcontent.com/pod-product-compliance
Lightning Source LLC
LaVergne TN
LVHW050759061126
851857LV00012B/611
9781402450068

L'exécution